Béla Estván

War Pictures From the South

Béla Estván

War Pictures From the South

ISBN/EAN: 9783337003326

Printed in Europe, USA, Canada, Australia, Japan

Cover: Foto ©ninafisch / pixelio.de

More available books at **www.hansebooks.com**

WAR PICTURES

FROM

THE SOUTH.

BY
B. ESTVÀN,
COLONEL OF CAVALRY IN THE CONFEDERATE ARMY.

NEW YORK:
D. APPLETON AND COMPANY,
443 & 445 BROADWAY.
1863.

ENTERED, according to Act of Congress, in the year 1868, by
D. APPLETON AND COMPANY,
In the Clerk's Office of the District Court of the United States for the Southern District of New York.

PREFACE.

I HAVE, as a refugee, for the second time set my foot upon the rocky shores of Old England, to complete, under the shelter of her glorious banner, a narrative of the remarkable events that occurred during a period of more than eighteen months' campaigning in America, the knowledge of which I acquired from my personal experience as an officer of the Confederate army.

Now that my book is ready, I can confidently place it before the reader, with the assurance that these "War Pictures" have been delineated not only to the best of my ability, but with a conscientious regard to truth.

Although circumstances led me to take service in the Confederate army—my long residence in the Southern States being, however, the main inducement thereto—I have not been the less disposed to do justice to both sides engaged in this lamentable contest. Thus, while ever ready to bestow my hearty admiration on all the instances that came to my knowledge of heroism, patriotic devotion, and high-principled conduct, whether displayed on the part of my own comrades or on that of their opponents, I have, on the other hand, not hesitated to lay bare the errors and blamable acts, by whomsoever committed, that have been conducive to so much disaster and misery, nor have I spared the wrong doers.

Having completed my task, my thoughts naturally recur to the land wherein this unholy war is raging. To America, my second home, whose image I cling to with fond attachment, I cannot look back without sorrow for her misfortunes. I there contemplate deploringly the spectacle of a people once united, now dissevered through mad dissensions—dissensions which, involving in their fatal course the principle of the defence and maintenance of sacred rights, have issued in a suicidal conflict. My memory, in reverting to the fearful scenes so recently witnessed, painfully recalls those sanguinary battle fields whereon many a gallant soldier breathed out his spirit, struck to death by the bullet of a man whom he had been wont to regard in the light of a brother. Again the gaunt spectre of discord rises before me, with lightning flashing from its eyes, and rancor foaming at its lips, as, armed with a scourge of serpents, it frantically urges on whole populations to mutual destruction!

Now that my book is ready, I dedicate it to the soldiers of the two contending armies, as a greeting from afar. I have only to add, that if some of my criticisms may appear too severe to those whose conduct I censure, I have, in making use of them, been actuated solely by a fearless resolve to tell the truth and state my honest convictions. In the exercise of this, which I claim to be an undoubted right, have I written my book.

THE AUTHOR.

Dover, May, 1863.

CONTENTS.

CHAPTER I.
Secession of South Carolina, ... 1

CHAPTER II.
The Riot at Baltimore, ... 36

CHAPTER III.
Destruction of the Fleet at Portsmouth, ... 42

CHAPTER IV.
The Battle of Bethel, ... 45

CHAPTER V.
Colonel Porterfield's Volunteers, ... 49

CHAPTER VI.
M'Clellan's Victory at Rich Mountain, ... 52

CHAPTER VII.
Movements on the Potomac, ... 61

CHAPTER VIII.
Bull Run, ... 65

CHAPTER IX.
The Battle of Manassas, ... 71

CHAPTER X.
Richmond after the Battle of Manassas, ... 103

CHAPTER XI.
Beauregard Commander-in-Chief of the Army of the Potomac, . . 107

CHAPTER XII.
The Campaign in Western Virginia, ... 110

CHAPTER XIII.
Operations on Gauley River, ... 114

CHAPTER XIV.
Camp Defiance, Cheat Mountain, Cotton Hill, ... 122

CHAPTER XV.
M'Clellan appointed to the chief command of the Federal Army, . . 131

CHAPTER XVI.
The Campaign in Missouri, ... 135

CHAPTER XVII.
The Battle of Carthage, ... 140

CHAPTER XVIII.
The Battle of Oak Hill, or Wilson Creek, ... 147

CHAPTER XIX.
A General without an Army, ... 151

CHAPTER XX.
Battle of Lexington, ... 155

CHAPTER XXI.
Recruiting at Richmond, ... 162

CHAPTER XXII.
Hospitals of the Wounded Prisoners, ... 165

CHAPTER XXIII.
The Prisons at Richmond, ... 169

CHAPTER XXIV.
A Christmas Eve, ... 171

CHAPTER XXV.
The Battle of Belmont, ... 176

CHAPTER XXVI.
Battle in East Tennessee, ... 186

CHAPTER XXVII.
Fort Henry and Fort Donelson, ... 195

CHAPTER XXVIII.
John Morgan, the Guerilla Chieftain, ... 208

CHAPTER XXIX.
Johnston on the Tennessee River—Floyd and Pillow, . . 214

CHAPTER XXX.
The Battle of Shiloh, ... 219

CONTENTS.

	PAGE
CHAPTER XXXI.	
Surrender of Cape Hatteras, ...	233
CHAPTER XXXII.	
Surrender of Roanoke Island, ...	235
CHAPTER XXXIII.	
General Wise, ...	246
CHAPTER XXXIV.	
The Battle of Newbern, ...	251
CHAPTER XXXV.	
The "Merrimac" and the "Monitor,"	261
CHAPTER XXXVI.	
Destruction of the "Merrimac,"	269
CHAPTER XXXVII.	
Siege of Yorktown, ...	275
CHAPTER XXXVIII.	
The Battle of Fair Oaks, ...	282
CHAPTER XXXIX.	
Battle of Seven Pines, ...	288
CHAPTER XL.	
Investment of Richmond, ...	297
CHAPTER XLI.	
THE SEVEN DAYS' BATTLE BEFORE RICHMOND : JUNE 25TH TO JULY 1ST. 1862 :	
I.—A Council of War, ...	310
II.—First Day : Commencent of Operations, ...	311
III.—Second Day : Battle of Gaines's Mill, . .	313
IV.—Third and Fourth Days : Battle of Peach Orchard, . .	318
V.—Fifth Day : Battle near White Oak Swamp, . . .	321
VI.—Sixth Day : Battle at Frazer's Farm, ...	323
VII.—Seventh Day : Battle of Malvern Hill, . . .	327
CONCLUDING OBSERVATIONS, ...	330

BIOGRAPHICAL SKETCHES.

General P. G. Toussaint Beauregard, ...	335
" The late Albert Sidney Johnston, . . .	336
" Robert Edmund Lee, ...	337
" Thomas Jefferson Jackson, ...	337
" Sterling Price, ...	342

	PAGE
General C. Frederick Henningsen,	342
" Joseph Eccleston Johnston,	344
" Edmund Kirby Smith,	345
" Braxton Bragg,	345
" James Longstreet,	346
" G. B. M'Clellan,	347
" Francis Sigel,	348
" Ambrose Everett Burnside,	349
" Don Carlos Buell,	349
" Henry Wager Halleck,	350
" Ulysses S. Grant,	351
" John Charles Fremont,	351

WAR PICTURES.

CHAPTER I.

SECESSION OF SOUTH CAROLINA.

Election of Mr. Lincoln—Excitement in the South—South Carolina secedes—Major Anderson destroys Fort Moultrie—Resignation of Secretary Floyd—Journey to Charleston—Commotion there—Fort Sumter—President Buchanan rejects the ultimatum—Major Ripley, commander of Fort Moultrie—Warlike preparations—General Bragg—Uncle Sam—Montgomery—Fort Pickens—President Jeff. Davis and Vice-President Alex. Stephens—Secession of the States of Mississippi, Alabama, Florida, Georgia, Louisiana, and Texas—Peace Congress at Washington—Complete rupture—Lincoln's installation at Washington—Danger of the city—The new Cabinet—Bombardment of Fort Sumter—Sham Fighting—Capitulation—President Lincoln's Declaration of War—Condition of the Confederacy—My return to Richmond—Virginia joins the Southern States.

As soon as the election to the Presidency of the Republican candidate, Abraham Lincoln, became known, the South at once made preparations to dissolve the Union, urged thereto by the conviction that henceforth it had no guarantees or safeguard for the preservation of its rights. SOUTH CAROLINA, the mother of the Southern States, took the initiative in this movement, with but little foresight, however, and with very inadequate preparations for an effort of such magnitude; but it had resolved to take up the gauntlet which it conceived had been thrown down by the North in the election of Lincoln; and, on the 20th December, 1860, proceeded to declare itself an independent sovereign State.

Patriots now poured in on all sides, eager to support the young Government, not only by their countenance and counsel, but by deeds, if needful.

Major Anderson, of the United States army, who was in command of Fort Moultrie, one of the strongholds of Charleston, evacuated that post, after burning all the Government stores, spiking the guns, and destroying everything he could; and embarked, on the 20th December, with his detachment of 132 men of the United States army, to take possession of Fort Sumter, erected on an islet in the middle of the bay. This place offered him greater security; and within its bomb-proof walls he would be able quietly to watch the progress of coming events.

The indignation of the inhabitants of Charleston was intense when the flames arising from Fort Moultrie made them aware of its abandonment and demolition by its late commander. A number of steamers were prepared in all haste, and ordered, with various companies of State troops, to take possession of both Fort Moultrie and Fort Pinckney; which double occupation was effected without bloodshed, the small garrison of the former having already been withdrawn to Fort Sumter.

On the 30th December, Mr. J. B. Floyd, the United States Cabinet of War, notified to President Buchanan his withdrawal from the Cabinet; and, leaving his office in the greatest confusion, hastily left Washington for his estates in Virginia. The secession of South Carolina from the Union, however, did not disturb the equanimity of the North, as the people of that portion of the United States were firmly convinced that the Government could easily put down the rebellion. But the events which occurred shortly after, apprized the North that the Southerners were not unprovided with ways and means to begin a war, and that in the coming struggle they would prove anything but despicable opponents.

Thus the first signal step toward disunion was taken; to

what it might lead, no one could then foresee, especially as the first hasty and somewhat imperfect preparations did not imply any very extensive plan of operations. Popular passions were violently aroused; but who could have guessed in those dawning symptoms of strife the disastrous consequences of a fratricidal war, which was destined to overwhelm alike friend and foe, and to undermine the prosperity and wealth of the whole community?

Scarcely had South Carolina seceded from the Union, when I received a commission from two of the most influential Southern leaders, with directions for me to proceed at once to South Carolina to superintend the military preparations going on there, and the arrangements for bombarding Fort Sumter, where Major Anderson had taken up his position, and where, under the banner of the Great Republic, it was expected he could hold out to the last extremity. My arrangements for departure were speedily made, and I was ready to start on my knight-errant's mission. On quitting Richmond, the dreary morasses and monotonous rice, cotton, and tobacco fields of Virginia and of North and South Carolina were quickly passed; for the railway runs in a continuous line through this unpicturesque portion of the South. After a twenty-five hours' journey, the train came to a standstill, and the voices of the guards announced to the drowsy passengers the welcome news that we were at Charleston. All was now life and bustle; we had arrived at the theatre of impending war.

An omnibus took me quickly to Mills' Hotel, the best in Charleston, and far surpassing those of Richmond. After I had made myself presentable, I proceeded to the dining room to restore my somewhat wearied faculties. Here I found at the well-supplied table a host of Southern cavaliers, who seemed to enjoy the good things before them with considerable *gusto*. The events of the day were loudly discussed among them, and strong words uttered against the Government at Washington. Several of these gentlemen had already donned brilliant uniforms; and as they clanked their spurs, rattled their swords, and made dashing inroads upon the viands before them, I could hardly fail to be impressed by such evidences of chivalrous courage.

As soon as dinner was over, I hastened to deliver my despatches to his Excellency Mr. Pickens, Governor of the State of South Carolina. In him I found a perfect gentleman, full of amiability and courtesy; and on my applying to him for the necessary information to guide me in my endeavors to ascertain the military resources of the State of South Carolina, he ordered one of his numerous adjutants to attend me, besides directing that I should be provided with horses and a negro servant. Captain Nelson, the officer in question, at once tendered his services with that urbanity peculiar to the planters of the South; and, much pleased with my reception, I left the Governor's headquarters to pay my respects to the Hon. William Porcher Miles. After passing through some of the principal streets, we came in view of the Bay of Charleston. The sight which now burst upon me was so enchanting that I stood on the shores of the bay gazing with delight upon the noble spectacle before me. It was one of those glorious visions of beauty which, once seen, can never be forgotten. The magnificent deep-blue waters of the bay lay slumbering before me, and from out their midst arose the unsightly, dingy walls of Fort Sumter, with its formidable-looking guns and casemates; whilst a gentle south wind caused the majestic flag raised in the centre of the fort to give its ample folds to the breeze, displaying the Stars and Stripes to the many thousand citizens of Charleston assembled on the beach.

There, in the middle of the bay, within that unseemly mass of dark-looking rock, was housed a small band, all, no doubt, trusty sons of that great Republ'c whose banner seemed to intimate unmistakably to the crowd of Southern loungers on the opposite shore their resolve either to maintain the post entrusted to their keeping, or to die as brave soldiers in the performance of their duty. On the left side of the bay stood Fort Moultrie, from the battlements of which was displayed the banner of the Southerners—the Palmetto—which the people glanced at with eyes beaming with proud satisfaction.

I tore myself away reluctantly from the spot, and in company of the officer appointed to escort me, I proceeded to the residence of the Hon. William Porcher Miles. This gentleman gave me a hearty welcome, accompanied with repeated offers of service. After a long visit, I and my companion took leave of him, and proceeded to the hotel, in the saloon of which we remained but a short time before retiring to rest. I had not, however, been long asleep, when I was aroused by a violent ringing of bells, and by the prolonged blast of trumpets. On hastening down stairs to ascertain the cause of this turmoil, I found unmistakable signs of military activity all around me, reminding me of scenes I had witnessed in Italy in the year 1848. Halls and stairs resounded to the clank of spurs and swords—music familiar to the ear of an old soldier; and in the great room below were crowded together military men of every description—grenadiers, hussars, and others; whilst a corps of cadets had mounted guard in front of the hotel. Moreover, troops of all arms were marching past, and artillery rattled heavily through the streets.

Captain Nelson shortly made his appearance, and with a beaming countenance informed me that orders had just been received for the bombardment of Fort Sumter. President Buchanan had, in fact, rejected the *ultimatum* of South Carolina: namely, the withdrawal of the United States troops from Fort Sumter; and the plenipotentiaries had returned with this virtual declaration of war on the part of the President. All the impediments that had hitherto restrained the impatient Southerners from giving full scope to their courage, vanished as the barriers which had hitherto existed between the belligerents were removed. Some hundred officers were soon assembled in the dining hall, and the hubbub received additional stimulus from the incessant drawing of champagne corks, while all present seemed animated with martial ardor. In a short time Captain Nelson arrived, with horses and servants, and we set out for Fort Moultrie, where Major Ripley, formerly an officer of the regular United States army, held the command, and where the ball was to commence. My charger was a quiet old nag, which never in its life had faced such an excited crowd as that now surging hither and thither. Poor fellow, after having for a long course of years quietly munched his oats and hay in peaceful security, it was now his fate to smell gunpowder all at once, and prove his nerve amidst the thunder of cannon. As if he had some foreboding of what was to happen, he pricked up his ears and cast shy glances at the military life teeming around us. Nevertheless, without needing the admonition of spur or rein, he readily carried me up the heights which led to Fort Moultrie.

It was a charming day. The sun shone, mild and smiling, upon the deep-blue waters of the lovely bay. The green hills on the shore were reflected in the crystal mirror below, and all nature seemed so happy and peaceful as to present to the mind a strange contrast to the spirit of discontent and warlike strife which then brooded in the breast of man. Leaving our horses, we went on board a steamer, which conveyed us to the fort.

Through my excellent Vogtländer telescope I saw many indications of great military activity in Fort Sumter; guns were being brought into position, and new works thrown up in front of the fort; in short, it was quite clear to my mind that Major Anderson was not only determined to show us his teeth, but to bite hard if necessary. I handed my glass to my friend the Captain, who was standing near me, drawing his attention to the preparations in active progress then making, by the commandant of Fort Sumter; observing that so old a fox as Anderson would hardly fail to receive such a distinguished party as ourselves with all due courtesy and attention.

"What the devil do you mean? the confounded fellow is surely not going to fire at us?" anxiously inquired my heroic companion, while his face became remarkably pallid, and his well-waxed mustache lost considerably in its warlike appearance.

"Believe me, Captain," I rejoined, "that all those preparations he is so busily engaged in making mean mischief, and denote his intention to make good use of his formidable guns."

At these words a slight shiver pervaded my companion's frame, and pleading sickness, he retired in a state of trepidation, to find a place of greater security behind the bulwarks of the steamer. The other bold sons of Mars who had accompanied me from Charleston, now all gathered around, and pressed me to give them some account of my former military adventures under similar circumstances, which request I readily complied with.

In the midst of my narrative the captain of the steamer shouted out, "Fort Moultrie, gentlemen!" and we all prepared to leave the vessel. On landing, we were warmly welcomed by a number of officers and soldiers of the garrison, assembled at the landing place, and we then proceeded without delay to the interior of the fort, where we found the commander, Major Ripley, surrounded by a crowd of negroes busy at work. As soon as I made myself known to the Major, he begged me to excuse him for a few moments, as he was anxious to give his final orders in person. It was evident to me at a glance that vigorous warlike measures were in active preparation in the fort. Guns of every calibre were being placed in position; furnaces to heat the shot were getting ready for use; ammunition was being brought to the different batteries, and shot and shell of all sizes piled up in symmetrical pyramids. A portion of the garrison was likewise under arms, in readiness for immediate service, if required; indeed, the whole scene convinced me that the officer in command was an excellent soldier, notwithstanding a few slight mistakes that I could not fail to notice, which showed that his work had come upon him rather suddenly, and that this was, in all probability, the first time in his life he had been on active service. For instance, the defensive works of the fort were of too weak a construction to offer any effectual resistance to the heavy guns of a bomb-proof fort like that of Sumter. A well-directed bombardment from its formidable batteries, by skilful and experienced gunners, would have knocked Fort Moultrie to pieces in a dozen hours.

One of the chief departments, moreover, that of the hospital, had been very badly provided for. There were no surgeons present, with their assistants, provided with instruments, bandages, ambulances, and other needful appliances, ready for instant attention to such casualties as might occur. There was an utter absence of the usual hospital details on the eve of hostile operations: no surgeons with sleeves tucked up, ready for their grave work, giving directions to their assistants, pointing out where and how their services might be required and turned to the best account. Nothing of the kind was visible, although such precautions were obviously of vital importance to the soldier about to confront a determined foe. The good-natured doctors in Fort Moultrie were strolling about the works in fine uniforms, as if it was an understood thing that there would be no wounded, and consequently no work for them to do.

As soon as I had made this inspection, which brought a smile to my lips more than once, I went into the inner court, where Captain Nelson imparted the very important news that Major Ripley was awaiting me with a capital bowl of punch. On taking the seat politely offered to me, I found the worthy commander of the fort sitting, like Bacchus, on an upturned barrel. His officers lay around him in picturesque groups, smoking their cigars, and eagerly awaiting the arrival of the punch, which was being brewed by a young cavalry lieutenant. I was most enthusiastically welcomed by Major Ripley and his officers, as I was almost the only European officer serving under their flag. We made ourselves as comfortable as we could upon the bales of cotton placed for our accommodation, whilst a host of slaves handed round the punch, together with excellent Havana cigars. The glasses went merrily round, and many toasts were drunk to the success of the Palmetto State. It was one of those martial orgies which only the hot-blooded Southerner can fully appreciate and enjoy. We were presently interrupted, however, in our unflinching attack upon the punch bowl, by the sentry on duty, who conducted an orderly from the Governor in charge of despatches for the commander of the fort. A dead silence now ensued, and all eyes were turned inquiringly toward Major Ripley. As soon as this officer had read the despatch he dismissed the orderly, thrust the papers into his pocket, and telling a young, active, woolly-headed negro to hand him a glass of punch, he thus addressed his companions in arms, who were waiting for intelligence in eager expectation:

"Gentlemen, fill your glasses! As regards the bombardment of Fort Sumter, it is all over for the present." (Great astonishment now manifested.) "I am to proceed at once to the headquarters of his Excellency," he continued; and then, raising his glass, he proposed a cheer for the Palmetto Republic and its brave sons. This was responded to by a round of cheers from the officers present, in which the garrison outside promptly joined. This scene, I confess, made me look at the Palmetto banner with thoughts of a rather serious nature.

Major Ripley then turned to Captain Lamb, and handed over to him the command for the day, while I and my companion started forthwith on our return to Charleston. On arriving there we proceeded to the headquarters of the

Governor, to ascertain the cause of the revocation of the previous orders. All the leading men of the State of South Carolina were assembled there.

We learned that after a lengthy debate it had been resolved to abstain from the bombardment of Fort Sumter, and that endeavors should be made to induce Major Anderson, by diplomatic means, either to evacuate the fort or to capitulate.

Major Ripley, Captain Nelson, and myself then adjourned to my hotel, to recruit ourselves after the fatigues of the day. On our entrance, however, one of the numerous waiters of the hotel handed me a despatch from Virginia, ordering me to start without delay, after my inspection was over, for General Bragg's headquarters in the State of Florida, in order to report upon the state of things there, General Bragg having already received orders to take Fort Pickens, which was held by the troops and fleet of the United States.

I was soon ready to commence my journey to Florida and Alabama, and took a hearty farewell of my comrades, whom I had learned to like during our short acquaintance; they made me promise that, should the bombardment of Fort Sumter actually take place, and I should receive information of the fact by telegraph, I would immediately return to be a witness of the valor and efficiency of the troops of South Carolina. We shook hands all round; and, accompanied by Captain Nelson, I proceeded to the railway.

Here I found my black servant, good old Uncle Sam, who, with his woolly head, came to me with a melancholy look, saying: "Massa Cornel take old Sam with him. Understand horses. Onkel Sam kill all mosquitos." I was really touched by the poor fellow's earnest entreaties as he chronicled all his good qualities, in the hopes of making a favorable impression upon me; so, shaking the old man's hand, I comforted him at once by telling him that he might come with me. He now gave vent to that unconstrained outburst of joy so characteristic of the negro race when any one of their wishes is gratified.

Pushing aside a young ebon-skinned negro who was standing near, gaping at us with open mouth and staring eyes, Uncle Sam exclaimed, in utter forgetfulness of his own coal-black hue, " Get out of the road, you dam black nigger; make place whar Cornel comes!" accompanying his words with a look of magisterial authority.

I requested Captain Nelson to allow me to take Uncle Sam with me as my servant, which he readily assented to. As the train did not start immediately, I sat down in the waiting room to read the newspapers. At last, when the signal for departure was given, Uncle Sam made his appearance, but completely metamorphosed. A pair of very scanty light-blue trousers encompassed his huge nether limbs; a light-yellow waistcoat brought his powerful chest into high relief; whilst a grass-green frock coat, adorned with gilt buttons, a black broad-brimmed hat—which also did the duty of an umbrella; a shirt collar—the ends of which nearly touched his eyes— and a Patagonian pair of boots none too big for his elephantine feet, completed his costume, of which he seemed ineffably proud. Uncle Sam, who evidently fancied himself irresistible in his new and rather "loud" style of dress, handed me with great dignity into one of the carriages, and then went to look after my luggage. He tramped along the station with that air of importance which negroes are so fond of assuming when they fancy their master to be a man of consideration.

When we were just about to start, Uncle Sam took good care to display himself in all his bravery on the platform of the carriage, that he might gladden the eyes of his admiring brethren, numbers of whom, hearing of his departure, had assembled to see him off. " Good-by, Bell; don't forget me," he shouted out to a thick-lipped, ugly negress, as she handed up some fruit. " Bob, don't forget you owe me ten cents." " Tim, my compliments to your lady. Onkel Sam is going to the wars, and kill many Yankees. Massa Cornel hab swords. Good-by, good-by;" and thus he took leave, perhaps forever, of his sable acquaintances.

My new journey was just as monotonous as that from Richmond to Charleston. In Augusta, in the State of Georgia, I made a halt to have an interview with the Hon. Mr. K——, to whom I had letters of introduction. I found this gentleman a devoted patriot of the great Republic. He shook his head sadly at the startling events in the Southern States, and emphatically condemned the inconsiderate, hasty action of the State of South Carolina, as likely to lead the country to ruin. On my observing to him that the whole of the Southern newspapers approved of the conduct of South Carolina, not a single dissentient voice having been raised against it, he replied, "Yes, yes, the newspapers join in this wolfish howl; but ask the people, appeal to the inhabitants of Georgia, and I will stake my head that four fifths of the population are in favor of the Union, and opposed to a separation from it. And this is not only the case here," he continued, "but you will find it to be the same in Alabama, North Carolina, and Virginia. But that portion of the community which has long been waiting for a pretext to get up this revolution has found an opportunity for commencing their odious game in the election of the Republican candidate, Abraham Lincoln."

I took a cordial leave of this worthy man and patriotic citizen, and continued my journey to Montgomery.

Some of the reflections I had just heard, I could not help fancying had already flashed across my own mind. It was intelligible enough that a factious party, actuated by ambition and restless discontent, with the press at their command, should persistently preach disunion, hoping by the overthrow of the existing state of things to bring about the accomplishment of their designs. I could not forget how majestic had been the growth of the Union, that vigorous plant which had been developed in such strength and power as to command the admiration of the civilized world. Each State was a glorious stem of this noble tree, and each leaf bore the words, Law, Liberty, Prosperity, Concord! These four elements of its flourishing condition were individually and collectively essential to its further development: a truth felt and cherished by the smallest member of the least part of this colossal Union. Why, then, were not the noxious insects at once crushed which had crept into the calyx of so fair a flower in order to destroy it? Why was not every rotten leaf at once cut off that threatened to poison the sap of the whole plant?

But who could have then dreamt that the small snowball moulded by the hand of discord would become ere long a mighty avalanche, increasing as it rolled on; would, in its destructive career, overwhelm thousands of the homesteads of peace?

MONTGOMERY, in the State of Alabama, was selected by the revolutionary party as the place best suited to concoct their schemes, and to lay out their plans in undisturbed security. On my arrival in this small town I found the greatest excitement and flurry prevalent amongst the citizens, who had assembled together by thousands. With some difficulty I procured a lodging for myself and Uncle Sam, and then hastened to the Capitol, where I had a short interview with some of the members of the Southern Convention, which was then holding a sitting. Without allowing myself any further respite, I proceeded at daybreak next morning to the seat of war in Florida, to investigate the state of affairs there.

At PENSACOLA, a miserable little town on the Mexican Gulf, in a sandy plain where yellow fever and alligators had it all their own way, was posted the army of the famous General Bragg, who, from this point, commenced operations to storm FORT PICKENS, situated in the middle of the bay, which post was then covered and defended by a United States' squadron and a small body of troops. Hitherto General Bragg had done nothing except to concoct and issue forth his pompous reports to the world. The impression he made upon me was precisely that of a strolling acrobat standing outside his booth, announcing the wonderful things that were to be seen within. It must be admitted, however, that his reports and bulletins were calculated to produce a telling effect in exciting the masses. Here is a specimen of the style of these precious effusions : " Prepare your cannon to destroy the world! I will disperse the dogs to the four winds! Not one stone of the fort shall remain upon another!"

In short, by such laconic proclamations he successfully courted the approval of the multitude, who began to fancy that Bragg was the only general in the world worth having— a second Alexander the Great. Indeed, if big words sufficed to make heroes, there would be no lack of supply in America; but as a makeweight they have happily a local proverb which teaches them that " Words are not cents!"

Bragg would not allow me to open my lips, but, in wild excitement, at once launched forth a vainglorious boast, that in less than four weeks he would capture Fort Pickens, put the garrison to the sword, and blow it in the air. " All this is very well, General," I quietly observed; " but what measures have you taken to carry out this great plan?" On this point, however, the gallant General declined to enter into any explanations; it was his wish, he said (pulling up his shirt collar at the same time, as if to give weight to his words), to astonish the public by his success. After this rather unsatisfactory interview, I proceeded along the shores of the bay to inspect his camp and the condition of his army. The defensive works were of the most primitive kind, and constructed with a carelessness which might have led to the supposition that we were in a state of peace, had it not been that a hostile fort opposite stood where the vigilant activity of the enemy was evident enough.

The sun's rays were so fierce that the dry sandy soil glowed with scorching heat. I therefore ordered a horse, and rode, accompanied by General Bragg's first adjutant, Major Self, through the camp. Major Self was a good-humored cavalry officer, who might be a good soldier, but he was rather too enthusiastic an admirer of GENERAL BRAGG, and was never tired of talking about the great things which the General *intended to do*. The troops assembled here consisted exclusively of volunteer militia, who had only been a few weeks in the service. They were a set of fine-looking young men. Camp life had given them much of the fantastical appearance of the French troops in Algeria, but they lacked their light-hearted good humor and ready wit; they seemed, at any rate, greatly to enjoy their military life: it was a relief from the monotonous routine of their plantation existence, and this change in their habits seemed to be not at all unpalatable to them. I had only been a few days in the camp when the news arrived that the Convention at Montgomery had elected JEFFERSON DAVIS as President, and ALEXANDER H. STEPHENS as Vice-President of the Confederacy. I took a hasty farewell of General Bragg and of the chief of the staff; ordered Sam to pack up my things, and on that same evening started on my way back to Montgomery.

In a very short time the circumstances of the South had undergone a great change. After the secession of South Carolina, that of other Southern States soon followed. Early in January, 1861, Mississippi, Alabama, and Florida seceded from the Union, and at the end of the same month Georgia and Louisiana did the same. Texas seceded in February. So that in less than three months after the election of President Lincoln all the cotton States had separated from the Union, taking, moreover, at the same time, the precaution to seize all State property, with the exception of the forts in Charleston Bay and Fort Pickens in Florida, which were held by the troops of the United States, who did not show the least inclination to give them up at the first bidding.

At the end of January the Legislature of the State of Virginia proposed a Peace Congress, to avert, if possible, the calamity of a civil war. This Congress actually met on the 9th of February at Washington, for the purpose of taking counsel to devise friendly and conciliatory measures calculated to quench the smouldering sparks of revolution, and Mr. Tyler, a former President of the United States, was elected to preside ; but after a few days' sitting the Congress broke up, as it was found impracticable to come to any understanding. The seceding States thereupon organized a Government of their own, and thus laid the foundation of the future Confederacy.

The delegates of the six seceding States met at Montgomery, and there, on the 8th of February, a constitution for the Confederate States was framed and adopted. The Congress then proceeded to the election of a President and Vice-President, and after some discussion, JEFFERSON DAVIS was, as already stated, elected President, and ALEXANDER H. STEPHENS, of Georgia, Vice-President of the Confederacy.

I looked forward with no little interest for the arrival of President Davis, who, I learned, was, on the news of his election, hastening to Montgomery to assume the functions of his office. On the 19th February he made his solemn entrance into that town amidst the ringing of bells and the roar of cannon. Followed by a host of office hunters, he found a still greater number of the same gentry awaiting his arrival. The 22d February was the day fixed upon for the installation of the President. The ceremony took place with all the pomp that was possible, under the circumstances. Bells pealed, salutes were fired, and military detachments from every part of the Confederate States came forward to take a share in the great show. But the whole thing was done in such a hurry that the election, arrival, and installation of the President were scarcely made public before they were accomplished. It almost seemed as if there had been a previous rehearsal, so rapid was the performance. On the 22d February, at 2 P. M., the Southern States possessed a President and a Cabinet, and the people stared at each other in amazement, not exactly understanding how this hasty election came about. A candidate for the Presidency had arrived in the night without the people knowing anything about it, without giving the citizens time to vote for or against him. Some politicians naturally took advantage of this to treat the citizens of this free country as serfs, and the latter, silently and without a murmur, put up with this contemptuous treatment of their rights. But not to allow them time to brood over their wrongs, the Government immediately took measures which were well calculated to completely bewilder them.

Forts Moultrie and Pinckney in Charleston Bay were taken possession of, as we have seen, as also were Forts Pulaski, Jackson, and Philip. The arsenals at Baton Rouge and Mount Vernon, the Custom House at New Orleans, and the Mint were also seized, the cash found there confiscated, and new officials appointed.

At this period the court of the newly elevated Jefferson Davis was thronged by all those who had contributed in the slightest degree to rend asunder the republic of the United States. It seemed as if from every part of the land the crows had flocked together to share in the anticipated feast. The ex-Secretary of War, Floyd, played no unimportant part here, as also a certain Mr. Tochman, formerly of the New York bar, who was at once appointed a general of brigade. A great number of former officials in the United States service, both civil and military, joined the new Confederacy. Many of these gentleman had a convenient elasticity of conscience, and understood perfectly well how to proclaim their love of country and disinterested conduct; while the Government which comprised within itself many similar elements, had naturally no cause to disavow this outburst of patriotic feeling. These men were, accordingly, received with open arms, and appointed to good situations.

Whilst the revolution was gradually preparing on a large scale in the South, the Buchanan Cabinet at Washington displayed an indifference which bordered upon insanity, to say the best of it. The relief of Fort Sumter, for instance, where Major Anderson was shut up with 132 men, was then apparently not even thought of; and the 4th March, the day fixed for the installation of the Republican President, Abraham Lincoln, was fast approaching.

To reach Washington, Lincoln had so many obstacles to overcome on the way, that probably some men in a similar position would have turned back; but quietly and calmly did this simple, clear-headed man pursue the course he had laid down for himself; and, despite all hindrances, not dismayed even at the pious wishes of the Southerners that he might come to serious grief on the road, he arrived safely at the capital of the United States.

The hour for his installation at last struck, and General Scott, commander-in-chief of the United States' army, received instructions to take all possible precautions to put down any attempt at an outbreak, as it was currently reported that a great demonstration had been resolved upon by the many thousand Southerners who had assembled on the occasion. The old General displayed the greatest activity on this occasion. He occupied the Capitol with regular troops; he ordered the by-roads which lead into Pennsylvania Avenue, the main street leading from the President's house to the Capitol, to be closed; while the flat roofs of the houses were occupied by riflemen, and large bodies of infantry and cavalry were stationed at various points, ready at a given signal to act in concert. Cavalry was ordered to form the advanced and rear guards of the Presidential procession, and to serve also as an escort. The marine brigade in the port was likewise ordered to be ready in case of any emergency.

A portentous cloud thus hung over the Capitol of the Union. Had a single unlucky shot been fired, the city of Washington was doomed; for General Scott was not the man to shrink at trifles, and would certainly have cleared the streets with grape had any mad attempt been made to oppose the installation of the President. When favorable reports from different quarters came in on all sides, the old General, addressing his officers, said: "Thank Heaven that I was not compelled to have recourse to force, for in that case it would have been a very sad business."

Merry peals of bells and the roar of cannon announced the ceremony of the installation. Thousands of people had arrived from all parts to see the old railsplitter of Illinois installed in one of the highest of earthly dignities, and I too formed one of the curious spectators. The procession which left the White House was headed by a number of volunteers, detachments of military, and various deputations; then came a plain carriage, wherein sat the ex-President Buchanan, and on his right, his successor, Abraham Lincoln. The President elect appeared pale and careworn from the fatigue and excitement he had undergone, and he cast a weary and cold glance at the moving mass of human beings at each side of the procession. Was he endeavoring to discover his Brutus among them?

Buchanan sat at his side with a beaming face; it was quite clear he was delighted at being relieved from the duties of his responsible position. The representatives of foreign States followed the simple carriage of the President in magnificent equipages, attended by the whole *personnel* of their respective embassies and consulates, in their official costumes.

President Lincoln made his inaugural speech—a serious and dignified oration—from the east portico of the Capitol. He swore solemnly with upraised hand that he would observe and defend the rights and laws of the United States, and that he would govern in such wise that he should be able one day to render a good account of his acts before his Supreme Judge. He declared that there was no necessity for the shedding of blood, or to have recourse to force, at least not *unless*—and he placed great emphasis upon that word—the insurgent people should drive the Government to it. He further declared that he should make use of the power intrusted to him by the majority of the people to maintain with a firm hand, under all circumstances, every town and citadel which belonged to the Government.

In the South, President Lincoln's speech was looked upon as tantamount to a declaration of war, especially when it was found that he had conferred the most important Government appointments upon the most determined enemies of the South. Thus he appointed—

>WILLIAM H. SEWARD, Secretary of State.
>SALMON P. CHASE, Secretary of the Treasury.
>MONTGOMERY BLAIR, Postmaster General.
>ANSON BURLINGAME, Minister to Austria.
>CASSIUS M. CLAY, " to Russia.
>C. SCHURZ, " to Spain.
>J. E. HARVEY, " to Portugal.
>CHARLES FRANCIS ADAMS, " to England.

In the Senate of Congress, Charles Sumner was appointed Chairman of the Committee on Foreign Relations; William P. Fessenden, Chairman of the Finance Committee; and Henry Wilson Chairman of the Committee on Military Affairs. Mr. Douglas, the leader of that portion of the Democratic party which still adhered to the National Government, paid great court to the President, and during the installation ceremony held his hat in his hand. At the ball which took place afterward he paid the greatest attention to the President, and to Mrs. Lincoln. Evil tongues spoke disparagingly of this, and attributed his conduct to interested motives: we prefer remaining silent on the subject.

On President's Lincoln's accession to the Presidency the condition of the finances was far from discouraging. In fact, the Government found itself in this point of view in a suffi ciently comfortable position. The War Department alone, under J. B. Floyd's administration, was found to be in a state of great disorder; the head of that department having thought the moment very opportune to join the banner of the Confederacy with all the material aid he could bring to them.

Meantime, the Confederate Government, stumbling from one step to another, burning all its bridges behind it, so as to prevent any possibility of a reconciliation, sent Mr. Crawford of Georgia, and Mr. Forsyth of Alabama, as delegates to Washington to negotiate the withdrawal of the United States troops from Forts Sumter and Pickens. Moreover, in consequence of the separation of the South from the North, they were to make proposals respecting a division of territory. Mr. Seward, Secretary of State, declined, however, to receive them as delegates from a sovereign State.

Whilst the greater portion of the population of the South anxiously watched the course of events, many still hoping for a peaceful settlement, I had long given up all such hopes, believing that the men who took the lead in the South were determined to oppose any attempt at reconciliation. Most of these men, it appeared to me, had little or nothing to lose, but hoped to gain a good deal, and, consequently, were decidedly in favor of forcible separation. As soon as the festivities of the installation were over, I started for Charleston.

Military committees now sat daily in Washington, under President Lincoln, to concert measures for sending reënforcements, ammunition, and provisions to Fort Sumter. These sittings lasted for nearly a fortnight, without any important decision having been adopted. The new Secretary of War at length took steps to be prepared for any eventuality. The regular troops stationed on the Southern frontier were recalled to Washington; the naval squadrons in all parts of the world were ordered to return home, with the exception of those vessels whose duty it was to protect the commercial interests of the United States at sea. Washington soon had the appearance of a great military school. These arrangements proved that the Government was aware of the critical state of affairs. In fact, it was high time that order should be restored out of the confusion which had arisen during the latter period of Buchanan's presidency, and that nothing should be wanting to show the firm resolve of the United States Government to bring back to the Union, either by conciliatory measures or by force of arms, those States which were declared to be in open rebellion.

On the other hand, the Confederate Government had not been idle. Three military bills passed the Congress sitting at Montgomery, which was also temporarily the seat of the Government. The first bill empowered President Davis to call out 100,000 volunteers for service; the second, to organize a regular Confederate army; the third, to form a local force. What, however, most alarmed the United States Government at Washington, was the fact that a great number of officers of the army and navy were leaving the service of the United States to join the Confederates.

At this trying time for the Government at Washington, many Governors of Northern States tendered aid in both men and money. It was also resolved that the Government should be empowered to employ the military force at its disposal, if no other means could be found, to suppress the rebellion of the Southern States. As soon as Lincoln's Government found that the Northern States intended to support it manfully with every means at their disposal, it was decided at once that reenforcements of men and supplies should be sent to Fort Sumter. With the view, moreover, of avoiding, if possible, even at the last moment, all aggressive measures, Colonel Lamon was sent to South Carolina, on a special mission to Governor Pickens, with the notification that the Government intended to send supplies to Fort Sumter. Governor Pickens listened quietly to the notification, but made no reply to indicate how the Government of South Carolina intended to act under the circumstances.

It was now resolved at Washington that not a minute should be lost in taking active measures. The Navy Department received orders to issue the necessary instructions to get the fleet ready at once for service. The greatest activity was displayed in all the dockyards, and in the arsenals of West Troy, where the works were carried on day and night. A great number of steamers and sailing vessels were purchased, large contracts entered into for war materials, and at last the Washington Cabinet showed the people that it was going earnestly to work. Recruiting for the regular army war carried out with no little success, so that in a very short time from 12,000 to 15,000 troops were assembled on Governor's Island.

On the 6th April, the naval officer in command of the squadron apprized the Secretary of the Navy that he was awaiting further orders.

The force ready for service consisted of—

The POWHATAN frigate, carrying 10 heavy guns, with a crew of 400 men;

The cutter HARRIET LANE, 8 heavy guns, with a crew of 100 men;

The sloop of war PAWNEE, 10 heavy guns, with a crew of 150 men;

together with the BALTIC, the ATLANTIC, the ILLINOIS, and other steamers; the squadron numbered altogether 11 ships, carrying 285 guns, and 2,400 men.

There was now no doubt that the first blow would be struck against Charleston. President Lincoln hesitated no longer, and showed to the world his determination, if all attempts at peace should fail, to have recourse to arms.

The Southern Government at Montgomery was, through its spies, kept perfectly well informed of all President Lincoln's measures, and appointed P. G. T. Beauregard commander of Charleston, with the rank of general in the Confederate army.

Beauregard had this appointment bestowed upon him without much being known about his military talents. The son of a rich planter in the State of Louisiana, he was educated at the Military Academy at West Point, and, on leaving that institution, he obtained a second-class certificate. When the Mexican war broke out, he is reported to have distinguished himself as a captain of engineers, and was twice honorably mentioned for his brave and meritorious conduct in the battles of Contreras and Churubusco. After the battle of Chapultepec, he was promoted to the rank of major. On the termination of the Mexican war, he received a commission from the United States Government to construct a mint and custom house in New Orleans; he was subsequently appointed Superintendent of the Military Academy at West Point, by President Buchanan. That appointment, however, was cancelled forty-eight hours after it had been made, and he then joined the army of the Confederacy, with the rank of general.

On my return to Charleston, I found a complete change in the aspect of the place, the whole town and its neighborhood having the appearance of a vast camp. An army of 30,000 men was assembling against Fort Sumter and its small garrison, just as if a place as strong as Gibraltar was about to be invested. Including the United States squadron, which was cruising in the vicinity, the enemy could not oppose to this force more than 2,500 men.

Beauregard displayed great activity in his operations. He ordered siege works to be erected on Morris and Sullivan's Islands, and batteries to be placed in position, many, indeed, without any apparent object. As soon as a mound of earth was thrown up and a gun mounted, a commander of a battery rose, like magic, from the earth. In a short time, no less than thirteen batteries were noted down in Governor Pickens's list, with Forts Moultrie and Pinckney, under the able management of Major Ripley, and there were also two colossal iron-plated ships. The preparations portended a tremendous siege and bombardment, and my curiosity was greatly excited.

To stimulate the energy of the troops, Governor Pickens visited the different quarters accompanied by his beautiful wife and his niece. Grand parades were held, flags presented to the different regiments by fair hands, and patriotic speeches made; in short, both officers and men declared that they were determined to conquer or die before Charleston. Oh, Sumter! poor Sumter! thy doom, thought I, is near at hand!

Whilst all these preparations were going on outside that stronghold, Major Anderson, within its walls, was not idle. When he took possession of Fort Sumter, it was in a very tolerable state of defence; according to the statement of well-informed Americans, the fort was bombproof. It lies about three English miles from Charleston, and is a prominent feature in the bay. It is built upon an artificial islet, having a foundation of sand and mud, which, by sunken blocks of stone and granite from the quarries of the Northern States, had been transformed into a hard and solid mass. Some idea may be formed of the cost and care bestowed on its construction, from the well-known fact that the foundation alone cost more than half a million of dollars, and took ten years in completion.

The walls, covered with slate and masonry, were sixty feet in height, and from ten to twelve feet in thickness, containing three galleries on the north, east, and west sides. Major Anderson found more guns and ammunition there than his small garrison needed. As regards supplies, he was equally well off, for since the 24th of December, 1860, the State of South Carolina had taken care to send them in regularly.

Nothing now remained to put these works and the skill of the commander to the test but a little real fighting.

On the 8th of April, an agent of the Government at Washington made his appearance at General Beauregard's headquarters, with the intelligence that the United States had despatched a squadron with supplies for Fort Sumter. General Beauregard at once forwarded the despatch to his Government at Montgomery, and shortly after received a despatch in reply from Mr. Walker, the Secretary of War, ordering him to demand, categorically, the surrender of Fort Sumter, and, in case of refusal, to commence the bombardment without delay. General Beauregard sent his first adjutant, as commissioner, to Major Anderson, and through him peremptorily demanded the surrender of the fort. The gallant Major smiled at so *naïve* a demand, and stated in reply that his honor and his duty compelled him to hold the fort for his Government. On being asked whether he intended to treat the unprotected city as a hostile town, he replied, "Only if I am compelled to do so." So ended the parley.

President Lincoln's message created a lively sensation amongst the good people of Charleston, especially as, at the same time, Governor Pickens issued an order calling upon all men from eighteen to forty-five years of age to assemble at the Capitol for the purpose of being formed into new regiments. Further orders were sent into the immediate neighborhood for the creation of four other regiments of infantry and two regiments of cavalry. It was not until then that *ambulances* were prepared for the wounded, and that the medical men of the town and vicinity were ordered to join the army. The Government, indeed, was intent on taking measures, as if some great battle was on the eve of being fought. When at last seven guns were fired as a signal for the men of Charleston capable of bearing arms to present themselves at the Capitol, the excitement in the population knew no bounds. Every man seized upon some weapon or other, no matter what, resolved to fight in good earnest.

It was a curious sight to see men carrying guns without locks, bayonets without muskets, Turkish sabres too, and some men even had old French cuirasses buckled on; all anxious to play a part in the attack on Fort Sumter, then quietly reposing three miles off in the middle of the bay.

Drums beat throughout the whole of the night, and the bells kept ringing so incessantly that Major Anderson and his little garrison must have been in an awful state of alarm. At the corner of every street, in every bar room, crowds assembled and warlike speeches were made, whilst cannon rattled along the pavement, and bodies of horse and foot marched past in rapid succession. The elder portion of the community took upon themselves the duties of police, whilst the blacks looked on with a shrewd eye to see if perchance anything might turn up in their favor. Every man was determined to do something, and these disinterested citizens made such a noise and confusion that one might have fancied they were so many Bedlamites. To add to the tumult, about midnight one of those terrible storms so common in the Southern States burst forth; the thunder pealed and roared to an extent that threatened to shake the earth to its centre, and the lightning flashed in forks of lurid light through the dark rolling clouds, until the storm terminated in real torrents of rain. It was a grand spectacle of Southern nature in one of its most striking aspects.

As early as half past four on the morning of the 12th of April, orders were sent to Major Ripley, at Fort Moultrie, and to Captain Wilson, commander of the battery on Cumming's Island, to open fire. The batteries soon commenced firing, and two hours afterward were responded to by the guns of Fort Sumter. Gradually every battery was engaged, and the air resounded with the prolonged roar of heavy guns. The whole population of Charleston was now in the greatest state of excitement. The church steeples and housetops were crowded by thousands of spectators, eager to see a contest of artillery, and watching with feverish excitement the progress of the struggle. At length all the forts, batteries, and ships were engaged; when suddenly a ship of war of the United

States hove in sight, on Charleston Bar. Shortly afterward a second ship made its appearance, and signals were exchanged with Major Anderson. Beyond this interchange of signals, however, nothing was done in that quarter; the ships kept at a very respectful distance from our land batteries, leaving Major Anderson to his fate. As evening came on, the fire from the batteries increased, but evidently producing little or no decisive effect. The firing was kept up by our batteries during the whole of the night, which not only afforded much harmless amusement to the good citizens of Charleston, but as much also to the contending soldiers themselves; for, despite the eighteen hours' bombardment, not one drop of blood had been shed in our batteries; and if Major Anderson had not suffered more from our artillery, he might feel satisfied, on this score at least, with the day's work. The reports received at headquarters, from the various batteries engaged after eighteen hours' bombardment, up to eleven o'clock at night, established the fact that no casualty had occurred: not one man was killed or wounded, nor was there a disabled gun.

General Beauregard, at the close of the day's proceedings, could therefore wipe, not the blood, but the dust from his sword, and complacently say, "Enough for to-day!"

On the following morning Major Anderson recommenced firing. The soldiers in our batteries had, however, already come to the conclusion that little harm would ensue, and, therefore, did not allow themselves to be disturbed in their usual avocations. Any experienced European officer could not fail, on taking a glance at our camp, to be considerably astonished at the Spartan self-confidence of our men.

About ten o'clock a dense pillar of smoke was seen to rise from Fort Sumter, whilst the flag was lowered half-mast high, as a signal that the fort was in distress. The United States vessels, which had drifted away during the storm, had again collected together near the bar, and made signals to Fort Sumter. Major Anderson returned the compliment by telegrapihng back to them that he stood in need of speedy help. Meanwhile the fire which had broken out within the fort had spread to the barracks and officers' quarters. The sudden cessation of fire from its batteries was hailed by a loud cheer from our troops, for all now anticipated the moment when Major Anderson and his garrison would surrender unconditionally to the triumphant Beauregard and his valiant army.

Notwithstanding that the firing from Fort Sumter had ceased, our troops kept up theirs with renewed energy, as .if they feared that this harmless amusement would too soon be over. As the smoke and flames in the fort increased, General Beauregard, true on this occasion to his chivalrous character, despatched one of his adjutants, bearing a flag of truce, to Major Anderson, with the message that he trusted the latter would not take it in bad part if he had done him serious damage, and that in case the Major could not master the fire in the fort by the unaided efforts of his men, he should be most willing to send him a detachment of his own troops to help him to do so.

Major Anderson now thought fit to discontinue further resistance, and ordered the white flag to be hoisted as a sign of capitulation.

I confess that at this moment my sense of military honor suffered a keen pang on beholding the flag of the United States lowered, and supplanted by the little flag of the Palmetto State of South Carolina.

In this manner did Major Anderson surrender a stronghold of the Republic, when he ought rather to have buried himself under its ruins than have given it up in so pusillanimous a manner. What could have been the motive that impelled him to commit so disgraceful an act I could not possibly conceive. His garrison, during a thirty hours' bombardment, suffered no loss in either killed or wounded; he had ammunition and provisions enough for full twenty days; the works were in a good state of defence; moreover, outside the bar was a squadron of United States ships of sufficient force to give him confidence and eventual succor.

That little Armada could undoubtedly have soon found a favorable moment to get in motion, and enable him to obtain better conditions than an unconditional surrender.* He could indeed have claimed more favorable conditions from any enemy, however powerful, if he had but resolved to decline all proposals for at least a week, and with the advantages he had, he could have defied superior numbers for that space of time. But the commandant of Fort Sumter, by thus prematurely yielding—uncrippled as he was, except by his own want of resolution—degraded himself in the eyes of all military men—in Europe at least.

Meantime the news of the capitulation spread like wildfire through Charleston, and, as may be imagined, created the greatest sensation. The church bells began to peal, and the cheers and shouts and the bombastic boasting and speechifying of men in a condition of mind more like that of lunatics than reasonable beings, produced a most disagreeable impression upon me.

Couriers were despatched with the astounding news of the fall of Fort Sumter throughout the length and breadth of the land, and drove the excited population everywhere into a state of frenzied delight.

When Major Anderson left the fort, where he had sullied his military reputation, he delivered up his sword to General Beauregard, who, in the politest manner, returned it to him with some well-turned complimentary remarks upon the gallant defence he had made. The Major and the whole of his garrison were allowed free passage to New York, and on their leaving the fort the United States flag was saluted with a salvo of fifty guns. It would seem as if enough powder

---

* The fort was surrendered because the provisions were exhausted. The command took their arms and all private and company property, saluted the flag as it was lowered, and were conveyed to any Northern port they desired.—*Am. Ed.*

had not been already wasted in this sham fighting affair, and so it was deemed advisable to get up a sort of spectacle at the conclusion.

Whilst this complimentary salute was being fired, two of the guns burst, thereby causing four of Major Anderson's men to be mortally wounded. This was the only blood shed during the whole of the operations connected with the capture of the redoubtable Fort Sumter.

This siege and bombardment of Fort Sumter will occupy a conspicuous and not very enviable space in military annals. It will, hereafter, surely be deemed incredible that a bombardment which lasted forty-eight hours, and in which more than 500 missiles from powerful guns were fired, came to a close without causing a single casualty on either side!

The fall of Fort Sumter did not produce the slightest effect upon President Lincoln and his Government; on the contrary, he, as well as the population of the Northern States, thought fit to pay the highest honors to Major Anderson. The President promoted him to the rank of brigadier-general, and his friends hurried in crowds to pay their respects to him.

Some two years have elapsed since that disgraceful capitulation. The name of General Anderson is all but forgotten; and he has not again appeared on any battle field.

On the 14th April, 1861, President Lincoln issued his declaration of war. It is couched in earnest and dignified terms, and runs as follows:

"Whereas, the laws of the United States have been for some time past, and now are, opposed, and the execution thereof obstructed in the States of South Carolina, Georgia, Alabama, Florida, Mississippi, Louisiana, and Texas, by combinations too powerful to be suppressed by the ordinary course of judicial proceedings, or by the powers invested in the marshals by law;

"Now, therefore, I, Abraham Lincoln, President of the

United States, in virtue of the power in me vested by the constitution and the laws, have thought fit to call forth, and hereby do call forth, the militia of the several States of the Union, to the aggregate number of seventy-five thousand, in order to suppress said combinations, and to cause the laws to be duly executed.

"The details for this object will be immediately communicated to the State authorities through the War Department.

"I appeal to all loyal citizens to favor, facilitate, and aid this effort to maintain the honor, the integrity, and the existence of our National Union, and the perpetuity of popular government, and to redress wrongs already long enough endured.

"I deem it proper to say that the first service assigned to the forces hereby called forth will probably be to repossess the forts, places, and property which have been seized from the Union; and in every event the utmost care will be observed, consistently with the objects aforesaid, to avoid any devastation and destruction of or interference with property, or any disturbance of peaceful citizens in any part of the country. And I hereby command the persons composing the combinations aforesaid to disperse and retire peaceably to their respective abodes within twenty days from this date.

"ABRAHAM LINCOLN."

In my opinion, this proclamation did not protest vigorously enough against the conduct of the Southern seceding States. President Lincoln ought to have seen, from their energetic preparations, that Jefferson Davis and his supporters were exerting every nerve to do battle with the Union. He ought to have called out for active service, not 75,000 men, but half a million, and another half million as a reserve. By so doing, he would have given a guarantee to some hundred thousand of dismayed Unionists in the South that he was resolved in earnest to support and protect all loyal subjects throughout the Union.

At Montgomery, President Lincoln's proclamation was received with contempt and derision; illusion reached so far, indeed, that it was rumored the seat of the Confederate Government might shortly be transferred to Washington, as it was confidently hoped that they would make very short work with the United States. Disaffection to the Union now spread rapidly, and one State after another refused passage to the forces of the United States. Maryland alone, of the Southern States, represented by Governor Hicks, promised the President to support him with troops, in his endeavors to compel the seceding States to rejoin the Union by force of arms. At the same time, Governor Hicks issued a proclamation to the citizens, calling upon them to await quietly and patiently the course of events, as he would soon give them an opportunity, through the election of members for Congress, of expressing their opinion whether they wished to remain true to the Republic of the United States, or whether they wished to range themselves on the side of the Confederate Government.

My mission in South Carolina having terminated with the fall of Fort Sumter, I returned forthwith to the State of Virginia, to watch the course of events there.

On the 15th of April, after nearly three months' absence, I arrived safely at Richmond. The appearance of the good old State of Virginia had undergone a complete change. As I entered its capital, my attention was at once attracted to the motley mass of adventurers who had flocked here from every part of the Confederacy; Baltimore, especially, being well represented. These gentry had positively taken possession of the city, as well as the State, and were powerful enough to overawe the Government.

The fall of Fort Sumter, and the bombastic reports issued in all quarters, glorifying the bravery of the troops of South Carolina, under their great leader, Beauregard, put these vagabonds into the greatest state of ecstasy. They compelled the inhabitants to illuminate the city in honor of the renowned victory, under the threat that all windows not lit up were to be smashed, and the occupants of the houses ill treated and handed over to the tender mercies of the rabble. Money and promises from the Government at Montgomery were not wanting to aggravate this sad state of things. At every corner of a street, bar-room brawlers, seasoning their speeches with oaths and curses, might be heard prophesying that on the following day Virginia must leave the Union. An interview, which I had on the very evening of my arrival, with Governor Letcher, who had not escaped insult from the lawless rabble, and with the Hon. John Minor Botts, gave me some hope, however, that the Government of the State of Virginia would make an appeal to the loyal citizens of the United States. Meantime, all that could be done was to await quietly the course of events.

On the following morning, the 18th April, tumultuous crowds assembled at the Capitol, in the square in front of Governor Letcher's house, and, amidst shouts of execration and defiance, demanded the removal of the United States banner, and that the flag of the Confederacy should be forthwith hoisted in its place. One fellow in this unruly mob was too impatient to wait for formal compliance with this demand, so, rushing up the steps of the Capitol, and climbing on to the roof, he attempted to mount the flagstaff that he might tear down the flag of the Union, encouraged and cheered in his efforts by the tumultuous multitude below. He had nearly reached the top when he slipped, and falling on the roof, was severely hurt. This was a bad omen. Shortly afterward a detachment of soldiers was ordered to the spot to keep the crowd in order. In the afternoon, however, the mob increased to such an extent that the small knot of respectable citizens, who resolutely aided the soldiers in their efforts to keep order, were driven back, the Capitol taken by storm, the flag of the Union torn down, and that of the Confederacy hoisted.

I could not but feel moved at this outrageous act of the populace, in thus ignominiously hauling down the flag of the Republic, under which I had found a refuge and a home, especially when I saw how deeply affected were many of the bystanders of both sexes—loyal adherents of the Union—on witnessing the occurrence.

The separation of Virginia from the Union created the greatest enthusiasm amongst those States which had already seceded, for the Confederacy now counted ten States under its iron rule. By the secession of the State of Virginia,—which throughout the whole country, not only from its great extent and prosperity, but from its historical associations and the eminent statesmen it had produced, enjoyed so high a reputation,—the Government at Montgomery hoped effectually to supersede that of Washington. It was firmly believed, moreover, that the State of Maryland would take advantage of this opportunity to leave the Union, and that the Government at Washington would be compelled to remove its seat further northward. All the inducements held out, whether by bribery or otherwise, failed, however, to shake the stanch honesty and strong will of Governor Hicks, who was determined to remain true to the cause of the Republic.

CHAPTER II.

THE RIOT AT BALTIMORE.

Consequences of the secession of Virginia—The Confederate Government is transferred from Montgomery to Richmond—Riot at Baltimore—Movement of the troops.

It ought not to be matter for astonishment that the Government of Washington was greatly incensed at the secession of Virginia from the Union, for the consequence of that act was that the States of Tennessee, Arkansas, and North Carolina quickly followed, and thereby the Confederate Government was sufficiently strengthened to carry on the war on a grand scale. All the railways were voluntarily placed at the disposal of that Government; and it certainly made the best use of this generous offer. The Congress at Montgomery authorized the Government to contract a loan of five million dollars, which was subscribed for immediately. In all the States which had of late seceded, regiments were raised zealously and at much personal sacrifice. All the male population between the ages of eighteen and forty years pressed forward to be enrolled under the Confederate banner; and, indeed, many men of even sixty years of age would not be deterred from taking up arms for their new Government. It is at the same time true that many regiments were only thus suddenly raised because a number of dues and charges were bound up and connected with their formation. Everybody was enthusiastic in support of the war; in my opinion, however, not so much for the sake of fighting in defence of the Confederacy, as from the opinion that, their States having seceded, matters would be soon, if they were not already, arranged; and none looked forward to the terrible events which were to follow. A great many persons availed themselves of their military position in order to travel on their business avocations, or to make little pleasure excursions at the Government's expense. Equipped in stately uniforms, and armed to the teeth with excellent weapons from the military storehouses, which had all been seized by the insurgent Government, these gallant soldiers strutted about without any apparent fear or alarm. It was a kind of general masquerade or carnival. That this was to be succeeded by the stern reality of war, with its bloodshed and misery, never seemed to enter any one's mind. That a future was approaching replete with disaster to the country, which would break up all unity and concord, and lead to the derision of their enemies and the inexpressible sorrow of their friends, was not thought of.

After a while the Government began to put a little military order into this chaos, by placing detachments of troops in the forts of Charleston, Pensacola, Morgan, Jackson, Philip, and Pulaski; whilst all the forces of the different States belonging to the Confederacy were ordered to the State of Virginia, which latter had been selected for the theatre of war. On the 20th of May, the seat of Government was transferred from Montgomery, Alabama, to Richmond, Virginia; and Jefferson Davis, the benefactor elect of the people, made his entry into Richmond amidst the vociferations of his friends and worshippers.

Richmond, the capital of the State of Virginia, and, virtually, indeed, of the whole South, was at this time, as regards its resources in mechanical industry, quite in its infancy, particularly as respects the manufacture of arms, for which the Confederates would indeed have been badly off, had it not been for the opportune aid they received from J. B. Floyd, the late United States Secretary of War, who helped them in their dilemma, dexterously contriving to transfer 115,000 excellent muskets and rifles from the United States military stores at Springfield and Waterford to the camp of the Secessionists. Thus, at the commencement of the war the South had, thanks to Mr. Floyd's good offices, from 150,000 to 200,000 muskets ready for the equipment of their troops.

The Government at Washington was not idle whilst these movements were occurring in the South, and assembled large bodies of troops. And it cannot be denied that, during the confusion and disorder with which it was at first surrounded, the people of the Northern States generally manifested the same kind of patriotic devotion as had been shown in the days of the great Revolution. The men who first responded to the call of their President were the volunteer militia regiments of Massachusetts, who hurried to Washington for the protection of their President and the Republic. The first regiment, on arriving at the railway station of Baltimore, was obliged, in order to reach the station of the railway for Washington, to traverse the city; a portion of the regiment was then conveyed by the horse tramway, the rest being obliged to walk. On the news arriving of the approach of these troops, the vagabond population of the place, always ready for mischief, became highly excited; whilst the police, although well acquainted with the intentions of the mob, offered little or no opposition. This passive conduct of the police authorities can only be construed as actually favoring the riot. Encouraged by this inactivity, and excited by drink, the leaders of the mob proceeded to violent acts. The rails were torn up, and barricades erected in the streets; whilst a part of the rioters, with the Confederate flag at their head, threw themselves in the way of the military, in order to dispute the passage through the town; and stones were thrown at the soldiers, as they were proceeding quietly on their way. Although the officer commanding the troops exhorted the people to let them pass quietly and unmolested, his efforts were in vain, and he was received with groans, hisses, and abuse. This officer maintained perfect self-possession; but when the soldiers were assailed by the mob, and showers of stones increased, he ordered the drums to beat and the men to make ready; and presently, at the word "Fire!" a deadly volley was discharged at the rioters, who, armed with knives and revolvers, commenced a regular struggle with the military. The soldiers forced their way, despite repeated attacks, to the railway station, with the loss of but few men. There, however, they found awaiting them a still more enraged multitude. The directors of the railway had, meanwhile, not been inactive, having hurriedly collected carriages for the conveyance of the troops to Washington. Nevertheless, the train was stopped, and the scene at the station became terrific. The soldiers, having taken their seats in the carriages, the mob continued to abuse them, threatening them with their knives and revolvers, howling and cursing at them incessantly. The police at last made some show of interfering, but without effecting much good; and the people were by this time so excited, that any attempt at expostulation was more calculated to inflame than to soothe them.

The train got off at last, leaving the populace howling and raging at the escape of its intended victims; and to compensate for this they completely demolished the station. As the train was moving off, some soldiers fired into the people, who were collected on each side; and, as is but too frequently the case on such occasions, many fell who had taken no active part in the riot. Several respectable citizens of Baltimore paid for their curiosity with their lives, and many others were dangerously wounded. The revolutionary party in Baltimore, of which we have already had occasion to speak, now developed itself and proceeded to great extremities. The railway bridge over the Susquehanna was burnt down, and Governor Hicks forced unwillingly to join in the movement against the President and the Washington Government. He did not, however, allow himself to be led astray by these would-be representatives of the people of Maryland; and before long placed four regiments at the disposal of the Union Government. For a long while subsequent to these events great disorder and discontent continued to prevail at Baltimore.

Baltimore had to submit to the military power of the Union, whilst the revolutionary element migrated further south. The railroads were soon put in order again, and they enabled the Government to forward from 4,000 to 5,000 men daily to Washington. The Southern party in Maryland protested in vain against the passage of these troops, as also against the military authorities, who had now taken possession of Baltimore and its fortifications. President Lincoln let them protest as much as they liked, and quietly pursued his course. General Butler, who was named Military Governor of Maryland, was a proper man to reëstablish quiet and order after the riotous proceedings which had taken place. The mayor of the city of Baltimore and all the chiefs of the police were dismissed and sent into the fortress as prisoners, and all rebels and criminals brought before a military tribunal, so that in a short time peace and tranquillity were restored.

In the North nothing was heard of but preparations for the war, and "Down with the rebels!" was the general watchword. Nobody seemed, however, to take the trouble to solve the problem of how this end was to be accomplished.

To prove in black and white that the North had a greater population and more wealth than the South—that it possessed a navy—seemed to be every man's favorite occupation; indeed, the merchants in the North went so far as to announce as an unquestionable fact, that the South would surely be starved, if they resolved simply to withhold corn and other articles of consumption from them.

The warlike plans of the North at this time may be thus succinctly summed up:

Simply to send 25,000 men across the Potomac to march on Richmond; to send another body of 25,000 men to Cairo on the Mississippi; to close all communications with the West; and to keep 25,000 more men as a reserve force.

In short, the journalists of the North had planned their strategical movements with such nicety and military genius, that a mere parade and march was all that was required for the subjugation of the half-starved Southerners. Soldiers were only enlisted for three months; and it was hoped and expected that the whole campaign would be over in that time. President Lincoln, however, fortunately did not allow himself to be led astray by these newspaper vagaries; and issued a second proclamation, calling out a further body of 45,000 men to serve for the time the war should last; giving orders at the same time for ten additional regiments to the regular army, and for an augmentation of 18,000 men in the navy. From all this it was clearly to be deduced that President Lincoln fully foresaw the dangers and difficulties of the task he had before him. As soon as a sufficient body of troops had been assembled at Washington, they received orders to cross the Potomac immediately, and to proceed along the Orange and Alexandria Railway in the direction of Richmond; whilst another column was sent from Pennsylvania through Maryland into the valleys of Virginia. The first military act was the occupation of the not unimportant town of Alexandria, which was effected on the 24th of May; on which the Southern troops fell back to the Manassas Junction, General Bonham assuming the command of those from South Carolina.

CHAPTER III.

DESTRUCTION OF THE FLEET AT PORTSMOUTH.

Proclamation of President Lincoln—Virginia the seat of War—General Lee commander-in-chief—Destruction of Harper's Ferry—Establishments at Portsmouth—Burning of the fleet.

ON the 19th April, 1861, President Lincoln issued a proclamation, in which he declared all ports of the Southern States under blockade. Hostilities between the North and South had therefore regularly commenced; troops were drawn together on both sides, and Virginia was generally acknowledged to be the chief seat of the war. It now became the endeavor of both parties to inflict as much damage as possible on each other; and this frequently was carried out with such a spirit of Vandalism as to shock the civilized world. One of these acts was the destruction of the fleet at Portsmouth; and I will endeavor to describe this event in a few words.

Immediately after the publication of President Lincoln's proclamation, President Jefferson Davis appointed the *quondam* United States colonel of cavalry, Robert E. Lee, commander-in-chief of all the forces in Virginia. The troops of the United States army abandoned Harper's Ferry, one of the most important manufactories of arms in America, on the 19th of April, after destroying the greater part of the buildings and machinery, and retreated to friendly territory. This destruction of property was, however, carried out so hurriedly, that a great many most valuable machines fell into the hands of the Confederate Government almost wholly intact, and they rendered very good service subsequently.

Great preparations were on the same day made at Richmond for the purpose of attacking the harbor of Portsmouth, which is situated at the estuary of the James river. The officers and Government officials of the harbor, who were pre-informed of this plan, lost no time in consummating their preparations for the destruction of this, the greatest military port of the United States. The officers in command, instead of endeavoring to hold these works for their Government, seemed, to have become quite bewildered, and incapable of recognizing the great importance of their position; so in the face of the most favorable circumstances they condemned to the flames that fine military harbor, on which all the former Governments of the United States had spent millions of dollars in order to render it one of the first in America.

It was a grand and imposing spectacle to see the columns of flame ascending from the majestic ships at anchor in the port and in course of construction in the docks. Amongst the ships lying there were, the line-of-battle ship *Pennsylvania*, of 3,500 tons, carrying 131 guns (once the largest man-of-war in the world), the beautiful frigates *Columbus* and *Delaware*, and the subsequently so-dreaded *Merrimac*. The frigate *Raritan* and schooner *Dolphin* were consumed by the flames, and the docks, which had cost millions of dollars, were blown up. The signal for this general destruction was given at midnight; and in a few minutes these magnificent productions of the energy and genius of man were encircled by a girdle of flame; and a slight breeze which sprang up increased the conflagration rapidly. The naval workmen and the whole garrison were meanwhile busily employed in conveying valuables on board the two vessels, *Pawnee* and *Cumberland*, which were riding at anchor, and both vessels were laden to the very portholes. At four o'clock in the morning the tide turned, and a signal sent up by a rocket from the *Pawnee* announced to the men in the dockyard that the moment had arrived for consummating the work of destruction, and in a few minutes the dockyard was one blaze of flames—a truly grand but saddening spectacle. The crackling of the fire and rustling of the flames, the falling of the masts, the explosion of the ships doomed to destruction, the blowing up of the buildings, which had been undermined—in fact, the whole of this gigantic work of destruction—was a catastrophe on which I cannot look back, even now, after the time that has elapsed, without a shudder. It was one of those silly and cowardly acts of destruction which, while causing no harm to the enemy, crippled their own Government, and caused them irremediable loss. Had the commandant of this place, his officers, and the garrison of the naval dockyard of Portsmouth, understood how to preserve this valuable and important place to their Government and country, their names would have lived in history, and been gratefully recorded in the hearts of their countrymen. They might well have waited for the indulgence of this strange eagerness for destruction until the moment of attack, instead of forestalling that event by the premature sacrifice of the accumulated wealth of so noble a harbor. The military port and harbor of Portsmouth ceased to exist on the 20th of April, 1861, and the country around was lighted up for miles as the *Pawnee* and frigate *Cumberland* sailed down the bay, laden with the valuables saved from the fiery wreck, to seek shelter under the guns of Fortress Monroe.

CHAPTER IV.

THE BATTLE OF BETHEL.

THE Southern troops, about 1,800 strong, had, under the command of General B. Magruder, constructed defensive works in the vicinity of the church of Bethel: which place is about nine miles distant from Hampton, where the enemy's troops had established their camp. On the 9th of May, Major-General Butler, who commanded the Federal troops, sent forward a detachment of 4,000 men, who were to advance on Bethel in two separate columns, with the view, if possible, of driving away the enemy and destroying the defensive works which they had erected. The command was given to Colonel Pierce. The first column crossed the river a little below the Southern posts, whilst the second column effected a similar passage lower down. No opposition whatever was made to the landing of these troops; and while the first column was attacking the Confederate troops in flank, the second assailed them in front. A battery of Richmond mortars, under the personal command of Major Randolph (now Secretary of War) opposed the attack. On this day Major Randolph gave the first proofs of his undaunted courage, and gallantly maintained his post. In the meanwhile the Federal troops attacked with such resolution that they succeeded in gaining possession of the first outwork without suffering much loss, and our soldiers were obliged to retreat in disorder, and with the loss of two pieces of artillery. This impetuous attack of the enemy somewhat dismayed our young and inexperienced soldiers, who were frightened, moreover, at the numbers of the attacking force, and not considering that a covered position has a threefold advantage, they rapidly abandoned that position, throwing themselves into the principal work, which lay to the rear. The enemy took a firm footing in the stormed outposts; indeed, the Confederates were very near losing their whole line of fortified works, and the troops became so disheartened that the consequences would certainly have been most disastrous, had not General Magruder, with great presence of mind and calmness, ordered four companies of the 1st North Carolina regiment, under the command of Major Bridges, to retake the outwork at all hazards. This order was splendidly carried out by the four companies. They advanced with coolness and determination, in the face of a heavy fire of artillery, which assailed them from the front, and on arriving within sixty yards' distance of the outwork, with loud hurrahs, they advanced at a run to the attack, and dislodged the Federal soldiers who held possession of it, with the greatest ease, causing them to retreat in the greatest disorder, leaving what they had but just before stormed in the hands of the Confederates.

The enemy continued to keep up an uninterrupted fusilade, which, however, being directed in a most irregular manner, inflicted but little loss on the Confederate troops. Whilst we established ourselves again in the reconquered outwork, our batteries reopened their fire—not, however, with much effect, the enemy's position being too well covered. His right flank leaned on a small, but dense wood, and his left was closed by some houses. A twelve-pounder battery responded to our own; it was, however, so well hidden by the wood and the houses, that we were only enabled to guess its position from its fire. The enemy's battery sent forth a hail of projectiles at us from a distance of from five hundred to six hundred yards; but, fortunately for us, their practice was so bad that the damage occasioned by this continual fire was inconsiderable. General Magruder at the same time ordered the commander of our batteries only to reply to the enemy's fire with the utmost care, and when large masses of troops appeared in line of battle. A little after one o'clock a large column of the enemy was descried on the road from Hampton, hastening to reach a small bridge in our front. This column was under the command of Major Winthrop, the first adjutant of General Butler. Major Winthrop led his men on to the attack admirably, and they advanced boldly against our outposts, but were received with such a tremendous fire from the 1st North Carolina Infantry, that they were hurled back in complete disorder.

Our marksmen, who were under fire for the first time, occasioned us no small confusion. They were utterly wanting in self-confidence, and would inquire before each shot, "May I fire? I think I can hit him," &c. As the enemy was being repulsed, a ball struck Major Winthrop in the breast. He was one of the most meritorious officers of the United States army, and his gallantry earned for him the admiration of our officers and soldiers. Colonel Hill, commanding the 1st North Carolina regiment, paid a high tribute to the memory of this brave officer, in his report of the battle. Major Winthrop fell while vainly endeavoring, from a height, to rally his discomfited men. The United States lost in him a most excellent officer. During the hottest part of the fire, a small body of the enemy had ensconced themselves in a house to our left, and occasioned us much annoyance by their intermittent fire.

A company of volunteers was ordered to clear this house of its troublesome occupants, and to raze it to the ground. This work was performed with consummate coolness and energy. The volunteers boldly attacked the house, and dislodged the enemy, who availed themselves of every aperture to fire on them.

After a while the enemy ceased firing, and leaving their dead and wounded on the field, retreated in ·haste beyond range of our guns. The results of the battle of Bethel were of incalculable advantage to our troops, as it inspired them with great confidence in their own capabilities. Although our little army generally behaved well and gallantly in the face of an enemy double its strength on this day, yet the bearing of the 1st North Carolina regiment is especially worthy of praise, as it was the most exposed of all our corps to the fire of the enemy's artillery, and behaved with the greatest coolness and determination.

CHAPTER V.

COLONEL PORTERFIELD'S VOLUNTEERS.

Whilst the South was thus showing a front to the enemy in the Virginian Peninsula, and earning its respect, it met with a reverse in the West, which nearly obliged the Confederate Government to withdraw further south from Richmond.

Colonel Porterfield, commanding the Confederate forces at Philippi, received an order from General Lee, the commander-in-chief of the army in Virginia, to raise the volunteers to the strength of 5,000 men, and to act in concert with the officials of the Baltimore and Ohio railway.

General Lee had, however, quite misunderstood the character of Colonel Porterfield, who was one of that numerous class of heroes that discourse much and profess to execute all kinds of impossibilities, but are at a loss how to act in the first really serious encounter. Porterfield was truly a fine example of such heroes. He had no sooner arrived at the district in which he was to recruit, than he discovered that all the counties were very favorably disposed to the Union. His first move therefore was, to ensconce himself in a comparatively safe nook, and instead of proceeding to act with energy and circumspection, he addressed a most wonderful letter to General Lee. In this letter poor Porterfield described himself as surrounded on all sides by thousands of enemies, and begged the General to send him a sufficient military force, that he might be enabled to proceed effectively with the organization of the volunteers. It was only after receiving reinforcements, that Colonel Porterfield actually commenced organizing his army. This beginning, however, showed but poor results, and the general reply which he received to his invitations to join the Confederacy was given in the negative by the people, coupled with the intimation that if they did want to fight they should do so in defence of the Union.

Colonel Porterfield strolled through the mountains of Virginia, like a minstrel of the olden time, exhorting the population to join the gallant army to which he belonged, and to follow the banner of the exalted Government of the Confederation. After resorting to numerous expedients, he succeeded in gathering under his flag a wonderful assemblage of ragamuffins. In a short time his little army had increased to 200 infantry and 300 cavalry, and at Grafton he pitched his tents. As soon as the United States general was informed of the circumstance, he broke up his camp, and overcoming all difficulties, advanced straight against Porterfield's force.

When informed of the enemy's advance, Porterfield might have fallen back on Philippi, and he did actually order the destruction of the Cheat bridge. This order was, however, imperfectly carried out. Even his outposts were so carelessly placed, as to betray an utter ignorance of military tactics; thus it befel that the enemy came upon him like a thunderbolt, when he and all his men indiscriminately took to their heels.

Throwing away their arms, all Porterfield's levies fled for safety to the mountains, and the Colonel himself, who on this occasion displayed an activity of movement quite surprising, arrived at General Lee's headquarters more dead than alive. The poor Colonel had positively nothing to say either for himself or for his men, further than to affirm that his little force had been attacked by overwhelming numbers, and that they had fought like lions; that his army might be, for all he knew, cut to pieces. This was the sum total of the account he had to give of himself and his followers. The Colonel could not explain how he alone had managed to escape and reach headquarters. He was subsequently brought before a court martial at Richmond, but gave so clever an explanation of his conduct, that the members of that court, who, possibly from a fellow feeling for the accused, not only acquitted him of all blame, but also bestowed their praise upon him for his valorous conduct.

CHAPTER VI.

M'CLELLAN'S SUCCESS AT RICH MOUNTAIN.

State of affairs in Western Virginia—The Confederate army under General Garnett—M'Clellan's plans—The ground in Virginia—Strength of the Southern army—Attack—General Rosecrans remains behind—Colonel Pegram—M'Clellan's indefatigable pursuit—Retreat—Surprise—The engagement at Carrick's Ford—Colonel Tagliaferro—A mistake—General Garnett falls—Loss of artillery and baggage—Disorganized state of the Confederate army—M'Clellan's talents.

WHILST the events just described were taking place in Winchester and Manassas, a great change had occurred at the theatre of war in Western Virginia. What under all circumstances may be considered as a large army of the Confederates, had been collected, and the command intrusted to General Garnett, who at Rich Mountain, Randolph County, North-Western Virginia, took up a position admirably adapted by nature, from whence he could without any anxiety watch the movements of General M'Clellan, who was advancing on Beverley, and had not masked his intention to take up a position in General Garnett's rear, so as to cut off his communications with General Lee. No military man in Europe can form any idea of the position and circumstances of this Western campaign, unless he possesses an accurate knowledge of the *terrain* upon which the military movements took place. The whole of Western Virginia consists of barren, unproductive, mountainous tracts, intersected by strips of forest land. The roads and means of communication are of the most primitive description; and as regards supplies for his troops, the General is obliged to draw them from a long distance.

The strength of General Garnett's corps was from 7,000 to 8,000 men, infantry, 15 guns, 6-pounders and 12-pounders, and 6 squadrons of cavalry. The troops were well armed, suited for mountain warfare, and hardened to their work by long habit. As already stated, General Garnett's position was judiciously chosen and well adapted for an excellent defensive basis of operations, both by nature and as by the aid of art.

Colonel Pegram, with a body of 3,000 men, took possession of the district of Rich Mountain; whilst General Garnett, with the main body of his army, took up his position at Laurel Hill.

For this wearisome and tiresome campaign, the Government of the Northern States selected two of the best and most experienced officers of the United States army—Generals M'Clellan and Rosecrans. It was in this campaign that M'Clellan for the first time drew public attention upon himself, and won the hearts of his men by the circumspection as well as by the bravery which he displayed. It was he who shook the Federal army out of the lethargy into which it had fallen, and led it to a victory which, under other circumstances, would have put an end to the existence of the Confederate army in the West.

General M'Clellan, who was well informed of the position of the Confederate army, contemplated, by a determined blow, on the 5th of July, to annihilate our corps, and thus to put an end to the campaign in Western Virginia, which had become a very troublesome one for the Federals. At a conference between the two generals of the enemy's army, the following arrangement was made: That M'Clellan should undertake the front attack, whilst General Rosecrans, with his force, was to manœuvre in such a way to attack the enemy's army without delay, and endeavor to reach the main body of the army by the flank. By combined and energetic action in the execution of this plan, it was hoped that the campaign would terminate in the capture of the whole of General Garnett's division.

In this campaign, General M'Clellan for the first time appeared in the character of an independent commander; and we cannot refrain from bearing testimony in favor of a man who commenced his career as a leader in so brilliant a manner. M'Clellan's army was by no means in good campaigning order; it consisted of troops gathered together from all parts of the Union. Not only were the regiments collected and mixed up together from different States, so that the troops had scarcely any knowledge of each other, but they were also unequally and badly armed. Despite these drawbacks—so trying to an energetic general—M'Clellan by his prudence and precautions overcame them all.

With care and attention he endeavored to form the spirit of his troops, and to make them regardless of fatigue and privations. And as soon as he felt that he had gained the confidence of his officers and men, he did not delay one moment to carry out the plans which he had formed.

On the 8th July he commenced his march with his troops, and on the same day took up a position at Bealington, opposite Laurel Hill, then left a portion of his troops behind as a corps of observation, and advanced with the main body in rapid strides toward Rich Mountain. This march was one of those fatiguing operations which such a country as America can alone offer an example of. Through pathless woods, over high hills, through streams and rivulets, the soldiers had to force their way. Added to this, the rain never ceased to pour down. Despite all these obstacles the men kept on without murmuring; they overcame every difficulty with a facility which entitled them to an honorable comparison with the tried soldiers of Europe. M'Clellan himself was always at the head of his men, to whom he set a good example by cheerfully putting up with every annoyance and privation.

Early on the morning of the 11th July, General Garnett received a despatch from Colonel Pegram, reporting the capture of a United States soldier, who had given information that General M'Clellan, with nine regiments, had arrived near Rich Mountain, and had given orders for the attack to commence on the following day; further, that General Rosecrans, with 4,000 men, was manœuvring in his rear, to cut off any retreat that might be attempted on the part of General Garnett; that consequently he, Colonel Pegram, had ordered Colonel Scott's regiment to take up a good position, there to await the enemy's approach.

On the receipt of Colonel Pegram's despatch General Garnett sent him orders to hold his position against all odds, and to defend it to the last man.

Colonel Pegram had scarcely got his troops placed ready for action, when General M'Clellan's men, with a loud cheer, rushed forward from a defile and attacked the Colonel in his excellent position. At this moment the artillery opened fire, which was reëchoed by all the mountains round. It was a fine military spectacle. The thunder of the guns, the breaking of the branches of the trees as they were smashed, the cheers of the enthusiastic Federal troops, the crack of the rifles, the beating of drums and clanging of trumpets: in short, the whole battle ground and its vicinity offered a picture such as would be indelibly impressed upon the memory of a soldier. The battle had waged for nearly two hours on this side when Colonel Pegram began to feel that he could not hold his ground much longer. He therefore endeavored to retreat, as his men were tired and their ammunition nearly expended.

General M'Clellan, however, was by no means inclined to lose the ground he had already gained, and thus Colonel Pegram had no other alternative than to fall at his post or sur render. Pegram adopted the latter alternative, and surrendered his post with guns and baggage.

General M'Clellan, however, was not, as yet, satisfied with the result of the day's work. He hourly expected the advance of General Rosecrans, but he found that on this occasion he had overrated his activity. Rosecrans proved timid at this emergency: he was swayed by doubts; he first marched, then halted, as if he did not quite comprehend the completeness of M'Clellan's plans. If he had performed his part as well as that General did his, not one man of General Garnett's corps would have brought the news of its defeat to Richmond; the whole corps would have been annihilated or made prisoners.

As soon as General M'Clellan had made Colonel Pegram's troops lay down their arms, he proceeded to carry out his manœuvre without delay, without waiting for General Rosecrans, and accordingly advanced to attack the forces under General Garnett.

When General Garnett received the unexpected news of the capitulation of Colonel Pegram, he, fearing the energy and determination of M'Clellan, ordered the position on Laurel Hill to be abandoned, and in all haste fell back on Huttonsville. Colonel Scott, who, with his regiment, had received orders to prevent the advance of General Rosecrans, immediately on receiving intelligence of Colonel Pegram's capitulation, hastily left his position and withdrew to a more respectable distance from the enemy. Even now, if General Rosecrans had, in the spirit of a brave and intelligent officer, carried out the plan agreed upon, and advanced to the attack, there was still plenty of time for him to take a brilliant part in the conclusion of the action. Colonel Scott's rapid flight must have dispelled any doubts he might have entertained respecting the inexperience and bad equipment of his troops. There can be no doubt that the conduct of Rosecrans on this occasion offers a remarkable contrast to that of General M'Clellan.

General Garnett was placed in a desperate position by M'Clellan's bold advance and Colonel Pegram's capture. In his retreat on Huttonsville he found that, owing to Colonel Scott's somewhat too hasty retreat, he would have to force his way over the best practicable mountain passes to Hardy County.

The retreat was effected in some order, although the roads were scarcely wide enough to allow a cart to pass; and on the following morning, the army, after a most fatiguing march, reached Little Cheat, where officers and men laid down upon the grass to restore themselves, in some degree, from the fatigue they had undergone.

They had scarcely been encamped one hour, when a roll of musketry along the whole line of outposts announced that the indefatigable enemy was already upon them, and had renewed the attack.

Without allowing his tired soldiers a moment's respite, M'Clellan hotly pursued our army, and although continually checked and kept at bay, by our gallant reserve, still continued the attack with unabated energy. Without hesitation, he boldly gave battle at every point; and although the fighting cannot be called more than skirmishing on a large scale, it, nevertheless, lasted throughout the day.

In the evening the news came in that a company of a Georgia regiment had been cut off by the enemy and made prisoners.

This little episode is known by the name of Battle of Carrick's Ford. M'Clellan followed it up, and drove our troops from their covered position across the river, and captured the greater portion of our baggage.

The activity displayed by the General on this occasion is deserving of high praise. Nothing seemed to stand in his way; despite the heavy, intermittent rain, the execrable roads, his troops displayed a fortitude and an energy that commands admiration. For two days, with indefatigable determination, he followed close upon our heels. Whenever we sought a few moments' rest, we were aroused by the fire of his riflemen at our outposts; and the bullets, which were flying about in all directions, made our position anything but comfortable.

As soon as we had got our artillery safely over Carrick's Ford, Colonel Tagliaferro was ordered to occupy the high banks of the river with his regiment, and to keep the enemy occupied as long as possible, so that our troops, who were quite worn out, might get some rest. Colonel Tagliaferro had scarcely taken up his position when the advanced skirmishers of the enemy appeared in view. At first our men fancied that they were the Georgia troops supposed to have been cut off, and they welcomed them with a loud cheer; but when, instead of a courteous response to this compliment, an unfriendly shower of bullets was sent as a greeting, knocking over many of our men, the mistake was discovered somewhat too late; but the enemy's fire was promptly returned. The officer in command of the enemy's outpost now got one of his batteries into position, and hammered away at us most unmercifully. Twice he attempted to cross the river, but was each time driven back by our men at the point of the bayonet. Whilst this skirmishing was going on, General Garnett had ordered the guns and baggage he still had left to be hurried forward, and sent orders to the troops engaged to form the rear guard of the retreat.

Our retreat was effected without much opposition, as the enemy, probably exhausted by fighting and forced marches, and by our energetic resistance, needed rest. At the second ford, a short distance beyond the first, General Garnett was shot by one of the enemy' sriflemen. This officer had scarcely got his troops across the river, when he ordered a company of the 23d Virginia regiment to occupy the bushes along the bank, and promised that he himself would take the command of the company charged with the defence of the ford. At the same time, firing was heard in the rear of our army. The enemy must have outflanked us, and a panic ensued in our rear guard. General Garnett, however, remained calm and unconcerned. He ordered the soldiers to remain firm, and to retreat without fear. He had scarcely given the order when he sunk to the earth, shot through the body by a bullet. One of the enemy's riflemen had fired the fatal shot which deprived us of one of our bravest officers. The General's horse galloped off up the road, besprinkled with blood, announcing the sad news of the death of our leader.

General M'Clellan, who might feel well satisfied with the result of the day, here gave up the pursuit. Having defeated and demoralized our army, he remained master of a large number of prisoners, with the greater portion of our guns and baggage as booty. Verily could he report to Washington:

"Our success is complete; secession in this part of the country is stopped."

The loss of the battle of Rich Mountain was a severe blow to our young army, and created a painful sensation throughout the Southern States. If the Government at Washington had only had the sense to take advantage of this success, it would probably, in a short time, have brought back the whole of Virginia under its rule. Instead of staking its existence and intrusting the weal and woe of the country to the hands of inexperienced generals, it ought at once to have shown its appreciation of the talent and energy of General M'Clellan, and without hesitation have given him the command of the army on the Potomac. Had it done so, the disaster at Manassas, so detrimental to the Federal cause, might have been avoided; for, after the successes achieved by M'Clellan in the western portion of Virginia, he would have been received by the troops of the Potomac, not as a stranger, but as an old acquaintance, with confidence and enthusiasm. The soldiers would then have had a commander whose success and devotion must have inspired them with respect, and they would have fulfilled their hard duties with cheerfulness and zeal.

That the Government at Washington was aware of M'Clellan's talents is proved by the fact that, when seriously pressed and alarmed, the command of the army of the Potomac was offered to him at a time when that army was all but destroyed, and Washington itself in danger of being captured by the Confederates. Then, as we shall presently see, when no one had the courage to rally the army which had been so terribly cut up at Manassas, when many a bold hero shrugged his shoulders and kept aloof, he came forward as a saviour of his country's cause, to fill up the sad void caused by a disastrous defeat. By prudence and determination he soon succeeded in again forming an army which, by its extent and efficiency, created considerable alarm in the South. But the enemy they had most cause to fear was General M'Clellan himself, the ablest and best officer of the Union, whose military qualities commanded the respect of his opponents.

CHAPTER VII.

MOVEMENTS ON THE POTOMAC.

Harper's Ferry—General Johnston joins the Confederacy—Position of the troops on the Potomac—Harper's Ferry evacuated—The railway bridge blown up—Colonel Jackson operates against General Patterson—Battle—Patterson's cunning—Manœuvre to weaken General Beauregard's main army—Johnston's position.

THE war now began to develop itself with activity on the Potomac, especially in the vicinity of Harper's Ferry, which had been abandoned by the Federal troops. General Joseph Johnston, who previously had held the rank of Quartermaster-General in the United States army, tendered his resignation as soon as the war commenced, and placed himself at the disposal of the Confederate Government, which did not hesitate for a moment to accept his services, and intrusted him with the command of the important post of Harper's Ferry. On the 27th of May, 1861, General Beauregard was relieved of his command at Charleston, and was at first ordered to proceed on service to Corinth, in Mississippi; but whilst on his way to Richmond he received counter orders, and was appointed to the command of the Confederate army, known by the name of the Army of the Potomac.

General Johnston's whole force at Harper's Ferry consisted of thirteen regiments of infantry, ten companies of cavalry, and seven companies of artillery; doubtless a respectable force. His duty was to watch both banks of the Potomac, and to drive back any attempted advance of the enemy in that quarter. Having reconnoitred the whole neighborhood he resolved to maintain his position as long as the Government should deem it necessary for him to do so.

The demonstrations of the United States troops were chiefly confined to outpost skirmishes, and their plans depended upon the movements of General M'Clellan, who was to push forward with his *corps d'armée* into the valleys of Virginia. General Patterson, who was posted with his troops in Maryland and Pennsylvania, also waited for General M'Clellan's movements, previously to advancing by Harper's Ferry on Winchester, to form a junction with M'Clellan's army. On the 13th of June our outposts announced the approach of General M'Clellan's troops. A detachment was at once ordered forward to stop him in his advance, and on the 15th of June, early in the morning, the order was given to evacuate Harper's Ferry, and to fall back on Winchester. The day after the order had been given for the evacuation of Harper's Ferry, one of those painful catastrophes occurred, which always follow in the wake of war. All the able-bodied inhabitants took to flight, and preparations were made to give up the whole place to destruction. The first prey to demolition was that wonderfully constructed railway bridge which here spans the broad stream of the Potomac. At a given signal this structure was blown up into the air with a terrific explosion. All the buildings connected with it, the station, engines, locomotives, warehouses, as well as a flourishing town, with all its trade and prosperity, were condemned to destruction.

It was a sad spectacle to see the columns of flame and smoke rolling upward; and with a feeling of sadness I turned away from this deplorable spectacle of ruin, and rode after the troops, which in dense bodies were marching along the Martinsburg road. The object of this flank movement was to get between Winchester and the army of General Patterson, which was now crossing the Potomac at William's Ford. Patterson, hearing of our evacuation of Harper's Ferry, ordered his troops to cross the Potomac in all haste to see if he could not arrive in time to save something.

General Johnston quietly continued his march to Winchester, where it was very easy for him to hold General M'Clellan in check, as also to prevent any further advance of Patterson, whilst at the same time it was very easy for him to form a junction with General Beauregard, who was stationed at Manassas Gap.

Advices, however, which we received from Maryland, gave us certain information that General Patterson intended to make another manœuvre, and induced General Johnston to direct Colonel "Stonewall" Jackson to advance with his brigade to the vicinity of Martinsburg, to support Colonel Stuart, who, with his regiment of cavalry, was acting as a corps of observation.

On the 2d July, General Patterson again crossed the Potomac. Colonel Jackson carried out the instructions he had received to the letter, and retired with his troops. The advanced guard of General Patterson's division, fancying that Jackson's brigade had taken to flight, made rather too hasty a pursuit. Colonel Jackson took two battalions of the 5th Virginia regiment and a six-pounder battery, and placed them in a most advantageous position, where his small force was well covered. He then accepted the battle that was offered him, and it was not until he feared that his communication with the main army might be cut off that he retired, quietly and unmolested, taking with him fifty-three prisoners. As soon as General Johnston was informed of Colonel Jackson's combat, he hastened to offer General Patterson battle. He took up a position five miles from Martinsburg, which was occupied by the Federal troops, and waited patiently four days for the appearance of General Patterson. The latter, however, had neither the courage nor the inclination to return the compliment and accept the challenge of Johnston, although his troops numbered nearly double those of his opponent. After waiting in vain, General Johnston ordered his troops, who were eager for battle, back to Winchester. They had, however, scarcely reached their old quarters when the corps of observation of Colonel Stuart announced the advance of the enemy under General Patterson. Johnston, delighted, hoped now to cross swords with him. At Bunker's Hill, about seven miles from Winchester, Patterson again came to a halt, and remained there quietly till the 7th July.

General Patterson then made preparations as if it was his intention to attack our left wing, but General Johnston now guessed what his plans were, and saw through his subtlety. The sole object of the operations and movements of the enemy was to keep Johnston at Winchester, in order that General Beauregard might be exposed to the main body of the United States army, which, under the command of Major-General M'Dowell, was concentrated near Manassas. Johnston now placed his army in such a position that on the first notification from General Beauregard he should be able to advance directly on Manassas, and thus Patterson's very clever plans, on which he had so confidently calculated, were not attended with any result.

CHAPTER VIII.

BULL RUN.

Preparations of the hostile armies—Strength of the Federal forces—The decisive moment approaches—M'Dowell's attack—Inexperience of the artillery—General Bonham—Longstreet's brigade at Blackburn Fort—Energetic attack of the Federals—Progress of the fight—Object of the battle to try the strength of both armies.

AT the commencement of July, 1861, two of the largest armies which America ever beheld were ranged in hostile positions at a short distance opposite each other, and awaited with eager anxiety the approach af the sanguinary day when North and South were to measure their strength. The Northern troops thought themselves already sure of victory, as they fancied it would be an easy task to disperse the Southern army, and to advance victoriously without much obstacle to Richmond, there to hoist again the star-spangled banner of the great Republic. This opinion was shared by many members of Congress who, it may be supposed, ought to have exercised a wiser judgment. That the whole affair would be over in twelve or fourteen days was considered certain. As regards the equipment of the great Federal army, nothing had been neglected by the Government to place it upon the footing of any European army of the same size. It was provided with excellent artillery, and contained, moreover, bodies of regular troops which the Government had collected together from all its extended territories—the Rocky

Mountains, St. Louis, Jefferson Barracks, Fortress Monroe, &c.—and this fact gave a sort of *prestige* to this army.

As regards its strength, if we do not err, we should estimate it at 50,000 men, inclusive of nine companies of dragoons of the United States regular army, and a park of artillery, of between fifty and sixty pieces, nearly all rifled cannon.

This imposing force was placed under the command of a leader who throughout the whole of the United States enjoyed the reputation of a soldier of the highest military genius, General M'Dowell. This reputation having for its foundation the success he had gained at the Military College at West Point.

General Beauregard was perfectly well informed of all that was going on in General M'Dowell's army, and of the intention of the enemy to force their way to Richmond; every precaution had therefore been taken by him to prevent that plan being carried out. It was a most critical moment for the Confederate army; for, if they were beaten, they had no more resources for carrying on the war to fall back upon.

What Schiller's William Tell says to his arrow, Beauregard might well have said of his army—

> "Should it fall harmless from my hand,
> I have not a second at command;"

and, truly, if the army of the Confederate host were beaten they could scarcely manage to bring another army into the field. Moreover, what would have been the effect in Europe if the South should be defeated? The leaders of the Confederate army must have had an anxious moment when they considered all the circumstances which seemed to combine for their destruction! It must not be forgotten, too, that it was here for the first time that the *élite* of the two hostile armies stood opposite each other.

What changes had taken place in a short lapse of time! For more than eighty years these same enemies, who now looked at each other with feelings of bitter animosity, had led together the life of peaceful citizens, and had made themselves but little acquainted with the art of war, for the war in Mexico was comparatively insignificant. And now this people, who were bound together by brotherly ties, who had the same interests in common, are suddenly split into two factions, arrayed as mortal enemies against each other. "On to Richmond" is the battle cry of one party; "Independence or Death" that of the other.

At Bull Run these exasperated warriors met, indeed, but for a short time. The battle did not last long, but was fierce enough to show, on a small scale, how the hostile factions would exert their energies to make some future battle a decisive one. The engagement at Bull Run may, in fact, be likened to an overture before the great spectacle of war, which, in a short time, was to be performed at Manassas.

Bull Run forms the north frontier of the county which separates it from Fairfax, and on its smiling banks, three miles north of the junction of the Manassas Gap, and the Orange and Alexandria Railway, was fought this memorable engagement, on the 18th of July. Bull Run is a small river which, at this point, runs from west to east, and lower down joins the waters of the Occoquan river. Fine, open, cheerful roads intersect the country here, nearly in every direction. The banks of the river are rocky and steep, but provided with a great number of fords, which from olden time had always been in use. Mitchell's Ford is about halfway between Centreville and Manassas. Each road is about six miles in length.

To oppose the enemy's movements, who, as General Beauregard suspected, were operating on Manassas, he withdrew his farthest advanced troops from the lines of Bull Run more toward his centre. On the morning of the 17th July, Beauregard's troops had taken up a position from Mills Ford to Stone Bridge, a distance of about eight miles. On the following day, General M'Dowell made preparations to attack Bonham's brigade. He advanced large masses of infantry, covered by some batteries of artillery. At noon, the enemy opened a heavy artillery fire from rifled cannon. Owing to the inexperience of the artillerymen, who were now probably for the first time in action, they did but very little damage to our troops. It was only after they had fired some hundred aimless shots, that they began gradually to acquire coolness and precision in pointing their guns, and their fire then occasioned deadly havoc amongst our men. Our batteries, as well as our troops, kept very quiet, but nevertheless impatiently waited the moment for orders to engage.

After a few moments, a light field battery of the enemy advanced to within a much nearer position. At the same time, General Bonham ordered one of his batteries to drive back that of the enemy, which order was so promptly and energetically obeyed, that after a short artillery duel, it was compelled to relinquish its position in all haste. The bold attempt they had made was thus completely defeated by our troops. The wonderful coolness and self-possession which our battery displayed in this affair, excited the admiration of our officers, and General Bonham promoted the officer in command to the rank of Major on the spot. Bonham now promptly withdrew the battery from the position it had taken, and placed it at Mitchell's Ford, where its guns could baffle any attempt of the enemy to cross.

Whilst this little cannon duel was going on, General M'Dowell threw forward large bodies of infantry, cavalry, and artillery, upon Blackburn Ford, where Longstreet's brigade was stationed, with orders to hold the position. General Longstreet, informed of the advance of this large body of the enemy, withdrew his outposts quickly behind the ford, whilst he manned the whole length of the south bank of the stream with a thick line of sharpshooters. The enemy's masses, sheltered by the undulating ground, were enabled to come up within 100 yards of our riflemen, whilst the enemy's batteries attached to both flanks, allowed the masses of infantry to get up close to us, under the protection of their murderous fire. As soon as the enemy's columns had deployed under cover of a heavy fire of their guns, which they did with great coolness, although it was probably the first time these regiments had been under fire, they were formed into an attacking column, and with a loud cheer rushed on Longstreet's position, who, however, received them with equal coolness and bravery.

It was at this point that, for the first time, these two hostile armies actually came into contact. The conflict which now ensued became every moment more deadly, and the mutual animosity of the men was increased to fury. The fighting had lasted already two hours, and yet neither party had gained one inch of ground. Every tree, every rock, every hollow was occupied by our Texan sharpshooters, who poured their deadly bullets into the enemy's ranks with fearful havoc. At last, Longstreet's division began to show symptoms of fatigue, and slightly wavered. At this critical juncture, General Early's brigade came up in the nick of time, and by this needful reinforcement the balance in the battle was reestablished. Ere long, the enemy's general became aware that he could do nothing against our solid masses. He therefore retired his troops from the line of battle, and confined his action to an artillery fire, which now opened on both sides, and afforded us the opportunity of ascertaining our superiority over the enemy in this arm. The commanders of the batteries could only take as a guide for their aim the glittering bayonets above the brushwood, and our men kept up an incessant fire amongst these partly concealed foes with rifled cannon. But we had scarcely thrown the enemy's columns into some slight confusion, when a Rhode Island battery came up at a trot within 800 yards, and poured in a hail of projectiles upon us, with the most destructive effect.

Many of our best horses having now been killed, our batteries were withdrawn from this devastating fire, while those of the enemy still continued to pound away for a time; but gradually the fire slackened, and when night threw her veil over the earth, the roar of artillery had ceased altogether. Thus terminated the engagement of Bull Run, which I looked upon as the prelude to a greater battle that must need to be fought between the two hostile armies. The battle of Bull Run had no other object than an attempt on the part of the enemy's general to cross the river, and to try the mettle of his troops. Although he did not succeed in crossing the ford, he nevertheless acquired sufficient knowledge of the bravery and self-possession of his troops, and, at the same time, no little respect for his opponents, whom he could no longer look upon as a despicable foe.

Both armies retired as if to recruit their strength, and to nerve themselves to the utmost for the coming great struggle, which it was hoped would decide the question of the existence of the Confederacy. The game had begun in earnest; what would be the issue of the throw?

CHAPTER IX.

THE BATTLE OF MANASSAS.

Movements of the Confederate army—Patterson perplexed—Espionage—Federal camp scenes—Scott's inactivity on the Potomac—Morning of the battle—A glance at both armies—The Confederate generals—Strength of the two armies—The battle commences—Advance of the enemy's columns—Our left wing attacked—Fierce engagement on the plateau—General attack—Beauregard and Jackson attack the enemy—Retreat—Heroism of Johnston—Corcoran's Irish regiment—Generals Fisher and Barton are killed—A fruitless struggle—Once more at them—Stonewall Jackson—A fresh massacre—Retreat—All apparently lost—Arrival of Jeff. Davis—Jackson, why called "Stonewall"—Help at need: Kirby Smith comes up—The decisive blow—The retreat—The battle field—Wounded foes—A horrible scene—Hospitals and attendance—Plunderers—Results of the battle of Manassas.

It was on Sunday, the 21st of July, that General Scott issued the order for General M'Dowell to advance with his troops against Manassas. This plan of operations was no secret to us. For, despite the severe check the United States army met with at Bull Run, very little foresight was shown by the Cabinet at Washington. General Beauregard received the very earliest information from a friend of his there, and had plenty of time to make all his preparations. He promptly made General Johnston acquainted with the enemy's intentions, and requested him to fall back on Manassas with all his troops, to form a junction with his corps. General Johnston performed this march in the most masterly manner. In order not to betray his retreat to the enemy's corps under General Patterson, stationed at Martinsburg, he ordered Colonel

Stuart to make a reconnoissance with his cavalry, on a large scale, to induce the enemy to believe that Johnston had the intention of shortly offering battle. Colonel Stuart carried out his instructions with such intelligence that poor General Patterson was at his wits' end, so he reported Johnston's demonstrations to Washington, and pressed for reënforcements. General Scott gave credence to the views contained in this report, and chuckled at the idea that Johnston was thus seriously occupied at Winchester with Patterson, as he hoped thereby to be able to annihilate Beauregard's army at Manassas, and strike a terrible blow at the Confederate army. Johnston, on seeing the success of his stratagem, laughed in his sleeve, and quietly took his departure from Winchester for Manassas. Kirby Smith's corps alone, with ten companies of cavalry, was left behind, with orders not to follow till next day.

From the very commencement of operations the Confederates enjoyed a decided advantage on the score of intelligence; and so it now happened that while we were accurately informed of every projected movement of the enemy, Scott and M'Dowell on the other hand were almost completely ignorant of our plans and intentions. They had not the slightest notion that General Johnston's corps had two days previously formed a junction with the army at Manassas, for, had they known of it, the corps under General Patterson, near Winchester—who still fancied he was threatened by Johnston's army, and was anxiously expecting an attack—would surely have been immediately ordered to occupy that town and make a demonstration in the Shenandoah valley. Had this really been done, however, the enemy would have cut off all our supplies from that rich valley, and have obstructed our communications in that direction. But the United States at this period had thought proper to employ several generals who were content to draw their pay, without choosing to put themselves much out of the way in the performance of any duty that required exertion or the exercise of great precaution, so confident were these men in their own superior abilities.

General Scott's headquarters at this season had more the appearance of a great fair than that of a camp of soldiers. Thousands of spectators had thronged there with the view of witnessing the bravery of the Federal troops, and the inevitable defeat of our army. Senators, members of Congress, politicians, clergymen, journalists, and idlers of every description, even women (if we may dare to rank them under the latter category) had then and there gathered together to witness the spectacle of the grand struggle about to take place, the successful issue of which, and the glorious results that would ensue, every one of the motley assemblage confidently predicted. Nothing is so mischievous to an army in the field as to harbor in its midst so many useless and detrimental elements. General Scott, however, it is certain, took no sort of measure to prevent this encumbering crowd of visitors from swarming in his camp. He placidly allowed inquisitive ladies and gentlemen to stroll through the various encampments, where each of these amateur critics was eager to display his or her copious strategical knowledge. To listen to the boasting rhodomontade, and other absurdities of these people, one would have fancied that all the heroes of ancient and modern times had met together on the side of the Federals, and that our army was to be utterly vanquished and slaughtered without mercy, down to the lowest drummer boy. Every one of these declaimers fancied himself for the nonce a Hannibal or a Napoleon, and disinterestedly promulgated his ideas for the benefit of all. Whole wagon-loads of champagne and other wines found their way to the camp for the great jubilation that was to take place in honor of the victory. It need scarcely be remarked that all this was detrimental to the troops, as it loosened the bonds of discipline and strict subordination, and lowered the standard among both officers and men of those essential military elements, coolness, self-possession, and mutual reliance. The whole matter was treated by the generals and officers with dangerous levity. Buoyed up as they all were with the confident expectation—almost amounting to conviction—that the scales of war were already turning in their favor, they really seemed to be incompetent to look earnestly ahead, and to solve with anything like accuracy the problematical course of coming events.

If we compare with the above picture the activity and demeanor of the United States troops under the command of General M'Clellan in Western Virginia—who, when cut off from all communications, deprived of the means of correspondence, in a country where every rock and every hillock was turned into a fortification, were always ready for action, day and night, in spite of all sorts of fatigue and privation—what a contrast does it not offer to the army on the Potomac! Nothing was more noticeable there than indolence, with an absence of military order and discipline, unless it was the ostentatious display of a variety of uniforms combining the quiet costume of the rough hunter just arrived from the far woods of Minnesota, to fight for the stars and stripes, with the ridiculous uniforms of the so-called Turcos, Zouaves, Arabs, and other theatrical dresses which decked the persons of their strutting owners.

But a truce to this description of a scene of egregious folly; we have stated enough to lay bare the root of those weaknesses and errors which proved the destruction of the army of the Potomac, and will now resume our narrative of events.

It was, as we have already stated, on the 21st of July, that General Scott issued the order to General M'Dowell to advance with his army against Manassas. The sun rose gloriously in the cloudless heavens on this lovely Sunday morning, and its rays unmistakably indicated a coming hot day.

Our troops had quietly partaken of their breakfast; the clergymen of the different regiments had preached their sermons, and prepared the soldiers by impressive words for the dread doings that would be enacted on this eventful day. The few remaining moments were devoted to exchanging words of farewell with beloved relatives and friends. It was a sad and touching spectacle to behold sons pressing the hands of their fathers, brothers those of brothers, and affectionately embracing one another, perhaps for the last time! Many a blessing followed the departing columns; many a reiterated farewell was shouted after them; many a tear was suppressed. The troops assembled round their respective standards, and took up their appointed places. Everything was done earnestly and seriously, every one present feeling convinced that a great and decisive moment was at hand. It was an enlivening sight to behold the cavalry regiments rattle past, headed by their brave commanders, Stuart, Ashby, and Davis. The general officers had assembled round Beauregard and Johnston, the latter of whom was, in reality, commander-in-chief, but he nevertheless left the command to General Beauregard, as it was he who had prepared all the plans and made the necessary disposition for the coming struggle. The countenances of the generals were serious, and many a thoughtful glance did they cast upon the columns as they marched past. Finally, their horses were brought, and the chiefs mounted, dispersing in various directions, each to his own post.

Though prevented by a fall from my horse from taking any active part for the last few days, I could not resist the attraction of at least witnessing the battle. Accompanied by a comrade, Prince de Polignac, lieutenant-colonel of artillery, on General Beauregard's staff, I accordingly proceeded to a hillock where a heavy battery had been placed in position.

It was one of those clear days when the air is so free from mist or vapor, as to allow the eye to discern objects at the greatest range, and from our position we could distinguish the most distant objects.

In front of us was extended the vast plain of Manassas, covered broadcast with innumerable masses of gaily dressed soldiers. It was truly a magnificent sight. Stretched out before us lay the Federal army, its long wings resting upon great woods, whose dark green foliage offered a fine background to the varied uniforms and glancing bayonets arrayed in front. A slight breeze brought over to us the stirring melodies of their numerous bands, resounding cheerily in the morning air. This brilliant spectacle of warlike array beneath our feet had all the appearance of a painted panorama; and, fascinated with the scene, we gazed untiringly upon it, until the eager-looking faces around us, and the light from the gun matches in the batteries, aroused us to the knowledge that, in a very short time, the work of death would commence in earnest.

Signs of active movement were now visible in the masses below. Like swarms of bees, bodies of troops kept crossing each other; batteries, ammunition carts, ambulances, flew past, marking with a cloud of dust the road each had taken. The troops took up their ground and formed slowly, but steadily, in the positions assigned to them. The sun shone with increasing splendor on the scene, while a fresh breeze blew playfully over the plain; and the heavens looked down smilingly, as if utterly unconscious of the fearful havoc that must ensue from the sanguinary work about to commence. There stood, in the full possession of life and youth—their breasts heaving with hope and courage—thousands who in a few short hours would be swept away by the merciless angel of death—would breathe out their last breath—and with their hearts' blood stain the green summer grass.

The picture suddenly changes, and the poetical coloring which a moment before pervaded it vanishes before the roar of artillery, which now issues with fearful violence along the whole line.

General M'Dowell had received orders from General

Scott to let the men take four days' rations with them, on the 21st of July, preparatory to his taking possession of Manassas, which position he was to maintain by every exertion in his power, as he could then receive his supplies per railway from Alexandria. These were the first instructions of the Federal generals for the expected battle of Manassas.

Meanwhile great activity prevailed in the headquarters of the Confederate army. Our chief, Beauregard, did not exhibit his generalship to the best advantage, having proposed various plans to his generals, which they could not comprehend. Thus, when Beauregard learnt that General Scott had given orders to M'Dowell to take the offensive and offer battle, he himself wished to adopt that plan, and it was only by General Johnston's interposition that the idea of so injudicious a manœuvre was abandoned. Johnston advocated defensive tactics, and showed in the clearest manner that, owing to the actual position of affairs, we ought first to await the shock of the enemy before taking the offensive. Despite these arguments, Beauregard remained unshaken in his opinion, and this day placed his talents as a great commander in their true light.

General Johnston's troops advanced in dense masses through Ashby's Gap, establishing a communication with Beauregard's corps on the Potomac, the left wing of which it now formed.

General Bee then occupied the advanced posts with the 4th Alabama, 2d and 11th Mississippi, and the 2d, 4th, 5th, 9th, 19th, and 35th Virginia regiments, so as to allow the remainder of the army time to effect its movements unmolested, and take up its proper positions.

Ewell's brigade had taken post at Union Mill; whilst General Jones occupied M'Lane's Ford; General Longstreet Blackburn's Ford; and General Bonham, with his division, Mitchell's Ford. General Coke and Colonel Evans were placed at the extremity of the right wing, and Holmes's and

Early's brigades were held in reserve, ready to advance whenever their services might be required. The centre and flanks were covered by our heavy batteries.

The order of battle this day comprised, on the side of the Confederates, including Johnston's corps and General Kirby Smith's division, a force of 65,000 infantry, 4,000 cavalry, and a park of artillery of 68 guns, partly rifled and partly smooth-bored cannon. Thus we were numerically in greater force than the enemy, and it was only in the event of Patterson's corps coming up in time that the Federal army would have outnumbered ours.*

The Confederates held Bull Run river to the extent of from nine to eleven miles, and with eager impatience awaited the battle. As soon as the enemy's artillery opened fire generally upon our line, a number of their batteries were needlessly brought into play, their services not being yet required or likely to prove useful. But the men were animated with such ardor that possibly no counter order could have prevented them from firing. Perhaps these overzealous combatants fancied that the roar of their guns would give courage to the timid and hesitating. Many a wondering glance followed the balls as they flew over our heads, and it was almost ludicrous to see the men duck their heads at a given signal, and pay a respectful salaam to the iron missile as it overshot its mark.

After the batteries had maintained a steady fire for some time, without either army showing any intention of coming to closer quarters, General Beauregard rode along our lines urging the men to display unfaltering bravery. Just then a body of the enemy's infantry was seen to move rapidly from the centre, and to form into attacking columns: these troops

---

* In making this comparison between the forces of the hostile armies, it is only fair to state that about half of the Confederate order of battle as above computed—that is, Kirby Smith's corps of some 30,000 men—did not arrive in the field until near the close of the action.

being probably sooner tired than our own, of the cannonade, and were consequently impatiently eager to attack us.

This was a moment of exciting and painful suspense. The military bands of our foes struck up "Yankee Doodle" to encourage their advancing troops. The necessary dispositions having been promptly made, their columns advanced against a small group of houses that had been occupied by our men, under General Evans, to whom the command of the position had a few hours previously been transferred from the hands of General Bee.

About noon the enemy sent their sharpshooters forward in large numbers, and these kept up a well-sustained fire. Immediately afterward the heads of the attacking columns came into view, entering the battle field in tolerably good order, but not with sufficient rapidity; a few minutes later the battle raged violently in this quarter. By the side of the cluster of houses we had drawn up a battery of sixteen guns, and these dealt death and destruction amongst the ranks of the enemy. The Federal troops, however, stood our fire with great steadiness; they advanced boldly, and drove out our men from the houses in question.

Beauregard now sent Fisher with his brigade to support them, and he attacked the successful assailants with such determined spirit that he recovered possession of the houses, driving the enemy's troops before him. Surely, however, had our troops regained ground, when General Evans issued an order that Fisher's brigade on the right should manœuvre toward Longstreet's division, whilst himself would endeavor to maintain the position that had been recovered. But the enemy, now coming up with strong reinforcements, and supported by a battery of horse artillery, made a desperate onslaught on Evans's division. The battle at this point was now at its height. In vain did that General endeavor to maintain his position until reinforcements should arrive. The enemy's leaders were indefatigable in urging on their troops, and their attack was so overpowering that our men were at length driven back, and the cluster of houses once more fell into the hands of our foes. General Evans then withdrew reluctantly behind the batteries with his shattered force, to give his men time to draw breath and recruit themselves after their hard toil and desperate but baffled efforts to hold their ground.

Whilst this minor but deadly contest was going on on our left, General Beauregard about one o'clock gave the order along his entire line to advance. General Jackson, with his whole division, supported by that of Ewell, then made a desperate attack upon the enemy's centre. The collision was fearful. The Federal troops held their ground without wavering, and Jackson's close encounter recoiled before the dense mass of foes opposed to him. The desperation and endurance with which both sides fought at this point entitled them to high praise. Despite the most gallant efforts General Jackson was obliged to leave the field with his mangled division. At this conjuncture General Beauregard made his appearance, and in person led Bee's and Early's divisions in support; but the men now seemed discouraged, and advanced reluctantly. The enemy then attempted to strike a blow at our left, when Colonels Stuart and Ashby, at the head of their cavalry, dashed into them with a loud cheer, using sword and revolver with such effect that they cut quite through them. This dashing and successful exploit inspirited our troops with renewed courage. Meanwhile General Jackson had again collected his forces and made strenuous efforts to redeem his mishap. Like lions his men rushed headlong upon the foe, stemmed their advance, and recovered some of the lost ground.

During the progress of these operations, those of our troops on the left wing who occupied the cluster of houses before mentioned, had again lost their position. The enemy tried hard to derive still greater advantage from this further success, and accordingly constructed a masked battery upon the plateau opposite to the houses; and they succeeded, in the course of the day, in posting, at this critically important point, Rickett's and Griffin's batteries. As soon as the battery was planted, it opened fire, and sent forth a storm of projectiles amongst our unprotected men. The havoc which these guns caused in our ranks was most serious. General Johnston, feeling that the plateau was easily accessible, ordered up a battery of twelve-pounder rifled cannon from the reserve, and gave orders that the enemy should be driven from that point. With the greatest coolness and energy the commander of our battery set to work; but all his efforts failed before the activity of the enemy's fire, which had been concentrated upon our guns as soon as the commander of the hostile battery divined our intention. Their first shot killed the artillery officer in command, besides dismantling two of our guns and killing and wounding a number of the gunners. Our position at this part of the field was very critical. As often as our battalions were marshalled in order to advance to the attack, their columns were riddled by the enemy's shot, which was poured in with such deadly effect as to cause disorder and confusion in our ranks.

General Johnston repeatedly cast anxious glances toward that part of the field where Kirby Smith's division was expected to advance from Winchester. From the effect of five hours' almost incessant fighting his men had become sadly exhausted, and their distress was greatly augmented by the force of the sun's rays, which darted down so scorching a glare as to take away, for a time, what little strength remained to his wornout troops. There was yet no sign of Kirby Smith's advance, and a moody despair began to show itself in the men's countenances, as if indicating that their courage was about to droop from sheer hopelessness. In this state of matters General Johnston made another resolute attempt to rally his troops, and, seizing the flag of the 6th North Carolina regiment, conjured his men to stand by him and save the honor of the Confederate cause: then at the head of the above-named regiment, he rushed furiously on the advancing foe. Nothing could now prevail against these men, who fought with all the madness of despair. Nothing could stop their onward rush; they broke through the enemy's ranks, and a terrible hand-to-hand conflict ensued, to depict which adequately would be impossible. Who could relate all the scenes of desperate daring and almost superhuman bravery that were here displayed? Without stopping, Johnston, followed by the North Carolina regiment and a portion of Bonham's brigade, made a rush for the plateau occupied by the hostile brigades of Rickett and Griffin.

General M'Dowell, convinced of the importance of this post, had sent Corcoran's Irish regiment to its support. The latter had on the way thrown aside everything that could impede their movements, and, at the point of the bayonet, repelled, in splendid style, all Johnston's attacks. Johnston, driven to despair, and almost fatigued to death by excitement and exertion, now leaned against a tree, and unable to suppress his vexation, continually stamped his foot on the earth. The fighting here was truly heroic. Generals Fisher of North Carolina, and Barton of Georgia, fell nearly at the same time; and right and left the men dropped, bathed in blood—yet not an inch of ground was lost or won.

At this most critical moment of the day, a portion of General Jones's brigade now makes its appearance on the field, with a fresh body of troops from Texas, Arkansas, and Louisiana. With a loud "hurrah," these men throw themselves impetuously upon the enemy, already confidently exulting in anticipated victory. At the same time, in order to stem their farther advance, Johnston, with his aide-de-camp, hastens down to the thinned ranks of his fine division, and endeavors again to rouse the dejected spirit of his men. They respond to his appeal; although panting from heat and fatigue, the brave fellows cannot refuse to follow their beloved and gallant commander. Again his shaken ranks are formed into a compact column, and stimulated by the rallying cry of "Forward!" this heroic band, with their physical strength all but exhausted by their previous exertions, dash irresistibly into the battle, determined there to seek either victory or death.

Even the Irishmen, who had hitherto stood like a rock under their able colonel, Corcoran, could not withstand this shock. They, too, were dead beat by the incessant hard fighting. Thus we were enabled to gain a little ground, which served still further to rouse the courage of our men. Like two thunder clouds driven into collision by a fierce tempest, the hostile masses closed. "Hurrah for Jeff. Davis!" shouted our men, and "On to Richmond!" was responded by the foe. The Federal gunners were obliged to cease firing, in order not to mow down their own men, and sword and bayonet were alone used to do their deadly work in this murderous *mêlée*.

Gradually the resistance of our opponents slackened—they began to give way. One more attack—one more headlong wild rush, regardless of death and horrible mutilation—one more desperate grapple—and the enemy is hurled back. A loud cheer then burst from our ranks, accompanied with exulting cries of, "They give way! they give way!" and exerting their remaining powers to the utmost, our men make a final and crushing onslaught. The enemy is compelled to relinquish his hard-earned advantages, and seeks shelter behind his guns, which are brought up in all haste, but in vain.

The Confederates having become again masters of the important plateau, with a portion of the batteries posted there, forthwith turn the guns against the columns advancing to the support of the enemy, which are now exposed to a galling fire.

The battle on the left wing had thus terminated in our favor. Johnston had defeated all the attempts of the enemy to maintain the plateau and the group of houses, and drove them back, with a great loss in killed and wounded, on their reserve. We now stood in special need of a good body of cavalry. If Johnston, at the moment the enemy gave way, had been so fortunate as to have two or three cavalry regiments at his disposal, our success would have been a decisive one. Our infantry was so worn out with heat and toil, that the men were not capable of performing the comparatively light duty of pursuing the beaten foe. Our success was, consequently, not complete. Moreover, had we been better provided with cavalry, we might have effectually relieved our centre when it was so hard pressed by General M'Dowell.

General Johnston felt very anxious lest the enemy should become aware of our weakness and return to the attack. He therefore sent aide-de-camps and orderlies, in all haste, in the direction where Kirby Smith's division was expected. If his troops should arrive in time our men might get some of the rest they so much needed; but this hope was likely to prove a vain one: not a trace was to be seen either of Kirby Smith's or of any other fresh troops, and the mind of Johnston was sorely troubled at contemplating the dearly purchased advantages he had obtained with his gallant soldiers thus placed in jeopardy, as the prospect of maintaining the ground they had won and following up their success seemed to fade away.

Meantime, the battle had been raging along the whole line. General Beauregard, informed of Johnston's success on the left wing, did not wish to be behindhand on his part, and exerted all his energy to strike a decisive blow at the enemy. He therefore ordered General Longstreet to place himself at the head of the attacking columns, and directed a general advance. Admirably did Longstreet lead his men on, and he was followed by the brigades of Kershaw and Coke in support. The enemy's troops calmly awaited our attack, and from a masked battery opened a destructive fire upon Longstreet's corps. This, however, did not check its advance for one moment; on it dashed in utter contempt of death, with fixed bayonets, across the plain and over some small brushwood which separated it from the foe. At this moment the enemy displayed his front; various guns, hitherto unperceived, poured a regular shower of grape into our attacking columns, causing whole ranks to be swept down on the bloodstained field. The two supporting brigades, beholding this terrible havoc of their comrades, with cries of rage and anguish burst from their hitherto well-kept ranks, and rushed wildly across the plain to their aid; but before they could come up with them, they in turn fell stricken to the ground.

Our foes, confident in the ultimate success of a well-concerted plan of action, defended their position with great skill and determination. Longstreet, rendered desperate by the terrible loss sustained by his men, endeavored in vain to rally them and inspire them with new courage. His corps was almost annihilated, and many of his men became mixed up with the other brigades so inextricably that great confusion necessarily ensued, and it was scarcely possible to procure any obedience to orders. Soldiers no longer recognized their officers, nor the officers their men, so incurable was the confusion at that moment. Like madmen the men fired and struck at their foes without order. All the appeals of Beauregard and his officers were disregarded. The troops, at last, struck with a panic, quite gave way and ran across the plain which separated them from the wood. They had scarcely turned when some squadrons of the United States regular cavalry followed them in pursuit. Happily for our men the leader of these horsemen did his work inefficiently. Profiting by this, some companies which had hastily got together, somewhat recovered their order, making a sufficient show of resistance to lead him to suppose they meant to repel the attack; thereupon, he turned back and allowed the remainder of our dispersed troops to save themselves.

The disheartened soldiers had scarcely reached the verge of the wood when Colonel Ashby made his appearance with some companies of cavaalry, and under this welcome protecting cover many of the fugitives found safety.

The enemy now advanced slowly, but with evident distrust, whilst their artillery kept up a useless fire. Our troops were not disposed to make any further stand. Their great and unlooked-for losses had disheartened them, and it was only when Beauregard came up with a few fresh battalions and a battery that the officers could succeed in enforcing obedience, when they endeavored, to the best of their ability, to get the disorganized mass into some order and discipline. Beauregard looked sadly, almost beseechingly, toward heaven, as if no aid could be expected from any other quarter. The few battalions he had brought up were sent to the front and spread themselves out in an extended line of skirmishers, opening a brisk fire upon the slowly advancing enemy, who probably fancied that much larger reinforcements had arrived than was really the case. Had they known at this critical moment how to turn their advantage to account, there was no need for them to force Beauregard's centre, disorganized and scattered as it then was.

From the left wing there was no help to be expected; for General Johnston, with his wornout troops, was incapable of more work, and was only too thankful that he had succeeded in doing so much. The reserves had been so lavishly employed from the very outset, that there were none now available; consequently, our troops were wholly insufficient to resist a fresh atttack on the part of the enemy; and if to this be added the general discouragement and the wornout state of the men, we may infer that in a few minutes more the battle of Manassas might have been decided in favor of the Federals. But it was not to be so: thanks to the slowness of our over-prudent foes, we were saved in our hour of greatest need, and the mighty blow that threatened our destruction fell short of its mark.

Our brave sharpshooters were meanwhile busily annoying

the advancing enemy; and the few battalions we still had to cover us kept the enemy at bay, like well trained hounds when facing a lion; and profiting by his unaccountable inertness and overcaution, seized the opportunity to attempt, hopeless as the chance appeared, once more to restore our fallen fortunes.

At the very time these momentous events were taking place on the right wing and in the centre, President Jefferson Davis made his appearance on the field, surrounded brilliant staff. For a triumphant procession, he must have soon perceived that he came somewhat too early, as he rode in silence along the columns of the brigades. What a sight! The glorious army was, so to say, dissolved. The pride and the flower of the South lay bleeding and broken on the ground, and only a small body still rallied round its tattered banners. The hopes of thousands had been baffled, the joy of other thousands crushed; groans, lamentations, and piteous cries for help were painfully audible on every side. In the midst of the fearful, sickening sight that met the eye of the President, what must the proud heart of that man have felt at this spectacle of misery? What must have been his feelings when the corpses of his friends, Generals Barton and Fisher—men who had found the death of heroes—were brought in?

With an uneasy hand he clutched his reins, his eye looking dull and sad, his face twitching nervously, influenced perhaps by a painful feeling of responsibility on beholding around him on all sides the poor victims who had fallen in support of the cause identified so closely with his own ambition.

General Beauregard communicated to the President, in a few words, the details of the progress of the battle. The soldiers, meanwhile, stood around in silence, leaning on their weapons. There was something of discontent visible in their looks, which may have seemed to upbraid the President for the policy that had brought them to make such fearful sacrifices.

His Excellency, unable to dwell upon so painful a scene, hastily rode off toward our left wing, but only to see a repetition there of the spectacle he had just endeavored to avoid.

Scarcely had the President left with his staff, when the enemy made a show of ending by one blow the work that had had been so far advanced.

They came boldly forward, drove back our sharpshooters, and approached the spot where we had posted our reserve, our hospitals, and magazines. If our foes could have succeeded in establishing a footing here, all resistance must necessarily have ceased. At this critical moment, Beauregard ordered General Jackson to attack the enemy on the left flank, whilst he should attack them in the centre.

Poor Jackson was, on every occasion, the last resource, and was therefore ordered forward when any difficult or almost impossible work was to be done. But he was always willing and ready, and no one ever heard him utter a complaint, or grumble at any order, however unreasonable. And so it happened to-day: he was again to attack the enemy, although no division had been so hotly engaged and suffered so much already as his own. He stirred up the courage of his men, and with unbounded confidence, they prepared to follow him. A few moments after Jackson had received his orders he was again alongside the enemy, engaged in a desperate hand-to-hand encounter.

The Federal troops had just crossed a ditch, but Jackson drove them back helter skelter, and hotly pursued them. The enemy was startled at this forward movement of the Confederates, who scarcely an hour before had appeared defeated and about to retreat. They pulled up, however, at a small ravine, and then made so stout a stand that every attempt of Jackson to drive them from this post failed.

Generals Scott and M'Dowell, observing the fatigued state of our men, resolved at once to make a general attack upon our wornout line.

General Mills was sent with three brigades to Centreville, to make a demonstration as a feint upon Blackburn and Mitchell's Ford, with a view to mislead General Beauregard; and General Tyler was, meantime, to operate against Stonebridge; General Heintzelman to advance as quickly as possible against Red House Ford, and take possession of that point. General Hunter, with two brigades, was, in the interval, to clear the ground and drive back the skirmishers.

The enemy carried out this manœuvre with alacrity and a feeling of confidence, whilst our army, owing to the immense length of our line of battle, was so widely distributed that some portions were left unsupported. Our troops could not prevent the enemy from carrying out their operations, as there was scarcely any possibility of concentrating large masses on one point, an operation that would have been attended, not only with great difficulty, but with much loss of time. Owing to the concentration of the enemy, it was much easier for them to support each other. Without giving us time thoroughly to understand their plans and to counteract them, the enemy's troops now made a sudden and simultaneous attack upon our whole line. Generals Heintzelman and Burnside made a furious onslaught upon Johnston's wearied troops, and attempted to drive them out of the position they had gained with so much resolution and perseverance.

Johnston was well aware of the importance of his position, and saw at a glance exactly how he was situated. If the Federals were victorious here, the only chance for the Confederates was to fall back on the centre, in which case Johnston would have to advance his left wing toward it. But this would cut off the communication with Kirby Smith's corps, for the enemy could then occupy the position thus vacated, throw itself between Johnston and Smith, and capture or crush the latter, who would then have to sustain the attack of their main body.

The enemy's two generals exerted themselves to the utmost to effect their object; but Johnston stood as firm as a rock, and was determined to hold the precious ground he occupied with his troops, until the last man should fall. A conflict on a large scale was, meantime, raging along the whole line. The sultry atmosphere was almost unbearable, and the troops, heated by continual fighting, were tired almost to fainting. With difficulty Johnston gathered his men together, and brought them up, almost desponding, against the enemy. Both parties fought with almost incredible obstinacy. The cannon roared, the rifles cracked, and with wild hurrahs the opponents met in mortal fight. Clouds of smoke and dust shrouded the horrible scenes of butchery here displayed. More than once had they driven back the enemy's attack, when suddenly Hunter's division came up to the support of the latter, thus bringing fresh troops against our wornout men. This was too much. Despite the great disregard of death which Johnston himself had personally displayed—despite the most heroic attempts at keeping up the courage of his men, it was evident that the position could no longer be held. Attacked on all sides, our troops retreated gradually from their dearly bought positions, defending every inch of ground with their last remaining strength.

Johnston was now in a state of despair; all seemed to be lost, and the exertions of the whole day fruitless. Like a wounded boar, he rushed about, endeavoring to collect the last remnants of his defeated corps; and the tide of fortune was fast setting in against the cause of the Confederacy, when, as an expiring effort, Hampton's legion was now brought up to support Jackson. "You cover the retreat," shouted Jackson; "we are beaten, and must fall back. Then," added he, resolutely, "I will again show the enemy our bayonets." In a very short time he had formed his troops into order; and General Bee exultingly exclaimed, "Here stands Jackson like a 'stone wall,' and here let us conquer or die!"

The exclamation was received with enthusiasm along the

whole line. "Stone wall! stone wall!" shouted the men; and their courage was renewed as if by magic. Here it was that Jackson earned the imperishable term of *Stonewall* as a prefix to his name. Meantime the enemy was already in possession of nearly all the important positions. Jackson, fully aware of their value, turned his attention to that quarter. Making a furious rush upon the scared enemy, he attacks them in their centre, and endeavors to hurl them back. A half battery of 12-pounders did very good service here; and General Bee followed up with the troops of the other division. But all these heroic attempts proved fruitless; the enemy was too strong. Heintzelman and Burnside defended their position with great skill. Johnston tried a desperate flank movement; but the enemy was not to be deceived. They merely sent their disposable cavalry and a few guns to oppose him; and these troops, by their firm attitude, kept him at bay.

Jackson was finally obliged to leave Johnston to himself, and make a retrograde movement. As soon as the enemy observed this, they determined to annihilate us at one fell swoop. There was no time to be lost now, and only the most heroic resistance could save the fresh regiments that had come up.

The condition of affairs on our side was at this moment desperate indeed. Our left flank was overpowered, and without support it was impossible to do anything with the worn-out troops in that quarter. General Holmes with three regiments, and General Early with some others, and a 6-pounder battery under Captain Walker, accordingly advanced to the support; whilst the routed brigades of Bonham, Kemper, Longstreet, Ewell and Jones were ordered to make a general attack upon the Federal forces. By the greatest good luck, it so happened that at this moment a body of fresh troops came up from Virginia and Tennessee, and by their gallant bearing revived the drooping spirits of our men.

Beauregard and Johnston held a conference at Robertson's Farm, at which President Jefferson Davis was also present. But few words could have passed between them; they probably referred to what appeared to be our inevitable retreat. In a few minutes the generals galloped back to their respective posts. It was high time that they did so, for the enemy were pouring in on all sides, overthrowing Beauregard's line of defence. Once more Jackson gathered his men together, and led them on to fight; but every attack failed against the obstinacy of the foe, who resolutely frustrated every attempt made by our men. This hot and sanguinary day was already drawing to a close; the sun was murkily setting in the west, as if it had already witnessed too much misery; darkness was beginning to spread its merciful wings over the scene of battle, over the downtrodden, mutilated corpses, and over the numerous wounded that lay scattered over the vast plain. The position of the Confederates became gradually more untenable; and when stragglers from Beauregard's defeated division came hastily up, one after the other exclaiming, "Beauregard is beaten! Longstreet is killed! all is over!" even the bravest spirits gave way. The roar of cannon drew nearer and nearer, and announced that we really were defeated. Vain were all attempts to stop the confusion which ensued; preparations were made by many for flight, and some, indeed, threw away their arms, and fled.

Johnston and Jackson rode like madmen through the ranks of the disheartened soldiers, but their zeal was of no avail. The confusion increased, and masses of Beauregard's routed division came hurrying back, adding to the general bewilderment. All discipline was at an end; the enemy's bullets already began to shower in upon us, and the shout of "Run!" was raised. And now at this moment appeared in sight, at no great distance too, the advancing columns of the anxiously expected corps of Kirby Smith.

Like an electric shock, the words ran from mouth to mouth

through the ranks, " Kirby is coming ! " and a thousand voices thundered forth, " Kirby is advancing with 30,000 men ! " Each eye now flashed with enthusiasm, and each breast heaved with renewed courage.

It was now an easy task for the officers to restore order amongst their men. The newcomers are greeted with shouts of " Welcome ! " The help that was needed to save the army had come at last. Kirby Smith advanced at once to the attack, and every one felt that his opportune arrival had operated a miraculous change in the state of affairs. The loud cheer that rang along our broken lines now startled the elated, advancing enemy.

Like a thunderbolt Kirby Smith fell upon the foe; our men fought desperately; and in a moment the Federal troops, who had felt certain of victory, were everywhere driven back. Scarcely had they commenced retiring, when it became impossible to restrain our troops. A giant Texan, throwing away his rifle, took out his Bowie knife. With one blow he split the skull of a wounded man who had fallen to the ground; and this became the signal for a general butchery. Like wild beasts, the incensed soldiery fell upon their victims, hewing, stabbing and slashing like madmen.

A fearful panic seizes upon the Federal troops. Even the bravest fly before such an onslaught; they give way, and, in mortal fear, officers and men run for their lives like startled deer. Only a few regiments hold their ground, and amongst them Colonel Corcoran's Irish regiment, standing like a rock in the whirlpool rushing past them, and which threatened to carry them along with it. The Irish fought like heroes; and not until a great number of them had fallen, and their brave colonel had been made a prisoner, did they slowly retire. These poor fellows, who had certainly done their full share of the work, could not possibly understand that the day was to end to their disadvantage. The savage spirit of our soldiers now almost bordered upon the horrible. Beauregard took advantage of this vengeful mood; he ordered his whole army forward, and with wild exulting cheers fell upon the broken enemy. Stuart meantime had collected all his cavalry together, and swept across the plain like a whirlwind, clearing everything before him.

The enemy was now in full flight at every point, and so quick was our advance that all order in our ranks was lost, and no regiment kept in its proper position. A rumor suddenly spread among the men that Kirby Smith had fallen. A cry of anger and horror passed through the ranks of the whole army. Our troops, now maddened with rage, fell mercilessly upon their opponents, and a fearful massacre commenced. Scenes of horrible cruelty too fearful for description ensued. Our men were no longer human beings; covered with blood and dust, and gunpowder, they fell upon their flying opponents with ungovernable fury.

The whole of the enemy's army was dispersed, and retreated in indescribable disorder to Bull Run. The whole plain was covered with fugitives, followed by our men in hot pursuit. The victory we had gained was complete.

Scarcely was Beauregard informed of the unexpected success of his arms at every point, when he wended his way to the spot where President Jefferson Davis had posted himself with his staff.

"President," said he, "the battle of Manassas has been won by the indomitable bravery of the Confederate troops. The victory is ours!"

The President, with emotion, embraced the hero of Manassas; the Confederacy was safe now for some time to come, and with it the position of its President.

It was past midnight, and at headquarters nothing was yet known of the actual position and condition of the troops. In the wild, disorderly pursuit, all the regiments had become disorganized, and in many cases the commanding officers failed in getting their orders obeyed. The roar of cannon had now become fainter, and the sound of musketry had ceased altogether.

The destruction and devastation which this battle of nearly twelve hours' duration occasioned is beyond my powers of description. On the field lay by thousands the wounded, the dying, and the dead; groans and piteous cries for help echoed through the silence of the night, but few took any notice of the poor sufferers lying on that field of blood. The preparations for conveying and taking care of the wounded were so defective, the means for attending to their wants so insufficient, and the staff destined for this purpose so small, that but little real help could be bestowed. The sultry air was still insufferable, and augmented the pangs of the wounded; yet the surgeons had no idea of their duties, although the most energetic action on their part was so indispensable.

Beauregard and the other generals were fairly bewildered by the victory they had achieved. They already pictured to their fancy the Confederate Government safely seated at Washington, issuing decrees from the Capitol to the vanquished North. But where the army was that had to effect all this, no one knew. A great portion of it lay dead on the field of battle, while the more unfortunate wounded were abandoned heartlessly to their fate. No hospital accommodation had been provided; but little surgical attendance had been prepared for the wretched sufferers. With the greatest difficulty the quartermasters managed to find room for some 1,500 to 2,000 of our own wounded, while those of the enemy, in still greater number, required accommodation. But whose business was this? The greater portion of the army was busied in plundering; from which occupation many repaired joyfully homeward, refusing obedience to their officers, and inflated with pride at the valiant deeds they had performed.

Our army was just then *de facto* dissolved, and there were but few troops amongst them who could be counted upon. But in the sad scene that lay before me, I could not stand by unconcerned at the sight of so much uncared-for misery; my heart bled at the lamented cries for help of the poor fellows lying around me. I then proceeded to visit the prisoners, and on inquiring if there were no medical men amongst them, I found a few, and with these proceeded to our left wing, where the fight had been fiercest. It was a sorrowful kind of work we took in hand: as soon as we came to the scene of the struggle, friend and foe lay side by side in one undistinguishable mass, the dead and dying crowded together in a frightful heap, mixed with broken ammunition carts and fragments of baggage.

We set about putting the houses which stood near the plateau, that had been the scene of such murderous strife, into the best order we could. Riddled as they were, however, with cannon shot, they were now mere shells. Carpenters and joiners did their best to turn them into a sort of temporary hospital, but the darkness of the night much impeded our exertions, and it was not till three o'clock in the morning that our first preparations were completed.

At five o'clock I again visited the field of battle. Our generals had given up all further pursuit of the enemy, and were occupied in restoring order amongst the troops—order out of chaos indeed! The whole population of the neighborhood was collected together, partly in search of booty, partly to inquire after the fate of relations and friends, and being intermingled with the troops, the whole presented the appearance of a roving mob. No one seemed disposed to obey the orders of his superiors or attend to his duties; the commanders themselves relaxed their grasp on the troops, and were dragged into the whirlpool. Numerous bands of soldiers strolled about, howling and bawling, and otherwise misbehaving themselves. Many deserted, for discipline and subordination were at an end; and the army of the Confederates was virtually broken up, despite the victory it had achieved.

If General Scott had had a reserve at hand, behind the ranks of which his troops could have been reformed, he might easily have restored the fortunes of the day, and at any rate have deprived the Confederates of all the advantages of the victory. His cavalry had not suffered much, and he could have ordered up Patterson's corps in all·haste from Martinsburg by forced marches, and by displaying a little energy and presence of mind, have retrieved the disaster that had befallen the Union banner.

But, on the other hand, the disorder and panic in the Federal army must nevertheless have been very great. The whole line of road taken by the Federals in their retreat was strewn with weapons, dead and wounded horses, wagons, baggage, in sad evidence of their utter rout. At Cub Run Bridge, to all appearance, there must have been an awful crush amongst the fugitives, the main stream of which, being pursued by Early's and Stuart's cavalry, infantry, and artillery, hurried on in such a helter-skelter style to place the river between themselves and the pursuers, that the bridge was thoroughly blocked up by the jamming together of wagons and horses. In fact, confusion reached its culminating point at this bridge. In their frantic efforts to escape, the Union soldiers climbed over the obstructing carriages, some of which were overturned; while in the midst of all this tumult the first shots of Kemper's pursuing battery began to take effect, thereby increasing the panic to the most fearful height.

Hundreds of curious spectators, who had come in carriages and on horseback to witness the victory of the Federal troops, now added, by their useless and obstructive presence, to the disastrous effects of the retreat, beseeching the exhausted soldiers to help them, who could not save themselves; horses without riders, bespattered with blood and frantic from wounds, dashed into the human mass, and contributed another phase of terror to the deplorable scene. Self-preservation was now absolute in its sway. Every man sought to save his own life, regardless of that of his comrade, whom he savagely thrusts out of his way; for they well knew that the Confederate horsemen were at their heels. On they came, like the wind, sweeping all before them, and trampling many a poor wounded fellow to death. Nearer and nearer, too, the dreaded roar of the cannon reached their ears. Thus but one thought, but one idea, self-preservation, prevails with the tangled mass of hunted fugitives.

The flight of the Federal troops continued till they reached Centreville, where was posted Miles's brigade. There, in fact, were reserves which had not been turned to account in the action : reserves that might have done good service if made use of at the proper time and place; but it would seem as if every man lost both head and heart. The very thought of a retreat had never entered their minds, still less that of a defeat, with such confidence had the generals gone to work. But what is no less singular, no arrangements for the pursuit of the enemy in case of victory had been made. All things considered, it is impossible to avoid severely censuring the Federal commanders for their want of foresight.

Neither General Scott nor General M'Dowell had given any orders to Colonel Miles to be prepared with his brigade in readiness for any emergency, and consequently this officer found his efforts to check the torrents of fugitives, and to collect any of them so as to make a stand utterly futile : the panic was overwhelming, and the reserve itself was presently whirled away in the vortex.

Let us, in conclusion, bestow another glance on the field of battle. What a horrible, lamentable episode in this fratricidal contest did it not present to the mind; and the man who could, on beholding it, remain unmoved at the terrible scene must have had a heart of stone. The reader must forgive me if I now refer to details in which my own active participation became essential. My description is only meant to give a faint sketch of the utter helplessness and neglect of precaution that I was shocked to witness. Prompted by feelings of conscientiousness and humanity, I made it my duty to seek out and attend upon the wounded; and the more so when I found that the work of alleviating their sufferings was performed with evident reluctance and want of zeal by many of those whose duty it was to do it. I looked upon the poor fellows only as suffering fellow mortals, brothers in need of help, and made no distinction between friend and foe; nay, I must own that I was at times prompted to give preference to the latter, for the reason that some of our men met with attention from their relations and friends, who had flocked to the field in numbers to seek for them. But in doing so I had to encounter opposition, and was even pointed at by some, with muttered curses, as a traitor to the cause of the Confederacy, for bestowing any attention on the "d—— Yankees." To insure safety from my own comrades, I waited upon General Jackson, and explained to him the task I had undertaken. He shook me warmly by the hand saying: "You are right; as a European officer you must know what a new army most stands in need of. Act, therefore, according to your own judgment, and, if necessary, shoot any ruffians who may dare to interfere with you in your work of humanity."

Thus sanctioned, I returned and went cheerfully to work. I took up a position in the centre of the battle field; and from this, as a radiating point, sent my men out with stretchers, bandages, refreshments, &c., to succor the wounded. Many of our officers and men looked on with more than indifference at my exertions when bestowed on wounded enemies. But I persevered, and toward evening we had three hospitals: one for the slightly wounded, one for amputations and other serious cases, and one for those who were wounded beyond all hope. The picture of human misery displayed in these ill-provided asylums was a heartrending one. A young Federal officer especially engrossed my sympathy. Pale as death, he lay with his eyes shut and closed lips, whilst tears rolled down his cheeks. "Courage, comrade," I said, cheeringly; "the day will come when you will calmly remember this battle as one of the things of the past." Gradually opening his eyes, and holding out his hand, he pressed mine, and exclaimed, in a trembling voice, "Do not give me false hopes, sir: it is all up with me." In vain did I endeavor to cheer his flagging spirit. "I do not grieve that I shall die," he quietly observed; "for with these stumps" (and he lifted the coverlet, to show me that both his feet had been smashed by a round shot) "I cannot live long; but I weep for my poor, distracted country. But had I a second life at my command, I would willingly sacrifice it for the cause of the Union." Deeply moved, I stood by the couch of this gallant youth, who with his dying breath still spoke in the same patriotic strain. His eyes had again closed; a faint smile passed over his face, like the young dawn of another world. Suddenly he rose nervously in the bed, while his whole frame quivered; and after exclaiming in distinct tones, "Mother!—father!" he fell back. His features became rigid—his spirit had fled.

Here, amongst enemies, he breathed out his young life, far away from his beloved relations, and none of them will probably ever learn where and how he died. There was nothing to give us any clue to his identity, with the exception of a small locket with the portrait of a fair young girl, which he wore round his neck. I put it upon the dead man's breast, and took care to have it buried with him in the small grave that had been dug to receive his body, under the shade of a large cherry tree. How many must have died in a similar manner, far from their friends, without one word of consolation, without one friendly look to cheer their last moments!

But enough of this: I could describe a hundred similar scenes which I witnessed in the hospitals, but the liveliest imagination of the reader could not portray the sad reality of such pictures of woe and misery as it was my fate to behold.

If the great and powerful among men could but once make themselves acquainted, by personal observation, with such hospital scenes, they would shudder more than they are prone to do at the horrors of war, and would resolve never to draw the sword or advocate a resort to it for any light cause.

Our Generals did their best to reorganize the army, and proceeded to draw up a report of the battle, but this was but imperfectly accomplished. Johnston's and Longstreet's brigades had suffered most, as they were nearly the whole day under fire. Nearly every company lost from forty to fifty men in killed and wounded. The loss in officers especially was excessive, some regiments having nearly every officer *hors de combat*. The deaths of Generals Bee, Barlow, and Fisher were universally regretted. General Barlow fell at the head of the 4th Georgia regiment, and with his dying breath encouraged his men. Fisher had only arrived a few days previously with the 6th North Carolina regiment, and here found the death of a hero. General Bee, a former pupil at West Point, was much beloved by his men; he fell in the last attack, and his troops became almost frantic when they learned the death of their commander.

According to the report drawn up, the loss of the Confederate army was 879 men killed, and 2,963 wounded. The loss of the Federal army could not have been less—rather greater if anything. The brigades of Generals Tyler, Heintzelman, Hunter, and Franklin were fearfully cut up. These troops, officers and men, who held out to the very last, are entitled to the highest praise. Griffin's battery rendered admirable service.

The spoils won by the Confederate army were very considerable. Besides capturing 28 guns, partly dismounted, they took about 1,600 prisoners, including several officers, a quantity of arms, carriages, ammunition, baggage, &c.; amongst other things, a state carriage and pair, in the inside of which a pair of epaulettes were found, without an owner.

A rumor prevailed that this was the victorious car of General Scott, in which he had intended to make his triumphal entry into Richmond.

However, the severe blow dealt to the Federal cause by the defeat at Manassas, so far from discouraging the Union Government, aroused it to new activity. A desire for vengeance spread through the whole North. The greatest excitement prevailed; recruits poured in from all quarters; and in a short time a larger and more powerful army was collected and brought into training than ever before was seen on that continent. General M'Clellan was appointed to the command of this army, and it may be fairly asserted that if this general had held the command a few weeks earlier, the battle of Manassas would not have been lost.

In the South, on the other hand, matters proceeded more recklessly than ever. No attempt was made to remedy the confusion and carelessness that had got the upper hand. Our politicians were intoxicated with the success of our arms. They felt as if they could dictate to the world. "Had not the battle of Manassas," they reasoned, "shown that we possessed the best generals in the world, that every soldier was a hero,—in short, that the South must conquer, and that the subjugation of the North was at hand?"

CHAPTER X.

RICHMOND AFTER THE BATTLE OF MANASSAS.

Rejoicing in the town—Adventurers—Gambling hells—Provost-Marshal Winder—Secret police—John Minor Botts one of their innocent victims—His sufferings—Deplorable state of Richmond.

THE exultation at the defeat of the great Federal army bordered in Richmond upon the fabulous. The whole town was in a state of the greatest excitement, and this was kept up by the public press. Since the Government had fixed its seat at Richmond, a complete change seemed to have come over the population. The town was thronged with adventurers from every quarter; and the population, which was formerly 30,000, had greatly increased. A number of gambling houses from New Orleans and California had started into existence, and were plying their nefarious trade with an impudence that is scarcely credible. They seemed to spring out of the earth like weeds, so that Richmond in a short time counted no less than one hundred and seventy of them. Added to this, robberies of the worst description were perpetrated amongst our quiet population, so that the better classes began seriously to think of migrating from Richmond into the interior of the country.

The Goverument having lost nearly all power of control, appointed as provost-marshal for the State of Virginia, with the rank of a brigadier-general, a former colonel of the

United States army, J. H. Winder, of Baltimore. All the Baltimore men who had taken up their quarters at Richmond now fancied they could all have their own way, and scenes occurred which created the greatest alarm amongst the peaceable citizens. In the public streets, at the theatre, and in the boarding houses, men were attacked and murdered, and at night scarcely any one dared to walk in the streets. General Winder, who seriously intended to put down these disorders, formed a secret police, which, however, unfortunately consisted for the most part of banished Baltimore men, and, to their disgrace be it said, of a number of German Jews. A fearful state of things now grew up in Richmond. Assassinations and murder were the order of the day; all attempts of General Letcher and Mayor Mayo to restore the former state of order and tranquillity failed in presence of this secret police, whose first victims were a number of our most esteemed citizens—amongst others, the Hon. John Minor Botts.

The accusation brought against him was that he was in secret communication with the enemy, that he was a member of a secret society, whose object was to capture President Davis and his Cabinet, and to give them up to the enemy. To crown this act of villany, an individual from New Orleans, who had brought with him the reputation of a resurrectionist, and had only escaped imprisonment by flight, came forward as accuser. Despite the evident proofs of the falsity of the accusation, the secret police kept hold of their victim. These scoundrels wished especially to show the Government that they did not earn their pay for nothing, but that they had a care to the safety of President Jefferson Davis. The town, on the other hand, was not quieter or safer. Peaceable citizens, at their daily avocations, were attacked by armed soldiers, whilst drunken bands rendered the country unsafe for miles round. Against these scandalous proceedings the police took no measures; but worthy citizens not chargeable with any misdemeanor, except that of being loyal subjects and well inclined toward the United States Government, were brought before the Provost-Marshal and locked up.

Whenever the old State Government of Virginia made a show of punishing the real disturbers of the town, these men were forcibly rescued by the secret police and allowed to resume their villainous work.

For a long time did John Minor Botts, accused of being a traitor, remain a prisoner in durance; and it is almost a miracle that, in face of the mob, which was urged on by the newspapers, he escaped with his life. If ever the United States has to indemnify a brave patriot for ill treatment, John Minor Botts is the man.

Attacked and persecuted on all sides, unprotected by his own Government, placed at the tender mercies of an excited populace, he throughout displayed the calmness and dignity of a man conscious of his right, and claiming to be regarded as a free citizen of the United States. Declining all the proposals of the new Government, he remained true to his convictions.

The arrests at Richmond increased daily. An imprudent word heard by one of the secret police agents, who were always spying about to get men into their clutches, was sufficient to bring the speaker before the Provost-Marshal, and from thence to prison. Owing to the prevailing espionage, no one felt himself any longer free, or safe from his neighbor; even friends of long standing began to mistrust each other. A fearful state of things had befallen Richmond, which will ever be remembered by its inhabitants. In this city, as elsewhere in the South, trade and commerce came to a standstill, so much so that no man would buy or sell or barter. It was just as if the town had been occupied by hostile troops, bent upon doing all they could to effect its ruin. Richmond during this period, owing to the mismanagement of the authorities, friends, and protectors, lost all its former prosperity; and the once fine, flourishing town had more the appearance of a den of robbers than the chosen meeting place of the friends of their country. Many an honest citizen in this fearful time offered up a heartfelt prayer to Heaven: "Preserve me, O Lord, from my friends, for I have no fear of the enemy."

CHAPTER XI.

BEAUREGARD COMMANDER-IN-CHIEF OF THE ARMY OF THE POTOMAC.

The victors at Manassas—Inertness of the Confederates—Activity of M'Clellan—Beauregard fortifies Virginia—Disorders and sickness in camp—Beauregard goes to the Mississippi—The Army of the Potomac.

WHILST the enemy was working with the utmost zeal to remedy the losses which they had suffered, and whilst their whole attention was concentrated on improving the condition of their troops, carefully adopting every measure which tended to repair the injuries they had received, our generals did literally nothing in the way of preparation for the future. The genius of Generals Smith, Jackson, and Johnston had shone out brightly at the battle of Manassas. It was they who saved the honor of the day, and turned the balance of victory in our favor. Beauregard was, however, the ostensible hero of Manassas, the man, too, who took Fort Sumter; and whosoever entertained any doubts on the subject, had only to purchase, at the cost of two cents, the *Richmond Despatch*, where it was printed in black and white that the most victorious warrior of the age was no other than General Beauregard. It was really most surprising to observe the inertness which followed the battle of Manassas. Our War Department, our generals, our soldiers, were all reposing on their laurels, lost in the happiest dreams of their late success. Nothing was done toward insuring the fruits of this victory. The idea of having beaten the Northern army was so consoling, that the Southerners began to think that what every experienced military man urged—namely, that the soldier should be taught, as he had still everything to learn—was pure folly. "We have now," they said, "beaten the greatest general of the age," (for poor Winfield Scott was up to that time so regarded,) "we have destroyed his army, and consequently it would be a waste of time to drill, exercise, and do other things of that kind; they would now be superfluous."

"Europeans," they said, "who do not know how to kill time, and who are not made of the same stuff as we, who all are born heroes and soldiers, believe in all this nonsense. We need only draw our dreaded bowie knives, and every enemy who is able to run will do so."

These ideas predominated among the soldiers of the army of the Potomac, and the officers took no pains to counteract them. This was indeed a great pity, as the raw material existed, and every element was there for the creation of a firstrate army, if in the hands of a general competent to the task. When General M'Clellan was appointed to the supreme command of the Federal army, and set to work to strengthen his position by the construction of fieldworks, in order to be enabled to proceed the better with the reorganization of his forces, Beauregard at last began to bestir himself and to rouse his officers and men from their lethargy. Fortified works on a grand scale were now undertaken, and, indeed, the preparations were so extensive that it appeared as if the whole State of Virginia was to be fortified. No steps were, however, taken to provide for a winter campaign, for the erection of hospitals, the improvement of the roads, or the instruction of the soldiers. While the strict blockade maintained by the United States fleet deprived us of many necessaries.

We were especially ill provided with medicines and clothes, and the troops suffered greatly in consequence. Added to this, sickness broke out in Beauregard's camp. It was the more serious, inasmuch as our authorities had never directed their attention to any sanitary precautions. Wounded men and horses were alike treated in the most negligent manner, and the consequences were indeed appalling. Dead horses lay about in hundreds as they had fallen, and nobody seemed to care about it, or to take any steps to put an end to a state of things so detrimental to the health of the army. Before long, the hospitals in Beauregard's camp became enormously overcrowded, and the scythe of death reaped a large harvest in the narrow lanes of the camp, mowing down the lately blooming youth of the South. Happily for the army, General Beauregard received orders to assume the command of the Confederate army on the Mississippi, and he at once left for his new destination, to try conclusions with the Federal General Buell. It was, indeed, high time for a change in the administration of the army of the Potomac, as the demoralization, negligence, and the lax discipline which permitted the soldiers to assume a bearing which verged on actual insubordination, were becoming quite unbearable. Pale, haggard faces peered out upon you from the tents, and forms worn to the bone by hunger and disease tottered about. Nobody seemed to exert any authority, and nobody was disposed to obey. Like master, like man; no one cared for the other; no one looked to the future—all lived for the day, as if no to-morrow was to come, and there was no enemy to contend with. Beauregard left his army in the most deplorable condition, hurrying straight to the scene of his future defeat, a defeat which he had only escaped at Manassas by sheer good fortune.

CHAPTER XII.

THE CAMPAIGN IN WESTERN VIRGINIA.

Western Virginia—General Wise—General Henningsen—Headquarters, Charleston, Va.—The enemy crosses the Ohio—General Wise abandons Charleston, and hands over the command to Henningsen.

THE campaign which now commenced in Western Virginia offered features of peculiar interest. It is to be regretted that the Confederate Government did not sufficiently appreciate the value of this mountainous region. It was looked upon as a sort of Siberia, and the generals and troops sent there were regarded as exiles.

General Wise, who was feared on account of his upright and straightforward character, received orders to establish his headquarters in Western Virginia; to drive back the Federal troops, which had already crossed the Ohio; to keep the country clear, and to make a demonstration in the direction of Wheeling, in order to dislodge the Virginian Legislature, which still lingered there and remained true to the Union. This was no small task in itself; but the orders which had been given him with no friendly intent, did not daunt the old soldier. He inquired with quiet earnestness of manner, what troops would be placed at his disposal for the accomplishment of his task, and was told by the Secretary of War, that as the Government had principally to keep the Potomac in view, the War Department was under the necessity of sending all reinforcements in that direction; that he (General Wise) must endeavor to collect what troops he could in Virginia itself, and that the Government would take care that he should be well supplied with ammunition.

Any other general would, in all probability, have thrown up his commission. General Wise, however, politely took leave of the official authorities, and resolved to accomplish the difficult task allotted to him.

At Richmond his friends received him with the most hearty welcome. Officers and men tendered their services. General Henningsen, an Englishman by birth, well known in Europe, was one of the first to wait upon him. General Henningsen, a man gifted with a fine commanding exterior, and endowed with great abilities, proffered his services in the most handsome manner. General Wise, though suffering from ill health, then worked day and night in making the necessary preparations for the campaign. He issued a proclamation to the people of Virginia, which was heartily responded to. In a short time, having assembled a considerable force, he resolved to move his headquarters to Louisburg. From this point he proceeded down the Kanawha Valley, where he was received with great respect, not from his being a general of the Confederate army, but from the grateful sense entertained of his conduct when formerly acting as governor of that district.

The Virginian representative at Congress was George Summers, member of the Washington Government, who enjoined his constituents to remain true to the Union, or, at least, to observe a strict neutrality.

General Wise, without impediment, arrived at the small town of Charleston, and there established his headquarters.

In a short time his little army numbered 2,500 infantry, 700 cavalry, and three battalions of artillery. Colonel Tompkins, formerly in the United States army, joined him shortly afterward with a few companies, which brought up his effective strength to 4,000 men. As regards the Virginian recruits, or volunteers, they were scarcely of any use whatever. General Wise chiefly depended upon a small body of men, consisting of one company under the command of his son, and upon three to four squadrons of cavalry, and the artillery, which was deficient, however, in guns.

The Federal troops took up a position at Parkersburg and Point Pleasant, on the Ohio. Their commander having ordered his troops up the Kanawha river, in order to dispute the possession of the valley, General Wise directed Colonel Patton to drive the enemy from the river. An engagement ensued, in which Colonel Patton was severely wounded; but he succeeded partially in driving back the enemy.

It was at this juncture that the news arrived of General M'Clellan's success at Rich Mountain. General Wise thereupon, fearing an attack from superior forces, ordered defensive works to be constructed on Gauley river, and sent in a report of what he had done to the Government at Richmond, requesting reinforcements and supplies of arms and ammunition. Suddenly the news reached the camp that the enemy, after crossing the Ohio, had arrived at Marietta. General Wise immediately advanced against them. An engagement ensued, in which the enemy got the worst of it and retreated. The tide of battle, however, turned presently after, and after a brilliant cavalry engagement, General Wise found it advisable to fall back on Charleston (Va.). Colonel Tompkins, who commanded at Charleston, was ordered to send forward all the troops he could spare toward Ripley, while Colonel Richardson, who commanded the important post at Gauley Bridge, was ordered to keep a sharp look out for General Rosecrans, lest he should make a diversion on Gauley river, which would have placed General Wise in the predicament of surrendering at discretion to the enemy.

General Wise effected his retreat in good order. After

setting fire to Charleston he withdrew to Gauley Bridge. He sent his son, Captain Wise, to Richmond, to lay a complaint before the Confederate Government that he had not been properly supported, and tendered his resignation, offering the command to General Henningsen, which was accepted.

CHAPTER XIII.

OPERATIONS ON GAULEY RIVER.

General Henningsen assumes the command of Wise's legion—Floyd as a general. —Floyd and Wise—Awkward position of the General—Floyd is attacked— His defeat—Hasty flight—His report to the Ministry of War.

GENERAL HENNINGSEN is one of those men who speak little, but act quickly and with decision. He knew how to gain the love and confidence of his soldiers in the highest degree. As soon as he had reached the headquarters of General Wise, there to assume the command, after a short interview the two officers soon understood each other, and Henningsen, without loss of time, ordered a careful reorganization of the army, which had suffered considerably from fatiguing marches.

In a few days it was manifest that an able soldier had taken command; so that all the Government had to do was to send reinforcements, ammunition, arms, and money to pay the troops. The Confederate Brigadier-General Floyd, the former Secretary of War of the United States, who had taken up a position in Whiteville, near the Virginia and Tennessee Railway, received orders to hasten his arrangements, and proceed to the support of General Wise's legion. General Floyd, however, preferred a more quiet kind of life. He liked to receive his friends at his country seat in the vicinity, where they could thoroughly enjoy themselves at his well-furnished table, with his excellent wines.

Generals Floyd and Wise were bitter enemies. Floyd often laughed at Wise's mishaps, and when urged by the latter to hasten his preparations, he coolly replied, that as soon as he had assembled his troops he should move; adding that he would undertake to drive General Rosecrans across the Ohio in a fortnight.

Floyd was much given to expatiate on the great and mighty deeds that were to immortalize his name. He was liberal too in making presents. It is no wonder, therefore, that under such circumstances, he had many friends and admirers ready to sing his praises.

He remained, meantime, quietly at his country seat; and it was not until he had been repeatedly urged to move, that he resolved to start with his troops and afford relief to poor General Wise.

He now proceeded to organize his staff. For its chief, he appointed the editor and proprietor of the *Lynchburg Republican* (a paper said to be in Floyd's pay). His first aide-de-camp was the sub-editor of the same paper; chief engineer, a former mechanist; the leader of his cavalry, a farmer named Harnan, to whom he solemnly promised to bring back the cavalry precisely in the same condition in which it was on going forth to the wars: that is to say, without any loss whatever. Floyd must, therefore, have fully intended to spare his men as much as possible, and to avoid fighting.

These extraordinary arrangements having been completed, General Floyd resolved to commence his victorious career. He sent his baggage and guns to the railway depot, that they might be forwarded as far as possible by the train; but here he met with a sad obstruction. Nothing had been prepared for such an eventuality, neither carts nor horses; and although the great general had held his headquarters at Whiteville for three months, he was quite ignorant of the capabilities of the railway for military purposes. So he had to issue an order for the baggage and artillery to be taken on to the depot at Newbern, to have it conveyed from thence.

After a three days' march, the officers charged with the mission met with the same annoying obstacle, nothing having been done here to provide the means of transport. The wagons and batteries had, therefore, to return to Whiteville, and to proceed thence over the hills to the appointed place of meeting, White Sulphur Spring.

Floyd's brigade now began to move like a worm, whilst the chief of his staff and his aide-de-camp gave a grand account of the wonderful march in the *Lynchburg Republican*. The store of flour at Wolf Creek, which had been six months there, was found unfit for use; the bridges over the streams were broken down, and the roads in such a state that they were scarcely passable even for pedestrians, much less for baggage and artillery. At a distance of scarcely forty miles from the city, one of his 12-pounder rifled cannon fell down a declivity, killing men and horses. Thus his operations commenced with a bad omen. Moreover, on the road, many of his men deserted; and when, at last, after a most fatiguing march, the brigade reached the appointed rendezvous, instead of 3,400 men, with which he started, it numbered only 1,200. It is plain, therefore, that before having seen a battle-field, the precious management of the commander had ruined the efficiency of his brigade.

Meantime, Wise's legion, under the admirable management of General Henningsen, had undergone a complete metamorphosis, and, considering the few means placed at his disposal by the Government at Richmond, he had already effected wonders. Both officers and men placed the fullest confidence in him. Great as were his deserts, he was not properly appreciated by the Confederate Government—most probably by reason of his being a foreigner. This would have not prejudiced his chances of success, had he been inclined to take service in the Federal army.

After much delay, Floyd's brigade did at last make its appearance, and still later came the general himself. The meeting of Floyd and Wise was anything but amiable. General Floyd, as holding superior rank, received with a patronizing air General Wise's address, and his report on the state of the brigade and the measures he deemed advisable. It was really humiliating for the old officer, who had just gone through, if not a successful, at least an honorable campaign, to find himself the subordinate of a man whom he despised, and from whom, he knew very well, he had to expect every species of petty annoyance, for the mean gratification of showing off his superior rank. With a proud bearing, and earnest look, General Wise paid his visit, but declined the proffered hand, and in a few curt words said that he awaited his superior officer's orders. On General Floyd inquiring into the condition of his troops, Wise replied that he would order the chief of his staff to present him with the lists, and thus the two commanders separated as unreconciled as before.

On the same day, General Floyd received reënforcements from the 1st Mississippi, Louisiana, and Virginia regiments, and also nine guns from the regular army, which gave to his brigade a formidable accession of strength. On the following day a general order was issued by Generals Floyd and Wise for the troops to advance to Sewell Mountain.

Floyd then proceeded westward toward Sewell Mountain, where he was followed, a few days afterward, by Wise's legion; and after driving in the enemy's outposts, he rapidly approached his destination.

General Rosecrans now withdrew his advanced troops from Locust Lane and took up a position near Hawk's Nest, there to await the further operations of our generals. General Floyd, unmolested, reached Dogwood Gap, where the road from Summersville crosses that from Louisburg to Charleston (Va.) Here he placed in position a small battery of two guns to prevent a flank movement on the side of the Federal general Cox, who was at Carnifex Ferry with about 2,000 men.

The main body of the troops then took the direction of Picket's Mill, a few miles distant from the enemy's outposts. Scarcely had we arrived there when two orderlies hastened up to inform us that the enemy's generals, Matthews and Tyler, had made a show of attacking our rear. General Floyd immediately broke up his camp and commenced his march about midnight, to save his rear as well as his baggage, both of which were in danger.

Generals Wise and Henningsen were ordered to hold Picket's Mill at all risks, and to prevent any flank movement the enemy might attempt at Hawk's Nest. Floyd marched with his brigade rapidly on Carnifex Ferry, which place he reached about noon. He found on his arrival there that the United States troops had made a retrograde movement to prevent an attack by our troops on Hawk's Nest. General Floyd then resolved to raise the boats which the enemy had sunk, and therewith convey his troops to the opposite bank to take possession of the favorable position abandoned by the enemy. As soon as the chief of the engineers had informed General Floyd that he had completed that prodigious feat, which took him full twenty-four hours, whilst General Price, in half that time, took an army of 13,000 men across the river Osage, the troops were at once conveyed across to the other side. The infantry got safely over, but in conveying the cavalry, one of the large boats was upset, and six men and two horses were drowned. The unfortunate general now found himself in an awkward position: there he was with his infantry on one bank, whilst the whole of his cavalry and artillery remained on the other. The alarm amongst the infantry became every minute greater, for should the enemy get wind of the predicament in which the general was placed, they would not have failed to capture the whole army without firing a shot. The general shouted to his chief of engineers on the other side to construct boats in all haste; but it would have been just as easy for him to jump over the moon as to build a boat. He, therefore, did the best thing he could do; he mounted a horse, and set off as hard as he could go, to inform Generals Wise and Henningsen of the awkward position of their comrade, which news caused the greatest hilarity at headquarters.

General Henningsen, in this emergency, sent over his chief engineer, Captain Bolton,* who constructed floats quite capable of taking the troops across, although the river was now swollen by heavy rain.

Meantime General Floyd set earnestly to work to fortify his position, and sent out patrols, to ascertain the movements of the enemy. On the following morning, when all the infantry was safely over, news arrived that the enemy, in great strength, was moving down from Gauley Bridge, and had already occupied Cross Lane. The commander of the Federal troops had already been apprised of General Floyd's mishap with the ferry boats, and hastened to endeavor to cut off his infantry. Colonel Tyler, indeed, felt so certain of Floyd and his infantry that he did not go to work seriously enough. Instead of first ascertaining Floyd's real strength and the nature of his position, he was imprudent enough to place his outposts no further than 200 yards from his camp. Floyd, on being informed that the strength of the Federal troops did not exceed 1,200 men, resolved to attack them. The plan succeeded. After driving in the outposts by a sudden attack, he compelled the rest to beat a retreat. But this coup-de-main was not of much importance, for the Federal troops were driven back with very little loss; but the chief of the staff delighted the readers of his newspaper with a glowing report, as if General Floyd had achieved a great victory. Floyd could hardly have been ignorant of the motive for this attempt to glorify him; moreover, he loved to see himself figuring in print as a great general.

* An Englishman by birth, who had served in the British army.

This little affair made him, his officers and men feel quite presumptuous; indeed the idea was entertained of advancing between the forces of Rosecrans and Cox, so as to defeat the one in the vicinity of Hudsonville, and to cut off the retreat of the other on Charleston, and capture him; in short, General Floyd entertained great Napoleonic ideas. His quartermasters received orders to provide ten days' rations for the men, which was done; and his troops having gained some rest, he resolved to commence operations.

As soon, however, as General Rosecrans had been informed of the crossing of the Gauley river by Floyd's troops, as also of the mishap to Colonel Tyler, as quick as lightning he dashed forward on Floyd's flank, and before the latter had become aware of his presence he boldly attacked him, despite the fatigue of his own men, who had performed a march of twenty-five miles on execrable roads, without any opportunity of taking rest; it was only with the greatest difficulty that Floyd could maintain himself in his position. At nightfall General Rosecrans again led his men to the attack, and after a short engagement drove Floyd's army from all its positions. Without giving himself the trouble to look after his defeated men, or to attempt to organize an orderly retreat, Floyd, accompanied by his staff, was the first to reach the other side of Gauley river. Gradually his men dropped in with all haste to put the waters of the stream between them and their pursuers. That so many of them contrived to reach the other bank in safety, can only be ascribed to the fatigue of General Rosecrans's troops.

Yet scarcely had General Floyd recovered from this defeat and flight, when he must needs appear in a brilliant light before the world, and accordingly forwarded the following report to the Confederate Secretary of War:

"I am fully convinced that I should have driven back General Rosecrans on Toussansville, beaten Cox's army, then marched direct down the Kanawha valley, and have occupied Charleston, if the reinforcements which I had ordered General Wise to send me had reached me in proper time. I am convinced that if I had had 6,000 men instead of 1,500, I should have annihilated the enemy and taken the rest prisoners.

"J. B. FLOYD, C. S. A."

Now it is well known that as soon as General Floyd asked General Wise to send him reenforcements, he forthwith communicated with General Henningsen, when that officer started, in all haste, to join him with 2,000 men. Moreover, Henningsen left orders for two other regiments to follow immediately. Not only did the last-named general send off all the disposable troops he could, but he even sent more reenforcements to Floyd than he was justified in doing, in order that he might give him the utmost possible support. Unfortunately those troops arrived when the light-footed Floyd had already recrossed the river with his defeated soldiers, and had destroyed the timber bridge which had been constructed. It is likely enough that General Floyd in person accompanied the officer across the Gauley river who took the despatch to General Wise. He had no wish to be captured by Rosecrans and sent off to Washington.

Floyd managed to save the greater part of his brigade. And so it happened that, notwithstanding the simple, truthful report of this affair which Generals Wise and Henningsen sent in to the War Department, Floyd's report was believed, and he himself praised for the great bravery he had displayed.

CHAPTER XIV.

CAMP DEFIANCE, CHEAT MOUNTAIN, COTTON HILL.

General Wise proceeds to Fayette County—Vain attack—Floyd goes to Big Sewell Mountain—Henningsen and Wise intrench themselves in Camp Defiance—General Lee goes to Huttonsville—Floyd, Wise, and Henningsen operate against each other—Animosity of the two brigades—General Lee acts as conciliator—He concentrates an army of 28,000 men—Jackson's defeat at Cheat Mountain—Changes in the command—Floyd is appointed to the chief command—Wise and Henningsen are compelled to submit—Floyd breaks up Wise's legion and goes to Cotton Hill—Outpost skirmish at night—German soldiers and their songs—Rosecrans defeats Floyd—Floyd is transferred to Tennessee—Wise's legion at Richmond.

WHEN Floyd took post at Carnifex Ferry, General Wise marched down Big Creek to Fayette County, where the enemy's troops lay in considerable numbers. He had to outflank the enemy's position, and sent Colonel Anderson with his regiment over one of the narrow mountain passes to attack them on that side. The road was, however, so bad and impracticable that Anderson was soon obliged to return. Meanwhile serious fighting had taken place at Big Creek, between our troops and the hostile batteries, and our riflemen were briskly engaged with those of the enemy, without, however, any result being attained, and General Wise was compelled to fall back again on his old quarters.

Meantime General Floyd continued his retreat toward Big Sewell Mountain, where he reposed for a few days to give some rest to his men. He then held a council of war, at which it was unanimously decided to move still further back, and the army, consequently, retreated twenty miles more. Generals Wise and Henningsen declared to Floyd that he might retreat quietly to Meadow Bridge, but that they were determined to maintain the position which they held. General Henningsen ordered Captain Bolton to make an intrenched camp, which received the name of Camp Defiance. General Wise approved the plan of keeping a footing here, so as to maintain communications with General Lee in the northwest of Virginia, in order to carry out a plan mutually agreed upon.

In conformity with this plan, General Lee had received instructions to take the remnant of Garnett's corps, which had been dispersed by General M'Clellan, and with this force, aided by strong reinforcements, to clear the northwest counties, which were occupied in great strength by the enemy, and to bring them back to allegiance, as they were of great importance to the Government. This was Herculean work; but General Lee did not shrink from it. He commenced his march from Henfersville to Huttonsville, with the intention of cutting off the Federal general Reynolds, with his 6,000 men, posted at Tygart's river. He ordered General Jackson, stationed at Greenbriar river, to advance through Cheat Mountain Pass, rendered so celebrated by General M'Clellan, to outflank the enemy. General Jackson carried out his instructions to the letter, and, although the roads were in a dreadful state from heavy rains, he overcame every obstacle, and arrived at his destination. Here, however, he found the enemy well protected by blockhouses and intrenchments, and ready to resist any attack.

Not having received the signal agreed upon with General Lee, General Jackson, after much exertion, withdrew to his former position. Here he learnt that General Lee, with all his forces, had advanced into the Kanawha valley to relieve Generals Wise and Floyd of their respective commands, and to drive the enemy out of the western frontiers. He at once took the direction of Meadow Bridge, with all his troops, where General Floyd had established his headquarters, whilst Generals Wise and Henningsen held their position at Sewell Mountain.

General Floyd, who was greatly annoyed at his having gone so far with his brigade, ordered General Wise (on the strength of his rank as a full brigadier-general) to give up Sewell Mountain and to retire to Meadow's Bluff, as that position was a safer one. Old Wise, however, knew Floyd too well, and was aware that as soon as he obeyed the order, Floyd would take the advantage of the departure of his troops to gain access to his position by another road. Floyd would then have saved his reputation as a general, and held up Wise to the derision of the world for having taken flight. General Wise, therefore, resolved to remain in his strong position, and paid no further attention to General Floyd and his orders. Floyd thereupon sent a complaint to the War Department against Wise and Henningsen; and such a state of animosity grew out of this between the two brigades, that the enemy, had they only been made aware of it, could have annihilated the two separated corps.

At this juncture, General Lee made his appearance with a portion of his troops, and assumed the superior command. He fixed his headquarters near Floyd, and after a long conversation with the latter he hastened to the camp of Generals Wise and Henningsen to inspect the state of the brigade, and, if possible, to put an end to the misunderstanding which existed between Wise and Floyd and their respective corps.

General Lee is an open-hearted, honest soldier, free from all that pomposity which the younger generals are so fond of displaying. After Generals Wise and Henningsen had candidly and frankly communicated to him the details of their campaign, he, accompanied by these generals, inspected the state of the brigade and the intrenchments. After a careful inspection he expressed his full satisfaction at the excellent appearance of the corps, and then returned to Meadow Bluff. He next ordered Floyd's brigade forward to Big Sewell Mountain, and desired that general to take up his position there without delay. General Floyd, who had received large reinforcements, set to work at once, and had soon a line of defence to the extent of twelve English miles.

Meantime, General Rosecrans remained inactive at the other side of Sewell's Mountain, contenting himself by merely sending out a few detached companies to watch the movements of Floyd and Wise, without, however, firing a single shot to disturb them. General Lee's troops now advanced, bringing up the effective strength of the army in Western Virginia to about 28,000 men, with a very good park of artillery. General Lee had scarcely concentrated all his forces and made the necessary preparations for a general attack, when our patrols and skirmishers brought in the news that during the night General Rosecrans had assembled his troops and fallen back upon his position at Gauley Bridge. The expected battle did not, therefore, take place, for General Lee wisely refrained from pursuit.

General Rosecrans was no sooner aware of the presence of General Lee and his forces at Big Sewell Mountain, than he hastily gave up his post of observation, and proceeded by Gauley Bridge, Toussansville, toward Greenbriar river, where a corps of observation, under the Confederate General Jackson, was posted.

General Jackson had not the slightest notion of the storm that was gathering over his head. He was aware that both the enemy's armies were at Sewell's Mountain, and indulged in a feeling of perfect security. News of the movements of hostile troops on the road to Toussansville did not cause him the slightest alarm, and he laughed at the anxiety expressed by some of his officers. General Jackson had a number of officers on a visit at his house, and was enjoying himself in their society, while a violent autumn storm was raging outside. The company was startled in their revelry by an aide-de-camp suddenly rushing in with the news that large masses of troops were in rapid advance from Cheat Mountain. This information was received with some derision, but General Jackson ordered Colonel Rust to advance with a battalion to drive back the skirmishing force, as it was supposed to be, that had advanced so near. A moment after a heavy fire of musketry, accompanied by the sound of artillery, made the guests jump to their feet. They all rushed out uncovered to their respective posts; the enemy was then already debouching through the pass, and kept up a well-sustained fire, which caused the greatest confusion amongst Jackson's men, who were not at all prepared for this sudden attack.

In vain did the officers exert themselves to get their troops together and make them stand firm; it was impossible to bring the men, so suddenly disturbed from their rest, to any sort of order and steadiness, and General Rosecrans poured such deadly volleys into the assembling troops that they took to flight like a herd of startled deer. General Jackson, therefore, was soon compelled to abandon his position, and to retire to the mountains, where finally, after great loss, he succeeded in taking up a position at Ford Creek. The enemy, satisfied with the success that they had achieved, destroyed all the buildings, barracks, and fortifications, and, laden with a considerable booty, returned again to their quarters at Gauley Bridge.

General Lee never brought General Jackson to account for this mishap, as he himself was perhaps in some measure the cause of it. After the departure of General Rosecrans from his front, he must have known that that active general would not so willingly have left his position before Sewell Mountain unless he saw a certain chance of success in another quarter. He ought, therefore, at once to have informed Jackson of Rosecrans's movements, and urged him to be on his guard. General Lee, usually a most cautious general, did not on this occasion show sufficient prudence, and had to pay dearly for it. Happily, winter now set in in these mountains, and compelled the hostile parties on both sides to remain inactive. The Secretary of War, annoyed that General Lee should have allowed Rosecrans to escape from Sewell's Mountain, deprived him of his command, and sent him to Georgia and South Carolina. General Loring was ordered to Winchester to reinforce Stonewall Jackson, and the latter, after his mishap at Cheat Mountain, had to transfer his services to Louisiana. Generals Wise and Henningsen, moreover, were ordered to Richmond to defend themselves against the charges brought against them, and during their absence General Floyd was appointed to the chief command of both brigades.

It will be apparent from these alterations in the respective commands, that a complete change was effected in the Virginian army. General Floyd, on assuming his new authority, displayed his aptitude for command by contriving so to mix up artillery and cavalry, horses and harnesses, &c., that if General Wise had returned, he would have had the labor of a giant to perform, to put things straight again.

Winter having set in with great severity, General Floyd requested the Secretary of War to order him to proceed with his brigade to Cotton Hill, in Kanawha valley, as he should there have a better chance of encountering General Rosecrans. This request was granted, and one fine day, General Floyd took his departure, carrying with him everything that he thought might be serviceable, and leaving only a remnant of Wise's brigade behind.

Cotton Hill is situate in Fayette county, on the river Kanawha, just opposite the mouth of Gauley river. From its heights the enemy's camp could be seen, spread over the plain, which is there some miles in extent; General Rosecrans having his headquarters at Hawk's Nest, at the handsome plantation belonging to Colonel Tompkins, who was serving in our legion, while from the top of the house waved the flag of the United States, as if in derision of the owner.

After a very difficult march, General Floyd reached Cotton Hill, and his first step was to seize all the boats upon the Kanawha river. Shortly after his arrival, some sharp outpost skirmishing commenced. This, which is always the most unpleasant sort of fighting, was here particularly so, for rifle bullets kept whistling about in such numbers in the valley, that it was impossible to relieve guard in the daytime. The enemy's riflemen lay concealed behind every rock and tree, and wherever they saw the slightest stir, crack went their rifles. The *petite guerre* carried on in this quiet valley was rendered additionally fierce by mutual animosity, for our men did not wish to remain one jot behind the enemy in the rivalry of deadly strife. Even the river which separated the combatants seemed to partake of the turmoil that raged on its banks. And when the firing was over, as night came on, nothing was to be heard but the roaring of the waters, intermingled now and then with snatches of song from some of the German soldiers on either side, which produced a touching effect at such an hour. Ofttimes one of our Germans could be seen leaning on his rifle, listening to the sounds of his mother tongue as they were wafted over from the enemy's camp. At times, one of the sentinels would shout across, "From what part do you come, countryman?" "I am a Bavarian. From whence art thou?" "Halt! Who's there?" The dialogue is interrupted by bullets whistling by in all directions. Who knows that those two Germans, who, only a few minutes before, were talking peacefully together about their fatherland, may not be now lying dead far away from their native land? But such is a soldier's life!

Meantime a portion of the cavalry of Wise's legion came into camp; the General himself, who still at Richmond, had sent in a request to proceed with his legion to Roanoke Island, as the enemy was shortly expected there.

The Confederate troops remained for a long time confronting the troops of General Rosecrans, but all the fighting was confined to outpost skirmishing. General Rosecrans at last, weary of this inactivity, crossed the river Kanawha one fine winter's morning, with two or three columns, and suddenly attacked our position. General Floyd never expected such an uncivil proceeding on the part of Rosecrans: probably he did not expect to be molested at such a vile season of the year, in his by no means comfortable position.

Scarcely any preparations had been made for repelling an attack, as no one imagined that we should have to encounter a winter campaign. General Rosecrans, consequently, had it all his own way, especially as Floyd, as soon as he heard of the enemy's advance, pleaded illness and handed over the chief command to the head of his staff, who deemed the only safe course was to retreat. To fight shy at the approach of a resolute enemy, seemed to be a species of chronic disease with both Floyd and the chief of his staff. This time the retreat was so hasty, that a quantity of property belonging to the Government fell into the hands of the enemy. It was just as well, however, that we did make good speed, for Rosecrans's advanced troops had already attacked our rear and were with difficulty kept at bay. Our troops endeavored by clambering over stony paths to gain the crest of the mountain, and fortunately our rear guard was commanded by a brave officer, Colonel George Croghan, who manfully resisted all the enemy's attacks. For defence or attack, the colonel was always at hand, and the safety of Floyd's brigade was undoubtedly due to the resolute conduct of Colonel Croghan.

But my valued comrade did not live long enough to wear his laurels. A team of carts laden with provisions had been delayed, and ran the risk of falling into the hands of the enemy, who were almost at our heels, and already sending a few bullets amongst us to hasten our flight; when Colonel

Croghan, followed by twenty-five of his lancers, dashed down the road to check the enemy, with the view to save the carts, but he had scarcely reached the latter, when two bullets brought him to the ground. His men on seeing this immediately fled. In Colonel Croghan we lost a worthy, gallant comrade, and the State an excellent officer.

General Rosecrans pursued Floyd's troops for nearly twenty-five miles, and only gave up the chase on finding the roads so blocked up by broken carts, dismounted guns, and other obstacles; he then left the brigade to pursue its way unmolested. Floyd pulled up at the banks of Wolf's Creek, a rocky, uncongenial spot, and then endeavored to reassemble his scattered men. In a few days, an order came from the War Department, for General Floyd and his brigade to proceed to Tennessee, at the same time recalling Wise's legion to Richmond.

Joyfully did Wise's troops part company with Floyd's, and a few days after Richmond presented an exciting scene. With banners flying and drums beating, the remnants of this once fine legion entered the town, whilst thousands of citizens came forth to greet the warriors from the west; fair hands waved their handkerchiefs from the windows in token of welcome, whilst the populace vociferously cheered. Yet many an eye was dim, for the thinned ranks showed the loss of many a lamented relative. A carriage, with two ladies in deep mourning, moved silently along—conveying the mother and the intended bride of Colonel Croghan; they brought with them a handsome flag as a token of remembrance to his regiment of their late brave commander. In the evening a banquet was given by the citizens to the legion, and toasts drank in honor of Generals Wise and Henningsen, and to the glory and prosperity of the country.

CHAPTER XV.

M'CLELLAN APPOINTED TO THE CHIEF COMMAND OF THE FEDERAL ARMY.

M'Clellan appointed Commander-in-Chief of the army on the Potomac—Condition of that army—Its reorganization—The General beloved by the soldiers—His activity—His energy and talent.

AFTER the severe blows which the Federal army had received at Bull Run and Manassas, the eyes of the Government were opened to the fact that some other system must be adopted, and that men of talent were needed to carry out its views; it had to cast about for a general who should be found to combine in his person all the qualities necessary to shield the country from a repetition of such disasters. Now it happened that not long before, General George M'Clellan had, with a mixed body of troops, in a country which had offered every facility to the enemy to maintain a long and wearisome guerilla warfare, in a very short time achieved a victory which drew upon him the attention and favorable opinion of military critics both in his own country and in Europe.

A zealous sense of duty and an enthusiastic and patriotic spirit enabled him to overcome every obstacle that stood in his way. He understood, as his recent brilliant success over General Garnett amply proved, how to inspire his men with much of his own daring and energy, and they followed their commander, with devotion, in the path which rarely fails to lead to honor and victory.

When, as already stated, the Federal Government was anxiously looking around for an efficient general to organize as well as to lead an army capable of protecting the State and of winning victory back to the Union banner, General Winfield Scott, whose advancing years no longer allowed him to take the command himself, at once proposed George M'Clellan as the man who combined the requisite energy and talents for such a post. The Government at Washington followed his advice, and summoned General M'Clellan to the capital; without hesitation they intrusted him with the chief command of an army which, recently defeated and disorganized, had lost all confidence in its commanders.

The army that needed this reorganization and a competent chief to take it into the field was assembled at Washington and its environs. It was a difficult task for any one to attempt, that of imparting confidence to a body of men who, from recent disasters, had been completely discouraged. However, General Scott succeeded in overcoming all M'Clellan's objections to take the command, by promising to assist him with his advice; and he finally consented to undertake the thankless task.

When the official notification appeared that General M'Clellan, the hero of Rich Mountain, was to assume the command of the army of the Potomac, the intelligence was cordially welcomed by the troops. All were eager to serve under a commander who had given evident proofs of his military capacity. When he arrived with his staff in the midst of the great body of troops now confided to his command, he was welcomed by them, not as a stranger, but as an old comrade from the western mountains of Virginia, who had come to restore their lost confidence and to lead them once more to victory. Without being led away by the enthusiasm of the soldiers, M'Clellan went quietly and steadily to work to restore the spirit and discipline of the men, and to re-establish a good understanding between them and their officers. He neglected nothing to make himself thoroughly acquainted with the smallest details connected with the army. Unaffected by the high rank conferred upon him by his Government, and by the compliments paid him on all sides; but, like a skilful physician, he probed and examined into all the wounds, that he might know best how to heal them.

All the measures taken by M'Clellan proved that he was quite up to his work, and that he knew perfectly what an arduous task he had before him. He took care to see in person the wants of the men provided for; devoting his whole time to the most minute investigations; and thus, while reminding the men of the duties they had to perform, he was careful to set them a useful example himself. By such means, he soon gained the confidence of the whole army, was readily and cheerfully obeyed, and was looked up to as a leader capable of surmounting any obstacle.

By keeping his men hard at work, he strove to bring them into a state of good discipline, in order that they might be efficient on the battle field, and that they might get accustomed to the voice of their officers. The latter also, sharing in his own confidence, assisted him to the best of their ability; in a short time a complete change was discernible in the army of the Potomac. Fortifications, for the defence of Washington, arose on all sides. Sham fights, practice with the bayonet, cavalry manœuvres, daily took place. In short, General M'Clellan completely reorganized the army by his energetic reforms; and when he rode through the ranks back to his tent, he was always loudly cheered by the troops.

I willingly pay the tribute of my impartial admiration to General M'Clellan for the success of his zealous efforts in organizing, out of the raw materials at his disposal, so efficient an army; and no soldier, capable of forming an opinion on the subject, could refuse to join in that admiration.

The devotion of the army for their chieftain displayed itself again at a later period, when he was intrusted with the chief command at Frederick, in Maryland, on which occasion he was received with a regular ovation by the troops.

CHAPTER XVI.

THE CAMPAIGN IN MISSOURI.

Events in Missouri—German troops—St. Louis—Governor Jackson joins the Confederates—Troops assemble at Boonville and Lexington—Colonel Marmaduke —General Lyon—Cole Camp—General Price—Movement of the Federal troops —Hopeless condition of the Confederates—Sigel.

WHILST these events were occurring in Virginia, the other border States were not idle. The State of Missouri took the initiative. With the permission of the Confederate Government, a body of troops had formed a camp outside St. Louis. The captain in command of the Federal troops stationed there, did not, however, allow this germ of a revolutionary movement to grow apace under his very eyes. Relying upon the German population of St. Louis, as well as upon the loyalty of their feelings as citizens of the Union, he assembled some battalions of German troops, marched to the revolutionary camp, and, after an energetic summons, made them surrender. This gave great annoyance to the Confederates at St. Louis. The Germans were received with showers of stones and pistol shots, which unpleasant welcome was responded to by the poor fellows with a volley which killed some of the ringleaders. The excitement increased, and St. Louis, that beautiful and flourishing city, was on the point of becoming the scene of strife between two contending factions, which it only escaped through the presence of mind of Captain Lyon, of the United States army. To him it is due that St. Louis did not share the unhappy fate of Richmond. He placed a cordon of troops round the town, and handed over the ringleaders to the local authorities.

A few weeks after the capitulation of Fort Sumter, Governor Jackson of Missouri had thrown off his sheep's clothing and taken the side of the Secessionists, seeking a refuge at Boonville, whither he transferred the seat of the provincial government, there to carry out his further plans. One of his first acts here was to appoint his friend, Sterling Price, a major-general; he also appointed as brigadier-generals, Parsons, Clark I., Clark II., Slack, Stein, Harris, Raines, and Thompson; and he further issued a proclamation calling out 50,000 men. Major-General Price and the other newly created generals were ordered to levy troops as quickly as possible, and to send them on to Boonville and Lexington.

General Lyon resolved to crush the force already got together. Toward the end of June he assembled some thousand German troops, and after sailing to within a few miles of Boonville, he effected a landing, and proceeded to disperse the rebels, who mustered some 1,200 strong, commanded by Colonel Marmaduke. Whether Colonel Marmaduke was at heart true to the Union Government, or whether he did not put much trust in the courage of his followers, he, at all events, declared to them that, considering the superior strength of his opponent, he had resolved to abandon his position and take one up further back. His men, however, refused to obey him, and declared their intention of exchanging shots with the enemy. Colonel Marmaduke then left the place, transferring the command to Colonel Brand.

After a short, spirited engagement, in which both parties lost some hundred men in killed and wounded, the Secessionists dispersed in great disorder.

Generals Jackson and Price had their headquarters at Boonville, but as soon as they heard of the above defeat they embarked for Lexington.

The remnant of the body of men dispersed by General Lyon withdrew westward, commanded by Generals Clark and Parson, and accompanied by the majority of the officials of the different State departments. Their object was to reach Cole Camp, about twenty-seven miles further on, but General Lyon, convinced of the cowardice of the Government, sent 800 men to take possession of it.

Our troops had arrived within ten miles of the place, when they were startled by the news that the enemy was in the vicinity. In their hopeless position they were informed by a spy that Colonel Raines, with 700 men, was at no great distance, and was coming up to their support. It was then resolved to make a joint attack upon the troops under Colonel Cook. The scheme was attended with perfect success. The troops ordered by General Lyon to Cole Camp— a force of militia—fancied their work was done when their march was over; so, after having feasted themselves, they formed their camp without taking any precautions. Now, as their orders were to cut off the enemy's advance, they could hardly have been ignorant of his proximity. So confident, however, were they in their safety, that they retired to rest without even placing outposts, and the whole camp went unsuspiciously to sleep.

During the night our two divisions had formed a junction, and advanced with precipitation upon the enemy. The sentinels were cut down, and the slumbering troops aroused by the sound of musketry. Our men fell with a cheer upon the unarmed soldiers, and made short work with them. All that could escape did so, and amongst the first to run away, it is said, was Colonel Cook, to whom the whole disaster must be attributed.

Of course this small affair was trumpeted forth by the public press as a great battle. Governor Jackson now reappeared on the scene to take part, at least, in the last act. It was decided to attack Colonel Tatten. But Colonel Tatten having learnt the numerical superiority of our troops, fell back with the intention of forming a junction with General Lyon. The Confederate troops, thus thwarted in their intention, resolved to continue their march southward, to join our other forces there, which they succeeded in doing. As soon as a body of 4,000 men had been assembled, General Price took the chief command in person, and transferred his basis of operations to the Arkansas mountains, where Colonel Prince, of the Federal army, was stationed with a force of from 3,000 to 8,500 men, and made a show of cutting off General Price's retreat. General Price now resolved to make a retrograde movement, and, depite many obstacles, successfully effected this operation; so that on the 3d July, he was able to join the other troops in Cedar county.

In Cedar county the troops were formed into regular brigades. Generals Clark, Parson, Slack, and Raines were each appointed to a brigade of 1000 men, under the chief command of Governor Jackson. Before the troops had commenced moving, Governor Jackson received the information that the Federal troops, under General Lyon, were advancing on the north-eastern side, with a view to form a junction with Generals Lane and Sturgis, and then to fall upon his rear in large numbers.

Governor Jackson, seeing the dangerous position in which he was placed, exerted himself to the utmost to escape from this manœuvre of the enemy, which threatened him with destruction. He immediately set his small army in motion, and performed one of those forced marches which often have been the means of saving a whole army. By nine o'clock in the evening, after encountering many obstacles, he had marched twenty-three English miles, and could afford to allow his fatigued men a few hours' repose. On the following morning he received the certain news that a body of men, 3,000 strong, under General Sigel, had started for Rolla, by railway, and had already arrived at Carthage, a small town in his front, with the intention of giving him battle in a few hours, which, considering the fatigued state of his men, who were, moreover, but badly armed, was by no means a consoling piece of intelligence. Such was the predicament in which Major-General Jackson found himself and his Missouri army one fine morning: a strong body of the enemy in his rear, and General Sigel in front. He made up his mind, however, to attack Sigel, and after a forced march of sixteen miles came upon that general's outposts early on the morning of the 5th July, and found his army drawn up in order of battle on the slope of a hill.

CHAPTER XVII.

BATTLE OF CARTHAGE.

Attack of the Confederates—Sigel falls back on the town—Ben M'Culloch, the guerilla chieftain—Noble conduct of General Price.

As soon as the Missouri army debouched upon the open prairie it was immediately formed into line of battle. The infantry, in a compact body, was under the orders of Generals Clark, Parson, and Slack. General Raines took command of the cavalry, whilst Governor Jackson acted as commander-in-chief. The infantry took up a position at a distance of about 600 yards from the enemy, and the cavalry was placed on the right and left wings to attack the enemy's flanks, while the infantry was attacking him in front.

The few old guns our troops possessed were of little or no service. As soon as the Confederate cavalry deployed right and left, General Sigel poured a volley of grape, canister, and round shot into them from his excellent battery. Governor Jackson's guns replied as best they could, but with no success. In default of better ammunition the guns were loaded with broken pieces of iron and stones. Our cavalry made a vain attempt to capture the enemy's battery; but Sigel handled his guns so well that they were repeatedly repulsed with loss. This sort of amusement had lasted nearly two hours, when Governor Jackson, convinced that he could not do anything with his cavalry, resolved to storm the enemy's position with his infantry, the cavalry following in support at a short distance. The Missouri troops advanced courageously to the attack. With a loud cheer they rushed upon the enemy, and compelled General Sigel to yield ground and fall back upon Bear Creek, a river of some depth and width; after making his way across he destroyed the bridge, and finding that our troops greatly outnumbered his, he retreated about a mile, and then he made a halt. Then commenced one of those rifle skirmishes which so perpetually occur in American warfare. Weary at last of this sort of desultory fighting, which led to no great result, our troops cut branches of trees and made rafts, upon which they crossed to the other side; the cavalry swimming across. General Sigel, who was too far away from his reserve, now resolved to retreat to Carthage, about eight miles distant, and performed his retreat in good order, beating back our repeated attacks.

At Carthage he made a' halt to rest his men. After several unsuccessful attacks, Governor Jackson feeling that, notwithstanding his numerical superiority, he could do nothing, ordered the fighting to cease, that he might attend to his wounded, who lay in considerable numbers along the road. General Sigel then continued his march toward Rolla. Governor Jackson had reason to be well satisfied with his success, as it caused considerable sensation amongst the inhabitants of the prairie, who by hundreds left their families, and seized their rifles to join in the guerilla warfare. On the following day large masses of troops appeared in sight, which proved to be those of General Price, and the band of the famous guerilla chieftain, Ben M'Culloch. There were some thousands of these men, who, from their capability of enduring privation and hardship, were especially suited to this sort of warfare.

Sigel, who was also aware of the approach of these numerous guerilla bands, anxiously endeavored to save his little army. Great was the joy of the Missouri men on again beholding General Price, who had just recovered from a serious illness, but it became unbounded when the men of Arkansas and the men of Missouri mingled together. It was an exhilarating sight to see the bold hunters of the Western prairies and virgin forests, men who had waged war against the savage Indian, the wolf, and the bear, give their rough greeting to the sons of the sister State, and grasp the hands of many whom they had supposed dead, whose scalp they fancied hanging possibly at some Indian's girdle as a trophy; libations of whiskey and brandy, as may be guessed, were now freely indulged in by these swarthy warriors.

This was the first occasion on which the famous guerilla chieftain, Ben M'Culloch, made his appearance. He had been given the rank of a brigadier-general in the Confederate army, and it was extraordinary to see how the sunburnt sons of the plain, heedless of his rank and fine uniform, pressed around him, and with their brawny hands nearly crushed his in their friendly but eager gripe.

The festivities ceased; the shades of evening came on, and the stillness of night watched over the slumbers of the two armies. The sentinels alone crept about like snakes, or like spies on the trail of an Indian, to insure safety to their sleeping comrades. The god of dreams mildly swayed the thoughts of those sleeping warriors, drawing many a fanciful picture of future adventure. There lay those unconquered sons of America, their rifle by their side, calm, like children, dreaming some of their sweethearts far away, others of battle, or of booty, and they smiled as they slept. Yet many of them, perhaps on the morrow, would sleep the last sleep of death, with the long grass of the prairie for a tomb: struck by some hostile bullet—cut down like the ripe fruit from the tree.

On the following morning the troops were formed into divisions, and the march commenced for Conwoskin prairie, in M'Donald county, an Indian station at no great distance, as it had been ascertained that the enemy's forces, under

Generals Sigel, Lyon, Sturgis, and Sweeney, were endeavoring to form a junction at Springfield. Before, therefore, undertaking anything against the amalgamated forces, a halt was made for a few days at Croskin prairie, to bring more order into, and better to divide, the troops. The reenforcements, which hourly dropped in, brought up the effective strength of our army to 12,800 men. A council of war was now held. M'Culloch, as brigadier-general of the Confederate army, presided. After a somewhat lengthy debate it was resolved to follow the enemy to Springfield, and to give him battle. Preparations were immediately made to carry out this plan. General Ben M'Culloch took the command of the vanguard, and advanced toward Barry county, from whence the operations against Springfield were to be undertaken in common.

However, before the Confederate troops had reached Crane Creek, news was brought in that the Federal troops had abandoned Springfield. The enemy's outposts were seven miles distant from ours. Our forces were ordered to halt, and for some days the fighting was confined to outpost skirmishing.

After this mutual watching, and the inactivity evinced by the enemy's generals, who, probably, had delayed an attack until their plans were more mature and their artillery had arrived, General Ben M'Culloch suddenly lost confidence, and after a council of war it was decided to abandon our position, and to beat a retreat. The causes which induced Ben M'Culloch to take this step were the superior number of the enemy, armed with excellent weapons, and their greater number of guns, whilst his troops were badly armed, and not properly organized. Much of this, however, was untenable. First of all, the Federal troops did not outnumber ours; moreover, the enemy had commenced their military career at the same time that our men did, so that there could be no advantage in that respect; on the contrary, if there was any, it was on our side. As a set-off to the better arming of the Federal troops, it may be said, that they consisted chiefly of Germans who, when the war broke out, had left their peaceful homes to take up sword and rifle in order to fight for their adopted country : they had given up their quiet, industrial pursuits to undergo all the hardships of war. Whilst on the Confederate side, the elements of which the army consisted were men inured to warlike doings of every description ; who had been brought up to the use of arms from children ; and who, under able commanders, were capable of doing good service in the field. However, Ben M'Culloch took it into his head to retreat, and he was obstinate enough to carry out his will. In vain did General Price endeavor to persuade him to alter his mind. He proposed an immediate advance ; pointed out the enthusiasm which prevailed amongst the troops, and which ought to be turned to account to strike a blow against the enemy ; but it was like talking to the wind. As nothing could shake the obstinacy of M'Culloch, General Price asked him to give up the better arms which his followers possessed, and he (Price) would attack the enemy without him. But this he also declined, and General Price, much annoyed, left the tent.

On that same evening, whilst all the necessary preparations were being made to commence a retreat, an aide-de-camp arrived at the camp from Major-General Polk of the Confederate army, bringing the order for General M'Culloch to attack the enemy at Springfield without delay. As soon as he had read the despatch, he summoned all the generals together and communicated General Polk's order to them, declaring that he was ready to march at once on Springfield, provided he was given the chief command.

General Price nobly replied that it was immaterial to him in what capacity he fought, provided that he had an opportunity of doing service in the defence of his country, and that he was willing not only to give up his command, but his life if necessary. He then handed over the chief command to M'Culloch. These quiet, earnest words of General Price did not fail to produce a powerful effect upon the minds of the assembled officers.

Even Ben M'Culloch felt ashamed when his officers reproached him for his ambition. He advanced toward General Price, and held out his hand, but the latter drew back, and said, "Do your duty as the general in command, as I intend to do mine, and we will endeavor to forget what has passed."

Ben M'Culloch having assumed the command, his first general order was that all unarmed persons should remain in the camp, that those who had rifles or muskets should get them ready, should provide themselves with fifty rounds of ball, and. be prepared to march at midnight.

Ben M'Culloch now divided the army into three divisions. The first he commanded himself, and the others he intrusted to Generals Pierce and Price. About midnight, the troops quietly left the camp, leaving the sick and wounded, baggage, &c., behind, and commenced their march in the direction of Springfield. The men were all in excellent spirits and confident of success. They expected to come upon the enemy's outposts at about nine miles' distance from the camp; but when, after a fatiguing march, our troops reached the place and began to reconnoitre cautiously, they found that the enemy had decamped on the previous day, and were now retreating. Despite the great heat, our troops immediately followed in the enemy's track. As they had no canteens, they suffered considerably from thirst, but nevertheless advanced steadily until they reached Big Spring, about two miles from Wilson Creek, and about ten miles from Springfield, where they encamped that evening. Our troops, who had left all their provisions behind them, had not tasted food for twenty-four hours, and in their eager craving began to eat the green corn with which the fields were covered. They had neither tents nor blankets to protect them from the night air, and their clothing was in bad condition; indeed, nearly four fifths of the men were without shoes, yet they cheerfully performed this fatiguing march. The officers, too, were scarcely better off, with the exception of General Ben M'Culloch, who displayed his brilliant uniform to the admiring looks of our poor ragged fellows.

The army resumed its march on the following morning to Wilson Creek, and there encamped; the large fields of green corn they met with there supplying them with the only kind of food they had tasted for two days. At eight o'clock in the evening a general order was issued for the troops to be ready to march at nine against Springfield. After a council of war, General M'Culloch resolved to attack the enemy at daybreak, on four sides at once. The soldiers had already satisfied their hunger, prepared their ammunition, and were ready to march, when, owing to the heavy rain, a counter order was issued, postponing the attack till the following day.

CHAPTER XVIII.

THE BATTLE OF OAK HILL, OR WILSON CREEK.

The Federal troops under Generals Sigel and Lyon commence the attack—Sigel retreats—Lyon is obliged to give way—The Confederates are victorious—Death of General Lyon.

Before General M'Culloch's excellent plans could be carried out, and our troops put in readiness to attack the Federal General Sigel, General Lyon had already commenced an attack upon us, and our men had just got into position, when General Sigel also assailed us on our right wing and in our rear, while the artillery on both sides opened fire. General M'Culloch did all that was possible to keep his men in line of battle and repulse the repeated attacks of Generals Sigel and Lyon. The men of Missouri, under the command of their Brigadier-Generals Slack, Parsons, and Raines, had taken up a position in front, and were ordered by General Price to advance in all haste upon the enemy. After proceeding a few hundred yards, they came upon the main body of the enemy, under the personal command of General Lyon. Both sides immediately opened a brisk fusilade, the artillery being at the same time in full play; a Federal battery under Captain Tatten, and a Confederate battery keeping up a regular duel.

General Price then ordered two regiments—the Louisiana volunteers, and a regiment of dismounted chasseurs—to attack the battery in front. In a few minutes they were ready, when these wild sons of the prairie resolutely advanced with fixed bayonets, and attacked the enemy's left flank, posted in a large cornfield. Our two regiments were received with a terrible discharge of musketry, but persevered in their attack, and succeeded in repulsing the enemy, who had to fall back on the main body. As soon as General Lyon saw his troops thus retreating, he led forward in person one of the German regiments posted with his reserve. It was a fine sight to see these Germans rush on the advancing foe, and by their determined courage impede his further advance. Whilst the troops under General Price were nobly holding their ground in the centre, General Sigel observed that several Confederate regiments had assembled on his left flank, and threatened to attack this, his weak point. One of our batteries had already taken up a position to protect these troops with their fire, when General Sigel promptly ordered up some guns, and pouring a storm of grape upon the regiments who were preparing to advance to the charge, caused them serious loss.

General M'Culloch, observing the confusion among his troops, caused by the enemy's fire, ordered the mounted chasseur regiment under M'Intosh to their immediate support. This regiment was to the Confederate army much what the Old Guard was to Napoleon, and kept in reserve for any emergency. Such disorder had already spread among the Confederate forces, that it was indeed high time for the mounted Jägers to come to the rescue. Without losing precious moments in forming, they threw themselves headlong upon the battery which was causing such damage to our people, and in spite of a gallant defence, General Sigel was obliged to give way before superior numbers, and as the Texas and Missouri cavalry regiments threatened to cut off his retreat, in the event of his maintaining his ground much longer, he abandoned his position.

The Confederate forces having obtained these great advantages on their right wing, it became necessary for them to direct their attention to the enemy's centre, where the bulk of

General Lyon's forces were posted. General M'Culloch, therefore, directed the cavalry regiments of Colonels Embry and Churchill to dismount, attaching them to the infantry regiment of Gratiot, and adding M'Rae's regiment as a reserve; he ordered these troops to make a general attack on the front of the enemy's position. Our brigade was received by a tremendous fire as they advanced to the attack, protected by small columns at their flanks. Generals Sigel and Lyon defended their position gallantly, and in spite of the vigorous attack made by our troops, it was impossible to drive the Germans from their position. The German is a good and brave soldier when fighting from conviction, and for a cause which he loves. Quarter was neither asked for nor given, and the battle had already raged for several hours, without any particular advantage on either one side or the other. It was at this juncture that General M'Culloch assembled some regiments, and attempted to storm Captain Tatten's battery, which was causing such havoc among our soldiers. Our men attacked the enemy's battery with great courage; General Lyon, however, making a rapid flank movement, in his turn attacked our storming parties, inflicting great loss upon them by a well-directed fire, which mowed them down by columns. General M'Culloch's men were already beginning to waver, when, at this critical moment, three regiments of General Pierce's brigade hurried to his support, and he ordered up Reid's battery and the Louisiana volunteers, with which additional forces the struggle at the centre was renewed with desperation. The troops under General Pierce attacked the enemy with such determination that they began to falter and gradually give way. This retrograde movement of the Federal troops produced immense excitement among the Confederates, and the Missouri, Arkansas, Texas, and Louisiana forces threw themselves at once, with loud hurrahs, on the wavering line of the enemy, and drove him completely from his position.

The retreat of the Germans was, however, executed with

praiseworthy coolness, in the face of the furious onslaught of the Confederates. Generals Sigel and Lyon now perceiving the futility of trying further to repel the attacks of an enemy so superior in numbers, they issued orders for the whole army to retreat. Owing to the losses sustained by the Confederates, and their exhaustion, they could not molest them in effecting this movement. General Lyon fell at the close of the engagement, and the command-in-chief consequently devolved upon General Sigel, an able officer, who succeeded in withdrawing the Federal forces from the scene of action in good order.

Thus ended the battle of Oak Hill, as we named it, or of Wilson Creek, as named in the official report of General Sigel.

The battle lasted full seven hours, and our loss of 2,000 killed and wounded shows the desperation of this fierce struggle. Our trophies consisted of merely two dismounted cannon and some hundred muskets. The enemy lost in General Lyon a brave defender of the State of Missouri, and a good patriot. He fell whilst encouraging his men by word and deed; two bullets penetrated his heart at the same moment, causing immediate death. His doctor came to us after the battle with a flag of truce to claim his body, and General Price had the politeness to offer his own carriage for its removal. The body could not, however, on account of the heat, be conveyed further than Springfield, and General Price ordered Colonels Elgen and Mercer to provide a proper funeral, and a Mrs. Phelp, of that place, presented them with a coffin. A few days afterward the body was conveyed to his friends at St. Louis.

After the battle of Oak Hill, our generals found their division so cut up, that they were obliged to go to work very cautiously, General Sigel being just the man to give them but little leisure for recovering themselves. General M'Culloch determined to proceed to Arkansas with his forces; whilst General Price, on the other hand, advocated a continuation of the campaign in Missouri.

CHAPTER XIX.

A GENERAL WITHOUT AN ARMY.

Thomas Harris—His nomination as general—General Harris and General Price—Fort Scott—An abortive excursion to Warrensburg.

A MAN now appeared in the north of Missouri, with every intention of making a name for himself,—no other than Thomas Harris, who was on his way to the rendezvous of Boonville, with the intention of joining the Confederate army as a private. At Paris (a small hamlet in the county of Monroe), he was recognized by one of Governor Jackson's couriers, who forthwith handed him his commission as brigadier-general of the Missouri State Guard, with orders to undertake the organization of the forces in the northern part of the State with the utmost expedition, and to assume the defence of that portion of the State which was north of the river Missouri. At the time Harris received his commission and his orders he had no opportunity for expressing his thanks to Governor Jackson, as the latter had been defeated by the enemy's troops, and was wandering about the Western prairies without roof or resting place.

The unfortunate Harris, therefore, found himself all alone with his commission and the order to defend the northern line of the Missouri, without soldiers, without arms, without tents, and without money. He might have exclaimed like another celebrated general, " Can I make an army spring from the ground ?" Harris was, however, the reverse of a despondent character, and he tried his best to do honor to his exalted rank. He quietly pocketed his commission and his orders, and repaired to his native county. Immediately on arriving there he held a grand political meeting, described the position of Missouri in the most ghastly colors, and in order to increase the general effect he publicly took the oath of allegiance to the Confederacy; that solemn act being administered by a clergyman who happened to be present. Fifty-three persons at this assembly immediately joined him, agreeing to serve under him. General Harris then gave his future army the permission to go to their homes, provide themselves with arms, and then rejoin him at his headquarters.

The reader will perceive that this new defender of the country went to work with great circumspection, establishing his headquarters first, with the conviction that an army would ere long be got together.

Before his newly raised force of fifty-three men had, however, joined him, the rumor spread that a detachment of the enemy was approaching.

General Harris was not long in moving off to a more convenient spot, followed by his forces, then consisting of some staff officers and three privates, and proceeded with the organization of a band of guerillas. Wherever there is a chance of booty the crows will gather, and he managed in a very short time to get a body of men together, which would enable him to take a prominent part in the complicated events of the period. He soon collected 3,000 men under his orders, and it was on account of this force that General Lyon was at the commencement of his operations obliged to detach a corps to watch its movements. On General Price being relieved of his duties in the Confederate army, he advanced toward the river Missouri. No sooner did General Harris get wind of this, than he broke up his camp and marched a distance of sixty-eight miles in thirty hours in order to join him.

General Price was not a little pleased at being joined by

Harris and his forces, and received them with open arms. The two generals immediately determined to march on Fort Scott. After a tedious march they came in sight of Fort Scott—but only to learn that Generals Lane and Tennison had moved further westward with their forces; they then determined to proceed toward Lexington, as they had ascertained that some of the enemy were there encamped under Colonel Mulligan. Fremont had at this time been named by the Government at Washington to the chief command of the Federal army in Missouri. Fremont was the very man for this post. Immediately on assuming the command he issued a proclamation, threatening every traitor to the Washington Government with the confiscation of his property and the liberation of all his slaves.

As was to be expected, this proclamation created an intense feeling of indignation among the Southerners, and many of them left the army in order to save their property, whilst others, whose property was already greatly involved in debt, abandoned it on the plea of patriotism. The Confederate Government hastened to indemnify these latter by State bonds, and both parties became gainers by the transaction. The Government played a fatherly part, whilst the proprietors who were thus indemnified abused the Federal Government, and by extolling the Confederation, drew many persons to its standard. At the beginning of September, 1861, Generals Price and Harris, who were about to encamp, received information from spies that a detachment of Federal troops was proceeding from Lexington to Warrensburg, a small town in the vicinity, for the purpose of bringing away the Government moneys there, and the cash at the bank, to deposit them for safety at Lexington. This news spread like lightning through the camp, and in spite of the bad weather and the length of the march, the troops got ready with the utmost haste for the expedition.

The whole brigade appeared electrified. The prospect of

capturing some hundred thousand dollars worked wonders in putting the troops on their legs, and an immediate and general start was made, for fear that the booty might be lost. The men had never been so active before; indeed, the officers, although mounted, could hardly keep up with the briskly moving mass. Money is indeed a powerful magnet. Even the sick seemed to have suddenly recovered, and were not to be prevented from hurrying on with the rest, in the hope of sharing the spoil.

Although the troops had been much fatigued by the late marches, this was now quite imperceptible, and indeed when some of the officers wanted to rest they found it impracticable, as the men would not hear of dallying by the way. So on they went without stopping, until they reached Warrensburg. But here they were doomed to disappointment; the commandant of the enemy's forces had already accomplished his task the previous evening, and left the place with all valuables, breaking down the bridges behind him. The rage of the soldiers at the loss of the expected booty was indescribable, and became ludicrous when they saw the caricatures which the German soldiers of the Federal army had sketched on the walls of the houses, in anticipation of the arrival of the Confederates. On the bank itself there was an artistic charcoal drawing in crayons, representing an empty cash box, with a Confederate soldier peeping into it. All this caused bad blood among our people, and they cried for vengeance. The poor inhabitants had to suffer in consequence, and everything eatable or drinkable that was to be found in the little town was laid hands on by the soldiers, who were famished after the exertions of their long march. The generals resolved to assemble all their forces at this place. After a rest of two days the army moved on to Lexington, as it was known that the money had been conveyed to that place. The march was consequently willingly resumed, and on the morning following the advanced guard came in view of the enemy's outlying pickets.

CHAPTER XX.

BATTLE OF LEXINGTON.

General Price—Attack on Lexington—Colonel Mulligan's defence—Capitulation—Booty—Price's retreat—Secession of the State of Missouri—Fremont recalled.

AT daybreak a lively outpost skirmish commenced between the Missouri forces and the Federal troops. After a short engagement, General Price, finding that the enemy was too strong for him, ordered his men to retire and the whole army to fall back. He resolved first to await the reinforcements which had been promised him, and then to renew the attack. Like wildfire the news had spread through the country that General Price intended to make a small *razzia* to sack some cash, and hundreds flocked in to help him at this work. The numbers of the army increased hourly, and it was really amusing to hear the newcomers anxiously inquire if any booty had been made yet. On receiving a reply in the negative, their looks would brighten: they were elated at finding they had arrived in such good time. In a short time, the army of Generals Price and Harris had been increased by nearly 2,000 men, and a general advance was resolved upon. The enemy's outposts were driven back, and the attacking columns approached Lexington, where the Federal troops were strongly intrenched in a position where they were secure unless attacked by very superior numbers. There was one building especially, formerly a schoolhouse, which they had fortified with consummate skill.

General Price ordered up two batteries, and opened a heavy fire upon this post, but it was so well responded to by the Federal troops, that in all haste he ordered his batteries to retire out of range of the enemy's murderous fire. Generals Price and Harris, again losing confidence, withdrew their troops and retreated to Fair Ground, in the vicinity, there to await further reinforcements and fresh supplies of ammunition. In a few days they deemed themselves strong enough to renew the attack upon Lexington.

General Raines was ordered to attack the town on the east and northeast, whilst General Porter attacked on the south side, and all the guns were at the same time to open fire on the enemy's outworks in front. Swarms of sharpshooters were sent from both divisions to annoy the enemy by a continuous fire, and to cut them off from the place which provided them with drinking water. The riflemen did their work well, and in a short time took possession of the enemy's water station.

Immediately on arriving before Lexington, the fourth division, which in the absence of General Slack was commanded by Colonel Rivers, had been ordered to a position west of the enemy's fortifications, whilst a portion of M'Bride's and Harris's brigades was stationed near, to act in support. Colonel Rivers speedily commenced operations, and attempted to capture a steamer which was on the river, and to cut off a chance of retreat to the enemy. The Federal troops, however, poured in such a volley upon him from a house which was used as a hospital, and which had hoisted a white flag, that he had to relinquish the attempt. Shortly afterward, however, a detachment of Colonel Jackson's men, after a sharp engagement, captured the steamer and some small craft on the river, freighted with clothes, provisions, and ammunition, all of which things our troops stood much in need of. This capture was hailed, therefore, with great joy by our men, and spurred on their zeal. At the same time, Generals M'Bride's and Harris's troops took possession of the hills lying to the north of the building already alluded to as serving for a hospital. As soon as Colonel Mulligan, who was in command of the fort, was made aware of the presence of the Confederates, he made a *sortie*, with a view to drive them from the position they had taken. It is a pity that the colonel had not a larger body of men at his command, for he possessed many of the requisites for an able general. He was enterprising, and always ready to make a dash at his enemy when the latter least expected it, and was beloved and respected by his soldiers.

Fortunately for us, the advantages gained by the Federal troops could not be followed up for want of men, and the Confederates, though driven back at first, recaptured the position during the day, and effected this with the very same troops that had been driven back by Colonel Mulligan.

The hilly ground was now promptly placed in a good state of defence, so that the position was rendered strong enough to withstand any attack on a large scale. On the following day General Price erected batteries, and the serious preparations made by him to bombard the fort must have caused considerable anxiety to the garrison. Cut off from all help, short of provisions, opposed to a force more than three times its number, even the bravest might feel discouraged. But Colonel Mulligan met our attacks with undaunted bravery, and when we approached too near, he sallied forth and drove us back. It was only after fifty-two hours' uninterrupted fighting, when all its means were exhausted, that Mulligan, finding his small garrison worn out by exertions, and without a chance of relief, resolved, after holding a council of war, to hoist a white flag as a sign of capitulation. General Price at once ordered the firing to cease, and sent two of his officers to settle the conditions of surrender. The stipulations were soon made. The garrison, with their commander, were to lay down their arms and remain prisoners of war of the Missouri troops commanded by Major-General Price.

This surrender does not cast the slightest discredit on Colonel Mulligan, his officers and men. After having exhausted all their means against an enemy of three times their strength, they had no choice left but capitulation. The booty was considerable. In addition to arms, clothing, and ammunition, they took more than a million of dollars in hard cash. These dollars nearly rendered our fellows frantic, for this was the object which had induced the majority of them to take up arms against their former Government. General Price received Colonel Mulligan's sword, which he returned to him with a compliment: "I should be sorry," he said, "to see so brave an officer deprived of his sword." He offered to place Colonel Mulligan on *parole*, but the Colonel declined, as he said the Government at Washington did not acknowledge Missouri as a sovereign State. General Price politely placed his headquarters at the disposal of Colonel Mulligan and his wife, gave them up his carriage, and paid them every possible attention. It is thus that one brave man honors another, and by so doing honors himself.

The Confederate army had scarcely taken possession of Lexington, when a strong force of Federal troops showed themselves on the other bank, coming from St. Joseph, under the orders of Colonel Sturgis (of the cavalry), to support Colonel Mulligan. Had they come a few days sooner, a different result might have occurred. Colonel Sturgis, on hearing of the capitulation of Lexington, after the exchange of a few shots, returned to St. Joseph, there to form a junction with the army of General Lane.

Whilst the Confederates were celebrating the capture of Lexington, their generals in the southwestern portion of Missouri sustained a series of defeats. Generals Pillow, Horde, and M'Culloch were driven out of the field. This intelligence compelled General Price to relinquish the advantage he had gained, and to make a retrograde movement. Without losing time he commenced his retreat, and as he was badly provided with ammunition, he sent one of his aide-de-camps to Arkansas to arrange matters so that his wants should be immediately attended to, and the necessary ammunition forwarded under good escort.

General M'Culloch promised to escort the transport, but as soon as he heard of General Price's success he ordered the convoy to halt, on the ground that it might be dangerous to forward the ammunition, as General Fremont was advancing in the direction of Missouri.

Harassed on all sides, without ammunition, hated by Ben M'Culloch, General Price adopted the resolution of first reducing the extent of his army, and then of making a rapid retreat. His army before Lexington had swollen to 25,000 men; and this resolution of their honored general gave them great pain, and they did all they could to dissuade him from the step which he contemplated. General Price, after having designated what regiments were to accompany him, took a touching farewell of the remainder of his officers and men.

He now turned all his attention to his reformed small division. His task was not an easy one, and required good generalship. He could not count upon M'Culloch. Fremont had assembled his forces at Georgetown, whilst Sturgis was advancing from the north and General Lane from the west; and these three divisions were marching on Lexington to compel General Price to give battle. The plan was not a bad one; but General Price, fully aware of the position he was in, endeavored to counteract the enemy's plans. He sent all his cavalry forward, and ordered them to make a demonstration on the Georgetown road, to attract General Fremont's attention in that quarter, whilst he, with his infantry and artillery, would oppose Generals Sturgis and Lane. Neither of those generals was aware that Price's large army had been reduced, and that he had now only a small portion of it under his command; hence they were too cautious in their movements, and would not venture to undertake anything until the three divisions had approached closer to each other. Taking advantage of the slowness of the enemy, General Price made a rapid move southward, leaving orders to his cavalry to follow him and to cover his retreat. He reached the Osage without any obstruction, and crossed that river in boats with his infantry, the cavalry swimming across. Without any loss, either in time or men, he reached the other bank in safety. In military annals, this passage of a river by 13,000 men will figure conspicuously, as it was performed without pontoons or any other facilities, and, as already stated, without the loss of a man.

General Price continued his march without delay on Neosho, where the few members of the State of Missouri held their sittings under the presidency of Governor Jackson. General Price was received with marked honor by his Government; and found his comrade in arms here, General M'Culloch, with 5,000 men. The rivals met with great coolness. General Price had good reason to be dissatisfied with Ben M'Culloch's conduct; whilst the latter's envy was aroused at Price's victorious march. The members of the Missouri Government here resolved to send two of their members to the Confederate Government at Richmond, and General Price had the honor to celebrate the formal secession of Missouri from the Union with a salvo of 100 guns. After this harmless ceremony, General Price allowed his forces a respite to recover themselves from the fatigue they had undergone, and remained here fourteen days, when he resumed his march toward Pinéville in Macdonald county, there to reorganize his men.

Meantime Generals Sigel and Fremont concentrated their troops at Springfield, with the intention of putting an end to the war in Missouri. Sigel having proceeded from thence with the advanced guard to Wilson Creek, General Price ordered our troops to retire on the appearance of the enemy; but whilst about to carry out this order, our rear was attacked by Fremont's body guard, under the command of Major Zagony, formerly in the Hungarian service, doing us a good deal of damage, and compelling us to accelerate our retreat. On reaching Pineville, General Price made arrangements to await General Fremont's attack, and then to leave Missouri without once more trying the chances of a battle. He well knew how to inspire his men with confidence in his plans.

And now that General Fremont had caught us, as it were, in a net, what saved us? A battle? No: the Government of Washington at this juncture deprived Fremont of his command. This caused a complete change in the enemy's plans, and allowed our generals full scope to alter their position. The Federal army was now compelled to beat a retreat, abandoning the rich district of Springfield to General Price. The latter at once took possession of it, and settled himself down comfortably for a time in the position abandoned by the enemy.

CHAPTER XXI.

RECRUITING AT RICHMOND.

Stringent measures of the Government—Price of substitutes—The New Orleans Zouaves.

AFTER the unfortunate campaign in Western Virginia, and the reverses the Confederates had met with in Louisiana, Missouri, and Tennessee, the Government of Richmond resolved to take the most energetic measures to redeem its losses. A bill was passed by the Legislature, ordering all citizens, whether natives or settlers, to take service. All men capable of bearing arms, from eighteen to forty-five years of age, were called out. The Government was fully bent on being prepared for the winter campaign. Recruiting offices were established at every corner. General Wise's brigade soon received a large increase of men; for old Wise, despite his rough manners, always shared danger and hardship with his men, and was looked up to with respect. The system of paying for substitutes was now introduced, and a regular traffic in human flesh was the result; not a sale of blacks, but of whites. A portion of the rich planters of the South were discontented with the policy of President Davis and that of his Government, and were eager to leave a service which had lost all attraction for them, and the discomforts and hardships of which had become daily more distasteful. All such endeavored to get off, and the newspapers teemed with advertisements for substitutes, the price rising from the modest sum of 10 up to as much as 3,000 dollars. Agents travelled all through the South buying up substitutes, whom they disposed of at a profit. Soldiers, too, were induced to desert, and then drafted into another regiment. I know the captain of a small trading vessel, who within a fortnight disposed of himself twice in this way, and having pocketed some thousand dollars, succeeded in getting off to sea.

The Government endeavored to put a stop to this melancholy state of affairs, but it was too late, the evil had struck too deep a root, and could not be eradicated. However, to obviate it in some measure, the Secretary of War issued a decree, proclaiming the punishment of death as the penalty of those who dealt in this nefarious traffic.

Troops of every possible description continued to arrive at Richmond to take part in the war in Virginia. It was a fine sight to see them arrive. The North Carolina troops, especially, attracted the attention of the citizens by their frank and courteous bearing. It is true they did not boast of the fine names of their Southern brethren, such as "Tigers," "Wildcats," "Alligators," &c., their regiments being simply designated by numbers, but they were fine-looking, brave fellows. Then came the Zouave regiment of Colonel C——, formerly a noted professional gambler at New Orleans, who, when he found his trade spoilt, took to forming a regiment. With the sanction of the mayor of the city of New Orleans, he established recruiting booths in the different jails there. Each criminal was given the option to stay out the full time of his sentence, or join Colonel C——'s body guard. Hundreds took advantage of the offer to escape from prison, and in a short time the regiment was complete. The officer's staff consisted of noted gamblers of New Orleans, and this noble band started, not to fight for their country so much, perhaps, as in the hope of a little freebooting. In their wide red breeches, blue jackets, and capped with the Turkish fez, these men, bronzed by a Southern sun, made a warlike show, and excited much attention wherever they made their appearance. It was a strange, heterogeneous corps, formed of daring men from every country; but wherever a Zouave had been seen, something or other was pretty sure to be missed shortly afterward. Never, at any previous period, were so many robberies committed in and about Richmond, as during the stay of these defenders of their country. They laid their hands upon everything that came within their reach, and were the dread of the farmers all round. The poultry of the peasantry was carried off at night ; yet what were the poor Zouaves to do ? the officers kept back their pay, so they revenged themselves upon the population. It soon became necessary to assign them a separate encampment, as the officers and men of the other regiments would not mix with them. Strife and bloodshed were the order of the day : no man's life was safe who showed himself within the precincts of their encampment. Among other cases of lawlessness attributed to these men, I may mention that of a poor German gardener who lived in the vicinity, and who was compelled to abandon his house and garden, which was all he had to depend upon for his livelihood, owing to the ill treatment he received. The Government was at last under the necessity of ordering the Zouaves to leave Richmond, and sent them to the Peninsula, where they was soon dispersed, either by the enemy's bullets or through desertion.

CHAPTER XXII.

HOSPITALS OF THE WOUNDED PRISONERS.

Bad state of the hospitals—General Winder—Gross neglect of wounded prisoners—The want of surgeons—Humanity of Captain T——.

I TOOK a great interest in the fate of the poor wounded prisoners in the hospitals at Richmond,—firstly, because, owing to the animosity which prevailed against the Yankees, I fancied they would not be much cared for; and, secondly, because I was aware that, even with the best intentions, the Government could not do much for so many as 30,000 wounded men. Richmond, at that time, had the appearance of a great hospital. Every public building was filled with the sick and wounded. Many of the patients had never been in action. Bad food, insufficient clothing, and want of proper attention had brought them into a state of disease. Two surgeons to attend upon 600 patients were all I found in one hospital; happily, among the prisoners there were a few medical men, who did what they could to alleviate the suffering of their comrades. I shuddered at the spectacle I had to witness; the wounds of many had not been attended to, and maggots were eating into their flesh, whilst their clothing was stiff from clotted blood. I did what I could to improve their condition. I went from bed to bed, promising to exert all my influence in their favor, and many a poor fellow looked me his silent thanks.

I called upon General Winder to represent the case of these unfortunate men. Whilst every attention was paid to our own wounded and sick by the inhabitants, the unfortunate prisoners were allowed to rot and die. General Winder could not withstand my appeal, and promised me his assistance. I then appealed to the German and Irish population to come forward and do something for the poor prisoners, and in a few hours that appeal was responded to. I myself sent everything I could spare from my wardrobe. Many a bottle of wine and parcel of lint, prepared by German ladies, now found their way to the hospitals, and the Irish population, with their natural good nature, brought all the linen they could spare to the surgeons of the prisoners. When it is considered that the persons who did this ran the risk of being arrested by the secret police, the very smallest gifts rank as great sacrifices, for even a glance of pity at a poor sick enemy would have brought them under the suspicion of being traitors to their country. In a few days some sort of system was introduced into the prisoners' hospital. The sick were attended to and waited upon, received changes of linen, and were cheered with the hope of recovery. Many a tear rolled down their pale cheeks, and many a blessing was bestowed on me on the day when I took leave of them, and I left with the conviction that I had preserved the life of many a brave fellow. It is almost impossible to form an idea of the want of feeling of the population of the South. I will only mention one instance which subsequently came under my own observation.

It was after the seven days' fight before Richmond, and hundreds of wounded, friend and foe, were brought into Richmond, where for a long time they were left exposed to a broiling sun upon the platform of the railway station. I went with a friend of mine, Captain T——, son of an admiral in the Confederate fleet, to the station, to render help. Owing to the destruction of the Merrimac, Captain T—— was out of employment, and was in plain clothes. Captain T—— was a fine-looking man, had travelled far, and was a perfect gentleman. When we reached the station, the greatest confusion prevailed; groups of wounded lay in all directions; a number of benevolent ladies, with their black servants, were distributing tea, coffee, chocolate, and broth, to the wounded. I, however, soon observed that they took no notice of many of the sufferers. Some one touched my spur, and on looking down, I beheld one of those ghastly faces which can never be forgotten. It was that of a stately-looking soldier of the enemy, in full uniform. "You are a German officer," he said. "Yes, comrade," I replied; and his eye brightened. "Then I beg of you, most earnestly," he said, "to get me a cup of coffee." Both T—— and myself immediately went up to a lady who belongs to one of the best families of the South, and who had just passed the poor fellow by, without taking any notice of him. "Madame St. ——," I said, "will you give me a cup of coffee for a wounded man?" "Oh, certainly," she said, and her servant handed me a cup. I hastened back, but whilst I was stooping down to give it to the wounded man, some one pulled me by the sleeve, and to my astonishment, it was Mrs. St. ——, who, in a harsh voice, asked me if I was aware I was helping a miserable Yankee. "No, madam," I replied, "I do not know that, but I know that he is a brave soldier, as is proved by his wounds." At the same time I gave this prejudiced woman a look of scorn, which made her beat a hasty retreat, and I then gave the coffee to the wounded man. Tears ran down his furrowed, sunburnt cheeks, and having somewhat recovered himself, he whispered to me, "I am a Swiss; I served for ten years in the Kabermatter regiment at Naples, but never thought I should die in such a hole as this." I endeavored to console him as best I could. Captain T—— now arrived with a basket of strawberries, and pressing some between his fingers, put them into the poor fellow's mouth. Whilst thus occupied, a man seized him by the arm, and said, "I arrest you." It was one of the police agents. Captain T——— drew himself up to his full height. "On what ground?" he said. "Because you are helping the enemy," he replied, "and all the ladies here are talking about it." "Then tell those ladies that I have been taught to practise humanity, and do not act by their standard, and if it is your intention to arrest me, you can do your vile work at the American Hotel, where I am staying. My name is Captain T———." As if he had been bitten by a snake, the miserable wretch started back, pleaded duty and the instigation of the ladies as his excuse, and went away. Captain T——— looked both at him and the ladies with contempt, and continued his attentions to the wounded soldier.

Should these pages ever fall into the hands of Captain T———, he will see how keenly his noble conduct was appreciated by the writer, and he will, I trust, excuse that writer for pointing to him as an example of the contrast which exists between true humanity and the heartless feelings exhibited by the more prejudiced citizens of the South.

CHAPTER XXIII.

THE PRISONS AT RICHMOND.

Ill treatment of prisoners of war—Foul state of the prisons—Colonel Corcoran—A contrast.

WHEN the first prisoners taken from the enemy arrived after the battle of Bethel, a certain amount of pity prevailed amongst the authorities, but this, small as it was, soon disappeared after the murderous battle of Manassas, when they were brought in in large numbers. The strictness with which they were guarded was nothing to the severity that now took place. The prisoners were locked up by hundreds, without distinction of rank—officers and men huddled together in buildings formerly used as tobacco warehouses and factories, from three to four hundred in one room. Amongst others, the gallant Irishman, Colonel Corcoran. The foul air of the building was enough to poison the men; but the authorities seemed to take pleasure in exercising barbarous severity, and stuck to that principle. As, under a broiling sun, each of the buildings alluded to was the compulsory residence day and night of 400 men, it may easily be supposed that on entering it from the open air, the stench was overpowering. To get a breath of fresh air, the prisoners had to lean against the windows, where they were stared at and often hooted by the crowd below. The feeling of humanity sank daily lower at Richmond; and brutality increased so much, that at last it even reached the better classes. Pity vanished altogether; even women, who usually are so ready to give a helping hand to a suffering fellow creature, without inquiring who he is, became hard hearted. Colonel Corcoran put up with this undignified treatment and the insults of the mob with the greatest courage. He was ultimately sent to Columbia in South Carolina, where at least he found human beings, and where he was allowed to breathe fresh air without being stared at by a crowd.

How did the officers and soldiers of the United States treat their prisoners? When, in February, the greater portion of Wise's legion were made prisoners on Roanoke Island, General Burnside and his officers treated them with respect and attention. The officers of the Confederate army were allowed to go free on parole. Both officers and men of Burnside's army showed them many acts of civility, and gave them gold for their Confederate paper money, of little value there. In a few days General Burnside liberated all the prisoners on their giving their word of honor not to serve until an exchange had taken place. If either of the two Governments had a right to treat the prisoners as enemies, surely it was the United States Government, as the Southerners were the originators of this disastrous war. We were the rebellious sons of a worthy mother. She was not the cause of the war; it was we who had applied the torch and set fire to our once quiet and peaceful home.

Our men, when taken prisoners, were usually treated, not like convicts, but as misguided children. But the Confederate Government, which had already despoiled the Union of so many things, now wished even to deprive its adherents of the ordinary rights of humanity and respect.

It is true that many of our officers felt the injustice of the treatment inflicted upon the prisoners, but what could they do? Orders came from headquarters, and they were bound to obey them, for the first duty of a soldier is obedience.

CHAPTER XXIV.

A CHRISTMAS EVE.

Camp life in winter—Sad reflections—Petersburg—Christmas Eve—The Author.

On the 23d December, 1861, I rode back, after inspecting the outposts of our division of the Confederate army. It was a cold, dreary day; the snow fell in heavy flakes, so that my cloak soon had the appearance of ermine. Silently I rode along the banks of the New River, and the stillness around only seemed to make more audible the roar of the waters as they splashed over the rocks in the stream.

No joyous shout greeted me from the camp; none of the gay excitement of a soldier's life was visible. A few groups might be seen sitting silently and musingly round their watch fires, worn out and careless at what was going on or of what might happen next: most of the men were in their huts, and everything appeared cold and cheerless. Why so? Our proud hopes of victory were for the moment at an end; we were compelled to give way before the all-powerful enemy; we were beating a retreat—and the retreat of an army, even if performed in the best order, has, as every soldier who has been at the wars well knows, something discouraging in it. Winter added to the dreariness. Here, in cold and snow, were encamped the sons of those Southern districts, where the sun is always bright and warm; where the green meadows are never covered with snow or ice. Some cast dreary looks at the summit of Hawk's Nest, where the once beloved, now hostile banner of the Republic of the United States unfolded its stars to the wind. Many joyful reminiscences of home and former times were awakened in the breasts of the soldiers on beholding that flag, under whose powerful protection their own section of the community had also grown great and prosperous and they themselves had lived in comfort. Tattered and hungry lay encamped the sons of the South, here, in Western Virginia, deprived of their former prosperity and content, lying on the hard ground with their rifles by their side, eager to aid in lowering that flag for which their forefathers had shed streams of blood, perhaps to become, instead of free citizens, the subjects of some foreign adventurer or native despot.

My mind also was disturbed by these sad reflections; but a soldier's heart must not brood over sorrow, and I urged my horse to a quicker pace along the river side to rejoin my regiment. The dark night and the roaring stream were not congenial to lively thoughts; in vain did I endeavor to recall the happy dreams of my youth: they were dispelled by darker thoughts more in keeping with the shades of the night. How could it be otherwise? It was now thirteen years that I had been away from my native home, and now, drawn into the whirlpool of events, I found myself, almost against my will, serving in the ranks of a foreign army, and fighting for a cause with which neither my head nor heart could thoroughly sympathize.

Occupied with these rather depressing reflections, I reached my tent. I threw off my cloak and sat down by the fire; nature claimed her rights, and, with a physical enjoyment which for a moment set aside mental annoyance, I warmed myself at the glowing embers.

Suddenly I heard the voice of a friend calling out my name. It was General Henningsen, who soon joined me. "Here," he said, "are despatches for the Secretary of War, and which must be taken by a trustworthy hand immediately to Richmond. Will you take them?" I jumped up at once, ordered a fresh horse to be saddled, shook the General warmly by the hand, and, accompanied by an orderly, set out on my mission. "Keep a sharp lookout," shouted Henningsen after me, for he knew I had resolved to take the shortest road, through a defile which might probably be occupied by the enemy. A few shots, indeed, were fired at me from the heights; but, happily, owing to the darkness of the night, they missed their mark, and once through the pass we were safe.

It was only on the evening of the following day that I reached the little town of Petersburg. What a contrast it offered to the monotonous life in camp! Cheerful-looking houses, with well-lit shops, and busy people going to and fro, making purchases or looking in at the shop windows. Merry children, with their parents, buying Christmas gifts.

My path now took me through a dark street, where I was suddenly brought to a standstill. It was blocked up by a detachment of soldiers.

"What's the matter here?" I shouted; "why do you stop up the road?" "We are waiting for a sure conveyance," was the reply, "to send these d—— Yankees on to Salisbury, as they cannot march any farther."

I hastily got off my horse, ordered my orderly lancer to see the horses properly attended to, and accosted the prisoners. Here I found men of every nation, as is common in some regiments of the United States army. Germans, Poles, Hungarians, Frenchmen, Italians, and Irishmen were all mixed up together, each, in his own tongue, trying to describe his misfortunes, and beseeching my assistance. Many of the poor fellows lay wounded and footsore on the ground. It made my heart bleed to see them. What a contrast was this scene of misery to the gay shops of the town! What a Christmas Eve!

With a round English oath, I asked the officer in command of the detachment why he did not get shelter for his prisoners, for this one night, at least. He answered insolently, "That the vile dogs were not worth the trouble."

Convinced that if I was to give a distinct order it would wholly fail of effect upon so coarse a nature, and that the brutal officer would have found a hundred pretexts not to provide a shelter, I went myself in search of one, and succeeded in getting the large outhouses at the railway station arranged as best I could; and I then ordered the lieutenant to follow me with his men.

The prisoners, who numbered about 120 men, now lay down on benches and dry sacks, sheltered, at least, by walls, from the inclemency of the night. Good fires were lit, and the railway authorities sent in food for the hungry men. I gave twenty-five dollars to two subalterns, and sent them into the town for rum, sugar, and lemons, and the courage of the poor fellows gradually revived as the hope of better days dawned within them. On my taking leave they gave me a hearty cheer.

I remounted my horse, and was off for Richmond. I had spent my Christmas Eve!

Here I must be allowed to anticipate events, by introducing an incident that some time after pleasantly recalled this Christmas Eve to my mind.

Months had passed. Heaven had protected me. I had escaped without harm from the many sanguinary engagements which, as we shall see by and by, took place in the first half of 1862, when I was suddenly attacked by the yellow fever in the swampy ricefields of Savannah. With death in my heart, I had myself conveyed to Richmond for medical advice. The doctors were not wanting in good counsel; but the apothecaries' stores were exhausted. By the advice of my physician, I asked for leave and a free pass to the North, where the change of climate might restore me to health.

This being granted, I reached the outposts of the Union without difficulty, and received a hearty welcome from the general in command, who allowed me to continue my journey to New York unmolested. In fact, what was there to fear from a man who was more dead than alive?

I regained my health, nevertheless, in a wonderfully short time; and going down the railway one day, in 6th Avenue, New York, with a friend, I was suddenly addressed by a soldier with only one arm, with the question: " Are you not a colonel in the Confederate army?" "Yes, yes," I replied, hastily, fancying he wished to pick a quarrel with me, and seek revenge for his lost limb. "Well, then, Colonel," he said, "I am happy that I still have one hand left thankfully to shake yours, for I am one of the prisoners for whom you provided a never-to-be-forgotten Christmas Eve at Petersburg."

Much moved, I shook the brave man's left hand, and quickly left the carriage, around which a crowd had assembled.

CHAPTER XXV.

BATTLE OF BELMONT.

Kentucky remains neutral—Exertions of the Federals and of the Confederates—Violation of the neutrality by the Confederates—General Polk occupies Columbus—Appeal of Governor Magoffin—The Federal troops enter Kentucky—Colonel Tappon—General Grant commences hostilities—Pillow's division—Defeat of General Cheatham—The Confederates victorious.

MUCH to the vexation of the Southerners, who had always regarded Kentucky as one of their stanchest adherents, this latter State still continued attached to the Union. All the endeavors of the South to persuade Kentucky that its interests as a Slave State rendered it imperatively necessary for it to join those States which had already seceded from the Union, proved of no avail; the majority of the citizens of Kentucky declined to listen to any such overtures. After the election of Abraham Lincoln to the Presidency of the United States, the Kentucky Legislature resolved, by a large majority, not to secede from the Union, but to exert all its influence to restore the broken pact between the old Government and the States actually in rebellion. Should it not succeed in achieving this object, it was proposed that Kentucky should maintain a strict armed neutrality.

In reply, however, to the demand of the Washington Government for Kentucky to send its contingent to the army of the Union, the Governor of that State, Magoffin, declined to do so, and the Southern States exulted at this, as they fancied that this refusal was to be regarded as the expression of the sentiments of the people of that State. Subsequent events, however, soon showed that there was no foundation for their hopes. President Lincoln requested that a special Commission of the State should proceed to Washington, there to consider the measures the United States Government might think fit to propose, in consequence of the attitude Kentucky had assumed. In compliance with this request, the various districts of that State selected for commissioners men whom they knew to be averse to a separation from the Union. The result of the elections for the Legislature of the State were also in favor of citizens who were known to be loyal supporters of the Union.

The neutrality of Kentucky was first violated by the Confederate Government, which ordered a division of troops to occupy Columbus. General Polk, it is true, who commanded these troops, declared, in a proclamation which he issued to the citizens of the State of Kentucky, that the Confederate Government had been driven to this step because the United States Government had first violated the neutrality, by organizing a military force upon that neutral ground. It stated, moreover, that fortifications had been erected on the Mississippi, opposite Columbus, with the object of serving as a *point d'appui* for the United States troops which the Cabinet of Washington intended to despatch for the purpose of occupying Columbus. The object of the Confederate Government was forcibly to prevent the State of Kentucky from forming an alliance with the Union, which might have been fatal to the interests of the South, but all these manœuvres failed. The United States Government had ordered General Rousseau to organize a brigade in Kentucky, and to establish his headquarters at Louisville, which order he executed so well that in a short time he had collected together 10,000 men. Thus, after General Polk had occupied Columbus for a short time with his division, he found one day, to his alarm, the opposite bank of the river occupied by Federal troops, who, on his making his appearance, took up a threatening attitude, pointing their batteries toward Columbus. The citizens of Kentucky now sent delegates to Governor Magoffin, with an urgent appeal that he should order General Polk to evacuate the territory of the State immediately, which request the latter reluctantly complied with. Polk, indeed, at first signified his intention of only obeying the injunction on the condition that the Federal troops should abandon the opposite bank at the same time, and that the State of Kentucky should give a guarantee to his Government that it would refuse permission to any troops of the United States to enter its territory or occupy any portion of the same; but, as might have been expected, this attempt at interference with the rights of the State was indignantly rejected.

As soon as the Government at Washington was informed of this violation of the territory of a neutral State, it ordered the occupation of Paducah at the mouth of the Tennessee river. Convinced that the Confederate Government was exerting every means at its disposal to induce the State of Kentucky to join the revolutionary movement, it ordered large bodies of troops to be concentrated on the Ohio, so as not to abandon without a struggle this rich State to the Confederates. Preparations on a large scale were made to convince the enemy of the firm will and intention of the United States Government.

Meantime, General Polk had sent for General Pillow's division, in order that he might be enabled to offer battle to the enemy if necessary; and Albert Sidney Johnston, Commander-in-Chief of all the Confederate forces, so planned his movements, that he could operate in concert with General Polk. The hostile armies now took up positions on the Mississippi, on the banks of which river they resolved to uphold the flags of their respective Governments by force of arms.

Before daybreak on the 7th November, General Polk

received the information that a body of the enemy's troops under Major-General Grant was advancing in the direction of the village of Belmont, apparently with a view to give battle to the Confederates. On the other side of the Mississippi we had no other force than a single regiment under Colonel Tappon, acting as a corps of observation, and General Polk had not previously the slightest suspicion that it was the enemy's intention to attack that regiment before we could send reinforcements to its support. But now awakened to the importance of the position, he ordered Pillow, whose division was the nearest to Colonel Tappon's corps, not to lose a moment's time in pushing his troops across the river to the other bank. After personally superintending the crossing of his men, General Pillow with his whole staff passed over to assume the immediate command. The enemy lost no time in commencing the attack upon Colonel Tappon's regiment. The outposts and sentries were driven back upon the main body of the regiment, and Colonel Tappon found himself in a critical position, when Pillow's troops came up to his support. The attack of the enemy was repulsed, and the batteries opened a heavy fire, which must have convinced General Grant that General Polk was determined to maintain his position. The former, instead of needlessly exhausting his men by skirmishing, should, with his knowledge of the locality, have at once fallen upon us with all his disposable forces, and driven us Confederates back to the banks of the river. But as we have already said, instead of doing this, he contented himself with desultory outpost skirmishing, which gave General Pillow time to inform General Polk how matters stood.

The Federal gunboats having meantime taken up a position, they opened fire upon us, and a daring attack was then made upon our centre, after an attempt to outflank our right wing had been defeated by Colonel Betzhoven's battery. This officer handled his guns in such admirable style that the enemy's columns were compelled to fall back upon their centre. The attack upon our front was then carried on with such vigor and effect on the part of the enemy that they succeeded in breaking our line, and our men were for a moment thrown into some confusion. The troops then reformed in squares, as best they could, to resist an attack of cavalry. General Pillow now bringing up his reserve, consisting of two batteries and the half of another, was enabled to keep the advancing enemy in check and to restore the communication between his two wings; he then also ordered up Lindsay's battery, and placed it in a favorable position for raking the enemy's columns. All now went on well enough on our side, when word was brought that the regiments of Bell, Wright, and Russell had no ammunition left. This piece of bad news had scarcely reached us, when a message was received from Colonel Betzhoven that he too was out of ammunition, and must needs withdraw his battery. This was enough to dishearten most men, but General Pillow, fully aware of the critical state of the battle, displayed undaunted resolution on this emergency. After ordering Betzhoven to keep his battery in position, he formed the three regiments that had exhausted their ammunition into a compact mass, and boldly led them against the enemy with fixed bayonets. The Federals were now driven back to the edge of a wood, from the cover of which they opened a smart fire upon us to which we could not respond. Pillow then sent his aide de-camp, Captain Anderson, to General Polk to inform him of the predicament he was in, but the latter, uneasy for his own safety, hesitated to send reinforcements. To understand this, it must be stated that Polk had become fully persuaded it was the enemy's intention to attack Columbus this same day, although all our cavalry pickets sent in word that there was nothing to indicate any such intention on the part of the enemy, they having made no preparations for an attack. But Polk thought differently and was not to be undeceived, and consequently adhered to his own view of the matter, in order to show his Government that he was as good a general as he had been a priest.* So he allowed Pillow's troops on the other bank to be shot down, without taking any steps to relieve them from a position which was becoming every moment more critical. It was only after reiterated messages from General Pillow, and when our men had almost fired their last cartridge, that General Polk gave the order for a portion of his division to cross the river.

All this time Pillow had to withstand the incessant and determined attacks of the enemy. In vain did he display the most chivalrous bravery, and make the most strenuous efforts to maintain his ground; it was impossible for him to hold out much longer. General Grant, aware of the advantage he had already gained, vigorously renewed his attacks whenever he saw the Confederates endeavoring to rally. It was a sad spectacle to contemplate: the Confederates were gradually forced from all their positions by the fire of the enemy's batteries, and had no other resource left than to rely on the bayonet as a means of resistance; and in this plight were compelled, moreover, to abandon many of their wounded to the enemy. General Grant now got his most effective men together, and with these making another desperate onset, effectually broke our ranks, and drove us pellmell down the banks of the river. Pillow's whole division was disorganized and sadly cut up—not one company remained intact—and the men were huddled together in the greatest confusion. Although the Confederates were just then protected in some measure by a hill, numbers were picked off by the enemy's bullets, and there now appeared but two alternatives left to choose between: either to capitulate, or to fight to the last man. At this critical juncture, a Tennessee regiment came up to our support. In their eagerness to help their comrades.

---

* He was formerly a Bishop at New Orleans.

many of the soldiers jumped from the boats and swam ashore, and the moment they got across rushed forward to fall with fury upon the enemy. No quarter was asked or given, no orders obeyed; it seemed as if all the worst elements of human nature had been let loose, to indulge in a fiendish gratification. Additional troops from Texas and Louisiana successively arrived on the field of battle, which ere long attained its full development. The tide turned, and it was now General Grant's lot to be on the losing side. Attacked in front, flank, and rear, he exerted all his energies in vain to maintain the fortunes of the day. He found that he had a fierce and determined foe to cope with, and his men, disconcerted by the furious charges made upon them, began to waver; General Grant was unable to rally them; they were driven back from one position to another, until they fell back discomfited upon their reserve.

General Grant here halted to collect his men, and reinforced by some regiments, from his reserve, he ordered up fresh artillery from the same source and recommenced the contest. Observing that the Confederate General Cheatham was advancing in very careless order, he threw himself headlong upon him, and completely routed his force, capturing 300 prisoners and 2 guns; after which he made so dashing an attack upon our centre that he not only checked the advance of our troops, but compelled them even to waver. General Pillow now galloped along the line, bravely encouraging his men. Though nearly all his staff were by this time shot at his side, and his own clothes were riddled by bullets, the old general miraculously remained unhurt. The Federal troops continued their advance, steadily driving back our forces; and their general then, pushing forward his batteries closer to the river, opened a murderous fire upon our flank as well as upon the steamers which were bringing fresh troops to our assistance. General Polk now ordered Captain Smith to run up his twelve-pounder rifled battery to the bank opposite the battle field. Smith performed this duty in the most masterly manner, and in a short time the destructive missiles from his battery, flying across the broad stream of the Mississippi, were seen to plough through the enemy's ranks. General Grant on this immediately ordered up a battery of the same strength, and a very spirited cannon duel forthwith commenced. It was interesting to watch the precision and coolness with which the guns were handled: it almost seemed as if the batteries were simply engaged at target practice, and every shot told. A great deal of damage to the steamers now ensued, splinters of wood flying about in all directions, killing and wounding many men. Meanwhile fresh reinforcements continued to reach the Confederates, which enabled the exhausted men to take breath and recover their failing strength.

As soon as General Polk felt convinced that we were gaining the upper hand, he crossed to the other bank to assume the command at the conclusion of the battle, so that he might be enabled to despatch a victorious bulletin in his own name.

General Grant, finding that he could not hold his ground against the superior numbers now opposed to him, made his dispositions for a retreat: his troops had now been engaged for full seven hours, and he feared they could not withstand another attack. A previously planned movement, by which the Federal troops were to make a demonstration against Columbus, had not been carried out, and he was consequently exposed to a conflict with all General Polk's forces as they were successively brought up to the field of battle. His manœuvres at the close of the action betrayed his intention of reaching his flotilla, as he commenced his retreat in that direction. This was a sure proof to our men that the victory was ours; and accordingly with a cheer they threw themselves upon the enemy's retreating columns; but General Grant, who had already given so many proofs during this battle of his prudence and energy, successfully repelled the attack. We at last succeeded in taking possession of all his positions, and the depot where he had kept his stores and ammunition. Little remained there, however, for the victors to capture—only a few cooking utensils and a number of our wounded enemies. The surgeons of the Federal forces on this occasion evinced a commendable spirit of zeal and devotion to their professional duties by remaining behind to attend to the wounded. I grieve to say, that these worthy men were, in the blind fury of the final onset, attacked by our soldiers with sword and bayonet, and it was not until General Pillow came up that order could be restored.

General Grant had meantime succeeded in reaching his boats, and set about conveying his troops across; which operation had no sooner commenced than our men kept up a brisk fire on them, and this became hotter when the enemy's boats fairly got under way. Nevertheless, great order was maintained on board, although the vessels were exposed to our fire for at least a mile.

Our return of casualties after the battle showed a list of 680 killed, and 1,370 wounded—many of the latter severely. The battle of Belmont was won by the daring, personal bravery of General Pillow. General Grant lost it through the misconduct of the Federal general in command at Paducah, who, as we have already said, ought, in pursuance of a preconcerted plan, to have manœuvred so as to threaten Columbus, and hold Polk in check, whilst General Grant should make himself master of the river bank. Whatever was the reason that obstructed the execution of this plan on the part of the general at Paducah, it has not been ascertained. At all events, General Polk, as we have seen, was enabled to cross to the other side of the river with all his forces. Grant was, consequently, not enabled to offer further opposition to the superior numbers of the Confederates, and had no other alternative than to retreat. This operation he performed in a manner highly creditable to his talents as a commander.

It will be a long time before the battle of Belmont is forgotten by the soldiers of either of the opposing armies; it was so well contested as to make them practically acquainted with each other's bravery.

CHAPTER XXVI.

BATTLE IN EAST TENNESSEE.

General Zollicoffer—Rising of the Unionists—General Crittenden attacks the enemy—Midnight march—The fight—Death of Zollicoffer.

The consequences of the defeat at Belmont were most detrimental to the cause of the Union. Kentucky was placed by it in an embarrassing position, and the Southern newspapers took care to trumpet forth the victory as a decisive one.

Early in the summer, the Confederate Government sent Brigadier-General Zollicoffer with a force of several thousand men to East Tennessee, by way of Knoxville, as it was reported that Federal troops were advancing in that direction, through Cumberland Gap. Zollicoffer, acting upon the instructions of his Government, sent a telegraphic message to Governor Magoffin to the effect, that in order to protect Tennessee he had occupied the mountain passes of Cumberland, and the three long mountain ridges of Kentucky; that the Confederate Government had always maintained the greatest respect for the neutrality of Kentucky, and that if the Federal troops would give up their menacing position at Hoskins Cross Roads, he would immediately withdraw the troops under his orders.

A few days afterward, a detachment of General Zollicoffer's force proceeded to Barboursville, in the State of Kentucky, where, after a short engagement, it dispersed a small body of Federal troops. Encouraged by this success, Zollicoffer advanced on Somerset, where he hoped to meet with the same success. The Government at Washington, fearing lest General Zollicoffer should stir up a hostile feeling against them in Kentucky, issued orders for the concentration of a large force from the Western States of Ohio and Indiana, and gave the command of it to an ex-Hungarian officer, named A. Schœpf, with the rank of brigadier-general. The Government could not have made a better selection, as this officer possessed all the necessary qualifications of a general. As soon as Schœpf had collected his forces, and made the necessary preparations for so arduous a march, he lost no time in commencing operations. His plan was, first, to endeavor to defeat General Zollicoffer; next, to drive him back into Tennessee; and then to make himself master of Cumberland Gap, from which point he could always exercise a certain pressure upon Tennessee. He was advancing with quick strides toward Zollicoffer's position, hoping to be soon able to give him battle, when the news of the rapid advance of the Confederate General Hardee induced him to halt.

The advance of General Schœpf's corps had revived the hopes of the Unionists, who numbered largely in this quarter, and their leaders, Andrew Johnson, William G. Brownlow, and R. Nelson, confidently looked forward to the success of their party. These men had, despite all the dangers and obstacles they had to contend against, formed a conspiracy on a large scale, which extended its ramifications over the whole of the western portion of Tennessee, and into North Carolina, and were only waiting for a favorable opportunity to put their schemes into execution. Their chief plan, it should be added, was to destroy all the railway bridges in Tennessee, Virginia, and Georgia.

Scarcely had Brigadier-General Schœpf advanced through Kentucky, when the Unionist party took up arms, and proceeded to carry out their plan of burning or blowing up all the railway bridges, many of which had to be first captured; for instance, the bridge at Strawburg plain, where the officer in command made a stout resistance. This rising of the Unionist party, however, which threatened to be most serious for the cause of the Confederates, failed in effecting its object, in consequence of General Schœpf retiring, and the Government forthwith sent troops to arrest the ringleaders. General Schœpf having soon after formed a junction with General Thomas, they agreed to offer battle to General Zollicoffer, and commenced operations accordingly.

General Zollicoffer had, meantime, taken advantage of his opportunity, and had marched through Kentucky, where numbers flocked to join his standard from the towns and villages along the line of his march, which he continued as far as Cumberland river. Here he halted, resolving to take up a strong position on its banks.

He accordingly set actively and promptly to work to intrench his camp, in order there to await the course of events in Kentucky. As soon as his works were completed, he crossed the river, and commenced throwing up defensive works on the other side. He had scarcely finished this operation, and got his army into quarters, when Major-General Crittenden arrived to take the chief command.

When the war broke out between the Union and the Southern States, Crittenden was a captain in the United States army, and President Jefferson Davis rewarded him for joining the Confederates by conferring a high military rank upon him. The intrenchments of the camp, and the works on the opposite bank, were all that could be desired: great skill having been employed in their construction. The troops were tolerably well armed and efficiently organized, and were amply supplied with provisions; but their firearms were somewhat defective. Both officers and men were elated at the successful march they had just performed, and looked forward with confidence to victory. Thus, General Crittenden, on his arrival, found an excellent army, ready to fight zealously for the Confederate cause; the bad weather and the state of the roads being the chief drawbacks.

Generals Crittenden and Zollicoffer, having satisfied themselves of the efficient state of their troops, were prepared for the enemy's attack. Ere long the news reached them that the Federal Generals Schœpf and Thomas, despite the execrable state of the roads, were advancing from Columbus, and from their movements it was pretty evident that they were bent on attacking the Confederate forces on Cumberland river. General Crittenden accordingly hastened his preparations to meet the attack. The cavalry was sent out to forage, troops and batteries were held in readiness to march at a moment's notice; in short, everything indicated that General Crittenden was resolved to march against the approaching enemy, to anticipate his attack, and to fall vigorously on his two columns separately, before they could form a junction or receive reinforcements. Crittenden, convinced of the success of this plan, then commenced his march, contrary to the advice of General Zollicoffer. After one day's march, so much discontent manifested itself amongst his men, owing to the hardships they had to encounter, that it needed all the strictness of the officers to maintain order amongst them. The poor fellows, who were badly provided with shoes, could scarcely get along the execrable roads; whilst snow and rain continued to fall incessantly, turning the roads into a swamp. Crittenden was, from this cause obliged to abandon a portion of his baggage in the mud. Our troops put great faith in the artillery, and, according to the number of guns they had with them, so did their courage rise or sink. Therefore, whenever a gun stuck in the mud and the horses could not get it along, there were a hundred ready hands to perform the work. After a council of war, held during a halt, it was resolved to start again at midnight, so as to fall upon the enemy early in the morning, and surprise them by a sudden and unexpected attack. The plan was an excellent one, if well-disciplined European troops had been ordered to execute it, but was rather hazardous for recruits like ours. The resolution was, however, unanimously adopted, and a little after midnight the troops were called under arms. The men were literally soaked through by the rain; many amongst them, indeed, were already laid up by illness, and measures had to be taken to provide for their wants.

Zollicoffer's brigade being the first ready, commenced its midnight march; the other troops followed in silence; and the cavalry formed the van and the rear guard. The march was a most fatiguing one; the ground being so saturated and softened by snow and rain that it was difficult to get along, especially as we had to carry arms and provisions with us. Added to this, the night was so dark that we could scarcely see a hand's length before us; and the men were therefore obliged to follow close upon each other. Morning was beginning to dawn, the rain still continued to fall in torrents, and yet it seemed as if the weary march would never come to an end.

Suddenly the solemn sound of bells was faintly audible in the distance; some church or chapel was evidently not far off, and its bells were inviting the pious to prayer; it was Sunday morning. The effect produced upon our men was peculiar and striking. In the distance peaceful chimes betokened piety and prayer; while on the spot hostile columns were advancing in the dark, bent upon destruction; proceeding not to pray, like good Christians, but to slay and maim their fellow men.

Suddenly a shot was fired—then a second. A general halt was now made, and orderlies galloped about like gaunt shadows in the midst. In a few minutes a heavy roll of musketry followed. Like wildfire the news spread that the enemy had discovered the approach of our advance guard, and had fired upon them. The heavy sound of cannon soon added its deep base to the musketry. "Chapman's battery, forward!"

shouted the commanding officer, and our men pressed up close to the roadside to allow the battery and ammunition cars to pass; the lighted matches of the gunners looking like so many fireflies in the misty gloom of the atmosphere.

As soon as the battery had passed, the spirits of our men revived. Orders were issued with decision, and were promptly obeyed. General Zollicoffer alone seemed not to share in the general confidence displayed by the troops. Silent and sad, he sat on his horse at the mouth of the pass, casting an anxious look on the animated troops as they marched forward. Nothing seemed capable of rousing him. Like a statue he remained on one spot; indeed, had it not been that his black charger sent forth incessant volumes of steaming breath from his nostrils, both the rider and his steed might have been supposed to be cast in iron. Usually so cheerful, why was the brave general now so melancholy and sad? Suddenly he put spurs to his horse, and in a few minutes man and horse were out of sight.

In a very short time the Confederate troops were hotly engaged. The intention of their leaders had been, as we have seen, to make an unexpected attack upon the enemy, and the very reverse had happened; they had been anticipated. The whole air now resounded with the roar of cannon, the roll of musketry, and the cheers of the contending combatants. Zollicoffer, as was always his custom, headed the first attacking columns in person. Despite the snow, the rain, and the fog, which spread like a pall over the surrounding country, the spirits of our men were excellent. The different columns advanced cheerily to the respective positions allotted to them. As soon as it was sufficiently light to allow friend and foe to be distinguishable, General Zollicoffer, placing himself at the head of the 15th and 17th Mississippi regiments, addressed them in a few appropriate words and led them against the enemy. The first man to fall was the standard bearer, who, grasping his flag, sank mortally wounded. This somewhat disconcerted our advancing columns. Two or three men rushed forward to seize the flag, which was again raised on high. Our troops now boldly advanced against the enemy's well-protected position; they were received by a murderous fire which spread death and devastation in their ranks. The officers showed the most determined bravery, leading on their men with sword in hand. General Zollicoffer was aware that he must persevere in this attack without flinching, so as to allow the other troops sufficient time to take up their positions. The two Mississippi regiments fought with a courage which excited universal admiration, although their loss was most severe: more than half their number fell dead or wounded on the ground, but it was impossible to remove the latter in the heat of the fight. The enemy were well aware that, if once driven out of their strong position, there was but little chance left for them, as, owing to the state of the ground, it would have been impossible for them to manœuvre with any chance of success.

General Crittenden now ordered up Carroll's brigade to support Zollicoffer. These sunburnt sons of the West rushed furiously upon the enemy, Zollicoffer in person leading them on. His black charger was seen suddenly to leap a barrier, and at the same moment the general fell backward, horse and man rolling over together, both of them struck dead.

A cry of anguish and even fury ran along the ranks. "Zollicoffer is shot! Zollicoffer is killed!" Then using the but ends of their muskets, which were of little use as firearms owing to the wet, the infuriated soldiery rushed upon the foe, felling them to the ground right and left. The battle now became a regular melee; the Federals, overcome by the furious onslaught of the Confederates, gave way; their batteries were left unprotected, and as the artillerymen did not flinch, they were bayoneted at their guns. The attack and the defence were most obstinate, and the fierceness of the struggle showed that kindred blood ran in the veins of the contending foes.

The officer in command of the Federal batteries was cut down in front of one of his own guns, and a regular massacre ensued, which was only put a stop to by the arrival of the Confederate Colonel Morgan. The Federals made a hasty retreat toward the wood, but our men were too much fatigued to pursue them. General Schœpf got his troops together again, and having received reinforcements, attempted to recover the position which he had lost. A desperate struggle ensued, and our troops, despite all their efforts, were driven back over the hill, and lost the batteries they had captured at so heavy a sacrifice; the Federals poured an incessant shower of bullets into our ranks, and although General Crittenden did everything he could to rally his men, it was a useless effort. He ordered his cavalry to charge the enemy's infantry, but that, too, was unavailing. The death of Zollicoffer had caused a panic; the flight became general. To add to the day's disaster, the bridge over Big Creek broke down, and men and horses were precipitated into the stream. General Crittenden fell back upon his intrenched camp, pursued by the enemy. This, too, he was compelled to abandon, with the loss of his guns and baggage, and retreated hastily toward Monticello, where he hoped to find food and shelter for his troops. The poor inhabitants had nothing to offer, and the men had to satisfy the cravings of hunger with the standing produce of the fields.

The death of General Zollicoffer caused a painful sensation throughout the whole State. The remnant of his army reached Nashville in safety.

The corpse of General Zollicoffer fell into the hands of the enemy, who did not refuse a tribute of respect to the remains of the brave soldier. The Federal general in command had the body carefully washed and embalmed. The face of the dead soldier bore an expression of calmness and melancholy, and exhibited no traces of that animosity which commonly disfigures the features of those killed in battle—he seemed almost as if he slept. Who knows whether he was not happy at having thus met his end? A rifle ball had penetrated his heart, and his death must have been instantaneous. General Zollicoffer was one of those men whose bearing and manners make an impression not easily to be forgotten by those who have once seen him. He was adored by his men, and his State honored and esteemed him as one of her worthiest sons. As long as he was there to lead them, his troops would never have experienced any great defeat; but when they saw him fall they lost all hope of a successful termination of the battle, and their courage forsook them. His death was a heavy and irreparable blow to the whole army of East Tennessee.

CHAPTER XXVII.

FORT HENRY AND FORT DONELSON.

Retreat of the Confederate army—M'Clellan's plan of operations—Bombardment of Fort Henry—General Tilghman—Surrender of Fort Henry—Bombardment of Fort Donelson—General Floyd caught in a trap—Attack of the fleet—Pillow's activity—Iron-plated ships—Capitulation and surrender of Fort Donelson.

DESPITE the humiliating reverses which it had sustained, the Confederate Government, not dismayed at its waning popularity, was fully determined to persevere in the war, notwithstanding the imputation of being actuated in so doing by personal motives.

It had learned, through private sources of information, that General M'Clellan purposed making a flank movement with his army, with a view to transfer the seat of war to the Peninsula; nay, that he had even made all the preparations for doing so. This news had a powerful effect upon the Confederate Government and upon its generals. There can be no question, that if M'Clellan had been able to keep his well-devised plan a secret, he could have taken Richmond, and, with it, put an end to the war without much loss or sacrifice. But as soon as the Government of the South got an inkling of M'Clellan's plans, it at once issued orders for the withdrawal of its army from the Potomac. The plans of M'Clellan were so much dreaded that, despite the inclemency of the season, the Confederate troops were ordered to abandon their quarters without delay, and give up works at which an army of 100,000 men had been laboring for months; works which had cost hundreds of lives, and the erection of which was in direct proximity to Washington, had hitherto caused no little alarm to the inhabitants of that capital, who must have had their slumbers occasionally disturbed by the thought of having the Confederate army so near a neighbor. These works, which were on a very extensive scale, were all to be abandoned, in consequence of the Federal general's understood intention of attacking us at our weakest point. This fact alone entitles General M'Clellan to a page in history. Within twenty-four hours, he compelled an army of 130,000 men, posted within strong fortifications, to give up all the advantageous positions which they held, and to retreat one hundred and twenty miles back into the interior of the country, there to form a new basis for their operation. Surely this must suffice to prove that General M'Clellan's plan was a grand and skilful one. As soon as the Confederate army had commenced its march toward the Southern capital, Richmond, the Government ordered the now indispensable Beauregard to proceed to Tennessee, in order to concert measures with General Johnston for a plan of operations in that part of the country. But even before General Beauregard had started, General Grant, with a Federal army, was on his way to endeavor to drive the Confederates out of Tennessee and Kentucky. Moreover, the enemy's fleet had steamed up the Tennessee river, with a view to capture the fort situated on the eastern bank.

Fort Henry, the stronghold in question, was in an excellent state of defence, and was quite capable of giving a foe plenty of hard work. It was well provided with guns, and was commanded by General Tilghman, a brave and experienced officer, with a strong garrison under him. The United States general, Grant, armed with a powerful squadron and a considerable body of land troops, lost no time in going to work. The attack was commenced by the guns from the ships opening a continuous fire upon the doomed fort. General Tilghman responded to the bombardment to the best of his endeavors; and although his tents were set fire to, and the fort enveloped in smoke, he made a gallant defence. Shot, shell, and grape were incessantly poured into Fort Henry, whose brave commander, cut off from all retreat, adopted the resolution of defending himself to the last.

This determined conduct of General Tilghman and the garrison of Fort Henry, offers a striking contrast to the inglorious surrender of Roanoke Island.

It was not until more than half of his guns were disabled, and a great portion of his men killed or wounded, and that the conflagration inside the fort threatened to spread to the ammunition magazines, that General Tilghman reluctantly consented to hoist the white flag as a signal of surrender. The enemy's ships, seeing this, like a flock of birds of prey, darted forward to take possession of the fort. General Grant, actuated by a feeling of respect for the gallantry of its defenders, returned General Tilghman his sword and treated him with marked regard.

As soon as the Confederate General Johnston, who was stationed at Bowling Green, heard of the surrender of Fort Henry, he turned all his attention to Fort Donelson. He sent reinforcements thither, with exhortations to the officers to use all speed in perfecting their defensive works, so as not to be taken by surprise by the victorious enemy. General Johnston had scarcely issued all the necessary orders for the defence of the lines and of the fort, when the arrival of General Beauregard was announced. A conference was held between the two generals, at which Beauregard expressed his entire concurrence with all the measures taken by Johnston; he further promised the latter to exert all the influence he possessed with the Confederate Government to send him such reinforcements as they could spare, and to see that arms and clothing, of which the troops stood much in need, should be provided, and also that their arrears of pay should be forthcoming. General Johnston having ordered the chief of his staff to give General Beauregard a copy of his plan of defence, as also his order of battle, the two generals then shook hands and separated. Johnston now ordered General Pillow to take the command of Fort Donelson, and having impressed upon his mind the importance of that post, he ordered Floyd's brigade, which was encamped at Repelsville, to proceed to Fort Donelson without delay, there to receive further orders from General Pillow.

General Floyd reluctantly obeyed this order, deeming Fort Donelson, no doubt, to bear too much resemblance to a mousetrap, particularly as a Federal general was advancing with a large army for the purpose of taking the fort at all risks. General Floyd, who had a particular aversion to the Federal troops, preferred fighting in the open plain or in the mountains to being shut up in a fort, where the only alternatives before him were either to be killed or to become a prisoner of war. He advanced slowly with his brigade, hoping every moment to receive the news that Fort Donelson was invested by the enemy, and that thus his chance of entering it would be prevented. But his hopes were doomed to be disappointed. He arrived just in time to be able to enter the fort before General Grant appeared at the head of his army, accompanied by the naval squadron.

Fort Donelson was now blockaded both by land and water, and the ships forthwith commenced shelling the fort, until night put a temporary stop to hostilities. General Pillow took advantage of this lull to strengthen his defensive works during the night as much as possible. At daybreak the Federal ships were ordered to resume the bombardment; and in a very short space of time, Fort Donelson and the hostile squadron, which had approached so close as to bring its broadsides to bear, were hotly engaged in a cannonade that lasted till noon, when General Grant made preparations to storm the fort.

The Federal troops, elated by the capture of Fort Henry, advanced boldly up to the moats which were then full of water, and endeavored to carry the outworks, but General Pillow turning some of the guns he had been using against the ships upon his assailants upon the land side, poured a destructive shower of grape into their columns.

The havoc inflicted upon his troops by this discharge, compelled General Grant to order them to retire from the assault, a movement that was executed with some difficulty. General Pillow, up to this moment, had reason to congratulate himself upon this partial success. Despite the severe bombardment, the works of the fort had not suffered much, and the garrison worked manfully at the guns.

As soon as night set in, General Pillow again went actively to work with his garrison in improving his means of defence. He erected a new battery of seven 32-pounders, and made every possible preparation to annoy his opponents. General Grant, on his part, was not idle: he was quite aware of the serious position he was in, well knowing that if the siege should be prolonged until General Johnston received reinforcements, the latter would not hesitate to give him battle under the walls of the fort, which might, under such a contingency, not improbably terminate in a defeat of the Federals. Notwithstanding the wet and mud, his troops, who were ankle deep in water, set cheerfully to work, as the general had promised them that the flag of the Union should in a very short time float from the battlements of Fort Donelson. A siege battery was brought up during the night to a position within six hundred paces of the walls, whilst another was erected on the flank. When morning broke, the work had not yet been completed, and General Grant would not allow a shot to be fired till all was quite ready, so as not to expose a half-finished battery to the fire of the garrison. About noon he ordered his iron-clad ships to advance to the attack. In a few minutes these destructive monsters got up their steam, and on their approach General Pillow opened fire with his 32-pounders on the leading ship, but in spite of the heavy fire the iron-clad vessel crept closer, the shot flying off her sides like hail on the roof of a house. When within four hundred yards of the fort, she veered round and showed her broadside, the other ships following close in her wake.

Like a hut in a forest surrounded by famished wolves, so lay Fort Donelson, encircled by enemies on every side. As the besieging troops were not at that moment engaged, numbers of the officers and men lined the batteries to witness the fight between the fort batteries and the ships. About three o'clock the ironclads were nearly all in position, and at a short range opened a terrible fire upon the fort. As our 32 and 48-pounders seemed to have little effect upon them, General Floyd ordered double charges to be used, which was so far successful that it compelled the nearest ship to sheer off, a fact that gave occasion to a loud cheer from the garrison. A second ship was soon in the same predicament, and, finally, the officer in command withdrew all his ironclads from the contest, satisfied with the mischief he had inflicted upon our works. The Confederates were, on their part, not less satisfied with the result of their labors. The casualties in the garrison were few, and the men had got accustomed to the presence of the formidable ironclads. From hour to hour, however, it became more evident that (as experience has so often shown) it is almost impossible to resist successfully a series of energetic and simultaneous attacks by land and by water. Some of our works were considerably damaged by the cannonade from the Federal ships, and it was not to be doubted that when General Grant had completed his land batteries he would be able to carry the fort by storm. Timely aid by reinforcements from General Johnston could not be confidently reckoned upon, as he had already furnished all the troops he could well spare, and he must remain in observation at Bowling Green with the residue of his force. All these points were duly weighed by General Floyd, and with much anxiety he looked forward to the impending capture of the fort. In the evening he assembled his officers in a council of war, to deliberate upon the best means to be resorted to under the circumstances. After a long debate, it was resolved that a general *sortie* should be made on the following morning.

The officers forthwith received instructions to prepare everything for this desperate service. At midnight intense cold and a snowstorm set in, and the soldiers of the Confederate army, already greatly wearied by night watches, and enfeebled by the want of many comforts, had lost much of their energy. Moreover, the troops selected for the sally were soon covered with snow, then fast falling, which did not help to encourage them.

The following is an outline of the arrangements made for the *sortie*:

General Floyd, with his brigade and one battery of twenty-four pounders, was to endeavor to occupy the heights lying to our right, and, on driving the enemy from that point, to maintain himself there. General Pillow, with Baldwin's and M'Causland's brigades, was meanwhile to attack the centre of the besieging forces, and, if possible, to break through them; and then, if successful, by having the enemy between him and Floyd, to rout them or make them prisoners. Each brigade being required to tell off a sufficient number of men to defend the intrenchments.

The plan was a good one; detailed orders were not given, as the bravery of the troops was counted upon as much as the effect of combined action. The men assembled at one A. M., and had to endure for a tedious interval all the inclemency of the weather; they, however, stood cheerfully under arms, ready to obey to the letter the orders of their officers.

At three o'clock, in the midst of a heavy snowstorm,

they began gradually to leave the fort. The snow lay so deep that no noise of wheels could be heard, and the guns and ammunition vans moved silently along. The van of the expedition consisted of troops from Virginia and Mississippi. These trusty men could be implicitly relied upon, and they hoped to come upon the enemy unawares whilst wrapt in slumber. But they had miscalculated that enemy's watchfulness. At midnight, General Grant, anxious for the safety of his encampment, had visited all his outposts, recommending his officers to keep a sharp lookout. This indefatigable officer then made a personal reconnoissance of the ground round the fort. It was a bitter cold night, as we have said, with a strong northwester blowing, and the snow falling in thick flakes.

Grant, now fancying he saw a dark, solid mass moving over the snow, immediately ordered one of his regiments to prepare for an attack on the part of the enemy. He had scarcely given the order, when along his line of outposts the words "Halt! Who's there?" were uttered. Our men, who had hoped to force an entrance into the enemy's camp immediately after driving in the pickets, now found that the vigilance of their opponents had baffled them in that expectation: so they proceeded at once to open fire and to attack them resolutely. The enemy's pickets fell back, but without our troops gaining any marked advantage; while the regiment ordered up by General Grant soon made its appearance; and it was high time it did so, for the few troops engaged had a difficult task to hold in check our attacking columns.

Alarm signals having been promptly made, the Federal troops speedily took up their respective positions. The sound of heavy guns announced that the squadron of ships also was preparing for action. General Pillow now ordered his men to fix bayonets and charge, and by this succeeded in gaining some ground. The cold was so intense, however, that the men could not reload their rifles, and the fight was carried on solely with the bayonet and the but ends of muskets. It was a curious sight to witness the combatants struggling almost noiselessly in the middle of the night. Pillow had already pushed on so far that he hesitated about advancing farther, lest he should be too distant from Floyd's brigade on his right, and be left single handed to cope with the main body of the enemy. He therefore sent one of his officers to General Floyd to request him to form a junction with him as effectually as possible. But the latter had very difficult ground to get over, and endeavored to seize upon the road at Winn's Ferry, hoping from thence to effect a junction with Pillow's brigade. The enemy opposed his advance foot by foot, and when he had nearly reached the summit of the high ground, General Grant ordered a twelve-pounder battery to open upon his flank, which caused great havoc in Floyd's ranks and threw his troops into confusion. General Buckner, who commanded the reserve, immediately ordered up two regiments to Floyd's support; but Grant, observing signs of confusion amongst the Confederate troops, directed a general attack upon the enemy along the whole line. He, himself, led his men against our right flank, and drove us back from one position to another. Never, since the battles of Rich Mountain and Manassas, had the Federal troops displayed greater steadiness than they did on this occasion. Here was another proof how a popular general can influence the conduct of his troops. The struggle was a hand-to-hand one. The bayonet, the bowie knife, and the but end of the musket were the only weapons used. No quarter was asked—none given. Blood was shed in torrents, tinging the snow-clad earth all around with red patches. This conflict had now lasted nearly four hours, and numbers had fallen on both sides. At daybreak the ships opened the fire of their guns upon our troops, but soon desisted from firing, as friend and foe were so mixed up together that their deadly missiles would have been equally fatal to both. Our men were at last completely overcome, and many sank down in the snow from sheer fatigue, never to rise again.

Under these circumstances, General Pillow ordered a retreat to be sounded. To effect this was no easy task; and owing to the state of the roads, the wounded had to be left upon the ground. Pillow's sadly mauled brigade now retired hastily; Floyd's and Buckner's brigades bringing up the rear. Even the successful enemy seemed to have had enough of fighting, for he did not molest our retreat; the ships, however, continued to shell us, and immolated a few victims. About noon the last men of the Confederate army had re-entered the fort. Our troops were now convinced that the enemy was not wanting in courage, and that their general was not only prudent and cautious, but quite capable, by his resolute spirit, of repelling any attack. A horrible spectacle now presented itself. The whole plain around the fort was strewn with the bodies of the dead and wounded. Many of our wounded men held up their hands imploring help, as the snow continued to fall upon them. Some brave fellows ventured outside the fort, in order to rescue some of them, but they paid the penalty with their lives—the enemy being masters of the field of battle. For two whole days the Confederates could hear the groans of their dying comrades, without having the power to help them. Inside the fort the condition of the garrison was not much better. There were a great many wounded whose cases could scarcely be attended to; and many of the men had their fingers, toes, noses, and ears frost-bitten. Moreover, there was no adequate supply of provisions requisite for so large a force as 14,000 men. In the night, General Buckner, having assembled the officers of the fort at his quarters, plainly stated the condition in which the garrison was placed, and pointed out the impossibility of making a much longer defence: advising a capitulation. All had been done that honorable men and gallant soldiers could do; they were shut up in the fort, surrounded by enemies, and could not reasonably hope for any relief from General Johnston for six or eight weeks to come. In his opinion, it was advisable, therefore, to treat for honorable terms of capitulation. This explanation created a painful feeling amongst the officers, and a long pause ensued before any one would answer.

General Floyd at last declared that, as far as he was concerned, he should object to any capitulation, and would sooner try to cut his way through the enemy. That general had no particular wish to be taken to Washington as a prisoner of war, for he had rather an aversion to that capital. The ex-Secretary of War probably would have sooner encountered any risk, from cold, hunger, or other privations, than that of becoming a prisoner under the Federal authorities. Despite all the entreaties of General Buckner, Pillow agreed with Floyd's opinion, and the two set to work at once to arrange their flight. The latter picked out his best troops, and added to them a regiment of cavalry under Colonel Forrest. A little after midnight, this body of troops, under the personal command of Generals Floyd and Pillow, issued forth from the fort, to attempt to cut their way through the enemy. General Buckner, who had now assumed the command of Fort Donelson, listeen anxiously from the battlements for the expected sounds of the conflict. The whole garrison was on the walls equally anxious. A short roll of musketry, and then all was still. In a few minutes the sentries on the walls announced the arrival of some stragglers of Floyd's troops, who had lost their horses. The escaping force had cut its way through the enemy and escaped.

Early the next morning, General Buckner sent a flag of truce to the enemy's headquarters, to negotiate terms for a capitulation. General grant at once accepted the armistice proposed by Buckner. He expressed to the Confederate officer charged with the delicate negotiation his admiration of the bravery and firmness displayed by the garrison of the fort; entertaining the highest esteem for a gallant foe, and he should do everything in his power to make the condition of the prisoners as comfortable as possible. He then ordered the chief of his staff to accompany the Confederate officer back to the fort to settle the terms of capitulation with General Buckner, and at the same time gave orders to his own surgeons to attend to the Confederate wounded generally. The surrender of the fort was to take place that day before four o'clock. " If not completed at that hour, the bombardment would be immediately recommenced, and the fort razed to the ground." These words, spoken in a decisive tone of voice, did not fail to have due effect upon the Confederate officer. Whilst they were on the point of leaving, General Grant inquired how it came that General Buckner was charged with settling the capitulation, instead of either Generals Floyd or Pillow, both of whom held superior rank to him. On being informed in reply, that they both had escaped with a considerable portion of their troops during the night, he was fairly staggered at the unwelcome intelligence, and for the moment was compelled to lean for support against a table.

" What, Floyd escaped! " he exclaimed, as he struck the table furiously with his clenched fist. " Floyd escaped! the very bird I wished to catch! " It will be seen by this outburst of disappointment, that Floyd was not far wrong when he fancied that the United States Government was very anxious to have the pleasure of seeing him safe at Washington, when they would no doubt have clapped him in a very pretty cage. Finding that his coveted prey was lost, General Grant turned sulkily away, and ordered the chief of his staff to settle the terms of capitulation with General Buckner as speedily as possible.

At 1 P. M. the stipulations of surrender were so far settled that a Michigan regiment—a fine set of fellows—was allowed to enter the fort with drums beating and colors flying, then to assume the duty of sentinels. The Confederate troops assembled gradually, and, under the personal command of General Buckner, marched out. Once again the poor fellows crossed the battle field, where many a frozen patch of blood denoted the spot where their fellow comrades and themselves had struggled so manfully, though so unsuccessfully, in the great *sortie*. As they marched past in no cheerful mood, a cold winter sun shed its pale rays through a veil of clouds upon the scene.

At a given signal the Confederate flag was hauled down from the flagstaff of the fort and the remaining portion of the Confederate garrison laid down their arms. A salute of cannon then announced that the flag of the United States was about to be hoisted on the fort, and when the banner floated majestically in the air, the bands of the various regiments struck up "Hail Columbia," amidst the cheers of the Federal soldiers, proclaiming that Fort Donelson had fallen.

CHAPTER XXVIII.

JOHN MORGAN, THE GUERILLA CHIEFTAIN.

General Johnston, hard pressed by General Buell, retires to Nashville—Secret evacuation of Nashville—Fear and anxiety in the town—A general flight—General Floyd makes his appearance with the remnant of his troops—Entrance of the Federal troops—Order restored—John Morgan, the guerilla chief.

The surrender of Fort Donelson placed the whole of the State of Kentucky and a great part of Tennessee in the enemy's power. This was a most serious blow to the Confederate Government, as, independent of the great loss that thus ensued to the State, it left General Johnston opposed to the whole of the Federal forces under General Buell, who was advancing with 40,000 men to attack him. Johnston was, consequently, obliged to abandon his ground at Bowling Green; he took up a position opposite Nashville, there to await reinforcements and to watch the enemy's movements. But Nashville was as good as lost; on the day following his arrival he was obliged to fall back on Murfreesborough.

A scandalous scene now took place at Nashville, not easily paralleled in modern history. General Johnston, with the object of getting away with his troops unperceived, had quietly marched out in the night from that town. This sudden and unexpected departure created great consternation and confusion amongst the inhabitants; the tumult reached its climax when Governor Harris galloped through the streets announcing that the enemy was at hand, and that every man who was capable of doing so should save himself by flight. All the offices, courts of justice, house of legislature, where the members were holding a session, broke up; the whole population, in fact, was in a state of the most feverish excitement, and every one prepared to leave the town. The members of the State Government, and others high in office, were the first to take to flight. The hasty departure of the members of the Government to Memphis, and the retreat of General Johnston to Murfreesborough, added to the fear that the enemy would make reprisals, caused almost as great a panic as if an earthquake had taken place. Women and children ran wailing through the streets. Trunks, boxes, and furniture were thrown out of the windows, and lay scattered about the pavement. It was as if the whole population had gone stark mad. Every one was shouting and running about not knowing wherefore. In the midst of this scramble and hubbub a shout suddenly arose. "The enemy; the enemy is coming!"

On the heights above the town a body of troops was really in sight. They advanced slowly and cautiously, and entered the town. But these were no hostile troops; the newcomers proved to be Floyd with the remnants of his brigade. As cautious as an old fox who feared his snare, he made his approach. The noise and confusion, and the number of persons taking to flight had arrested his attention, and dictated prudence. As soon as it was known in the town that the troops which had entered were not those of the enemy, but Confederates, with the brave General Floyd at their head, the despair of the population was turned into the most ridiculous rejoicing. The Confederates were welcomed as victors; provisions and wine were brought out for their use; children danced in the streets, and many of the inhabitants, who had returned to the town, gathered round them to implore their protection. But when the soldiers, after having refreshed themselves with the good things laid before them, began to saddle their horses to proceed farther on their march, the astounded population discovered that these were not troops sent to protect the town, but that they were men who, themselves, were escaping from the enemy. Fort Donelson had fallen, and the enemy was advancing in great force on Nashville. Deep curses were uttered against Floyd and his men, and the population sought to make up for the time they had lost. The rabble of the town, who only awaited an opportune moment, now began the work of plunder and robbery. All the shops that contained food or drink were broken into; a regular scene of looting ensued. Women and children, laden with stolen goods, were running about in all directions, and gangs of drunken scoundrels rolled about the deserted streets. The black population streamed into the town to have their share in the general pillage, and, though more than one had his brains knocked out for his pains, many had the opportunity of making a large booty. Several adherents of the Union, who resided at Nashville, were in imminent danger of their lives, as they dreaded an attack from the mob. Millions of dollars worth of goods were destroyed or carried off during the night; and the stock of provisions which the Confederates had for months stored up here was sacrificed. In fact the total destruction of Nashville was imminent, if the Federal troops did not soon make their appearance to save it from so deplorable a fate.

In the night the news spread that the enemy's troops had arrived outside Nashville. All the peaceful citizens who had remained in the town looked anxiously forward for their entrance. Pistol shots were heard, and a detachment of United States dragoons galloped into the town, sabring right and left all whom they met in the streets. The rioters and pillagers fled in every direction, leaving the town in the possession of the troops and of the honest citizens who had not fled. A few hours afterward, large bodies of troops under General Grant entered Nashville, and soon restored order and tranquillity. With astonishment the Federal troops must have looked at the closed country houses and villas, which seemed quite deserted, and betrayed no sign of life within their walls. The owners of these had fled with the retiring troops of Floyd. While the Federal troops took quiet possession of Nashville, the partisans of the Confederates on the other bank were preparing for resistance, under the leadership of John Morgan, a man who had rendered himself famous by his extraordinary feats of daring.

Of vulgar extraction and of no education, but gifted with extraordinary courage and self-possession, John Morgan had formed a body of men of his own stamp, who preferred fighting, and the hardships of a roving life, to any peaceful occupation. His band roamed about the country with such audacity as to become a perfect dread to the enemy. Scarcely a day passed without some daring act being recorded of John Morgan and his horsemen. Although he and his band belonged, properly speaking, to General Hardee's division, and his duty was to watch the enemy's movements, he much preferred doing a little business on his own account.

One day he proposed to his men to make a raid upon the little town of Gallatin, twenty miles north of Nashville, then occupied by the enemy. The very idea of such an expedition created a joyful excitement amongst his desperate followers, and like lightning they fell upon the town and took possession of it. Whilst his men were robbing and plundering to their heart's content, Captain Morgan proceeded to the office of the telegraph in the expectation of finding important despatches there. The official on duty had not the slightest idea of what was going on in the town, and when Captain Morgan asked him with great politeness what news he had received, the agent took him for an officer of the United States army, and replied, "Nothing particular; but inquiries are being made continually respecting that rebel bandit, Morgan. But if he should ever come across my path I have pills enough to satisfy him!" pulling out his revolver as he said this, and flourishing it in the air before he thrust it back into his belt. As soon as he had finished, the strange officer thundered forth, "You are speaking to Captain Morgan; I am Morgan, you miserable wretch." The poor official sank on his knees, and with the fear of death full upon him, sued for mercy. "I will not hurt you," retorted Morgan, "but send off this despatch at once to Prentice :*

"MR. PRENTICE—As I learn at this telegraph office that you intend to proceed to Nashville, perhaps you will allow me to escort you there at the head of my band?
"JOHN MORGAN."

It is easy to conceive what a fright Mr. Prentice must have been in, when the authenticity of this despatch was proved a few days afterward.

After sending off this friendly invitation, Morgan hastened to the railway station to see the train come in. In a few minutes it came up, upon which Captain Morgan ordered one of his men, with pistol in hand, to take charge of the engine driver, whilst he examined the carriages, and proceeded to take five officers prisoners. He then had all the carriages set fire to, and filling the engine with turpentine, tow, and other inflammable matter, stopped up the vents, and sent it back on fire in full speed toward Nashville. The engine, however, exploded, after going a few hundred yards. After this exploit, Morgan and his men, with their prisoners, remounted their horses and gained the camp in safety, where they were enthusiastically welcomed by their comrades.

On another occasion he surprised a picket of six Federal soldiers, and made them prisoners. He was quite alone. On coming across them he went straight up to the corporal in command, and, passing himself off as a Federal officer, ex-

---

* Editor of a paper at Louisville, and a mortal enemy of Morgan.

pressed his indignation at their slovenly appearance, and ordered them to lay down their muskets, and regard themselves as under arrest. The order was obeyed; but when the men saw that he was taking them in a contrary direction, they observed that they were going the wrong road. "Not so," he retorted; "I am Captain Morgan, and know best what road you have to take." These little adventures, amongst many of a similar nature, made his name well known, and acquired for him a widespread popularity.

CHAPTER XXIX.

JOHNSTON ON THE TENNESSEE RIVER—FLOYD AND PILLOW.

General Johnston collects a new army—He occupies South Nashville on the Tennessee river—Outposts—Pillow and Floyd are brought before a court martial by order of President Jefferson Davis—Pillow's farewell to his troops.

MEANTIME, General Johnston was not idle; he gathered together the dispersed remnants of Generals Crittenden and Zollicoffer's forces, and also of what remained of Floyd's brigade, so that the army under his orders again numbered about 21,000 men, a force sufficient to enable him to take the field with some chance of holding his ground. The fall of Fort Donelson had compelled him to make considerable alterations in his previous plans, and to organize a new line of defence. Without deliberating long about it, he resolved to form a junction with General Beauregard, in Mississippi, and to undertake the defence of South Nashville, so as to keep open the southwestern railway for the use of the Confederate troops.

It was here, on the Tennessee river, that the most sanguinary outpost skirmishes occurred. North and South, with all the animosity which hatred and fury could excite, which cunning or deception could devise means for gratifying, endeavored mutually to destroy each other. Here is an example:

One day two sentinels were posted opposite each other. The one was a son of our sunny South, the other a moody

Northern. The Confederate lay behind a rock, and with the eyes of a lynx watched every movement of his foe, who was sheltered by a tree. The latter belonged to a regiment from the cold, frosty, western region of Michigan, and was a man of colossal stature, a fine specimen of a fearless soldier. For some hours the Northerner and the Southerner had been watching each other, without either having had a fitting opportunity for a shot. This wearisome inactivity at last annoyed the Southerner, who shouted to his foe to come forth from behind his cover. The latter obeyed the request, and coolly drew himself up like a tower, by the side of his tree. "Ping," and a bullet grazed his head without hurting him. "Too high!" he shouted back to his enemy; "it's my turn now." Like a snake the son of the South glided from behind his rock, and stood leaning on his musket as self-possessed as the other, opposite his enemy. Crack went the rifle.

"Too low!" shouted the untouched Southerner.

This game was carried on for some time, until a bullet from the Northerner grazed the ear of the Southerner. "Let us stop firing," shouted the latter, "my ammunition is out; let us go to camp for more." Whereupon both men shouldered their rifles and walked cheerfully away, the Northerner whistling "Yankee Doodle," and the Southerner his favorite tune of "Dixie."

General Johnston intrusted the joint command at Chattanooga to Generals Floyd and Pillow with their brigade; he, himself, taking up a position between the above-mentioned town and Memphis. One morning, a messenger arrived at Johnston's headquarters, bringing an order from President Jefferson Davis to the effect that Generals Floyd and Pillow should be deprived of their command, and that those two generals should proceed forthwith to Richmond, to explain their conduct when in command at Fort Donelson, and to give an account, before a court martial, of behavior which threw such discredit upon the Confederate army.

Whatever might have been thought of Floyd's conduct, there was, surely, no blame to be attached to General Pillow. This latter general, by his conduct at the battle of Belmont by the energy he displayed in the *sortie* from Fort Donelson, had given sufficient proofs of his zeal and courage. It was very disheartening for so honorable and brave a man to find that the fussy officials at Richmond should challenge his conduct, as every one of his acts had been performed with the welfare of his country in view, for the glory of which he had often faced death, and shed his blood upon the battle field. And yet the all-powerful President must needs bring before a court martial a man universally honored and respected by his countrymen. Rather an unfavorable prognostic for the future Confederate Republic, should it succeed eventually in achieving its independence! General Johnston himself did not fail to see the risk the Government incurred by such conduct; and other excellent and experienced officers, on hearing of what had occurred, frankly declared they would no longer serve the Confederate cause, if they were to be subjected to any such treatment at the hands of their Government. A formidable agitation pervaded the whole camp, which hourly became more serious; the feeling of indignation which had been aroused among the officers being shared by the men. All concurred in denouncing Benjamin, the Secretary of War, and the inflential adviser of the President, as the evil genius of the Confederate cause, and the source of more mischief than the loss of many battles. In fact, the discontent in the camp increased to such an extent that an outbreak was apprehended.

General Johnston was placed in a most critical position. In front of him he had an enterprising enemy flushed by recent success, and behind him a mutinous army. In this dilemma, he requested General Pillow to exert himself to calm the excitement that existed amongst the troops, and that zealous officer, true to his duty, immediately issued an order for all the men of his division to assemble at his headquarters, as he wished to take leave of them. Like a raging sea lashed into fury by the wind, with its waves breaking violently on the beach, the troops proceeded, in a grumbling mood, through the avenues of the camp, while here and there groups of the more discontented might be seen standing at different points discussing, in angry tones, the events of the day. A great number of men belonging to other divisions joined in the crowd to hear General Pillow's farewell address to his faithful soldiers. The excitement amongst the troops, in their eagerness to hear what the general had to say, reached its highest pitch; and, had some energetic leader just then come forward to denounce the Government, it might have fared ill with the cause of the Confederacy.

Had President Jefferson Davis and his *fides Achates*, Benjamin, made their appearance at this critical moment, I doubt very much whether their high position would have shielded them from the insults of the incensed soldiery.

At last a roll of drums, and a flourish from the staff trumpets, announced that General Pillow was about to take leave of his troops. Like a swarm of bees, all rushed eagerly forward to get as near to the general as possible.

Pale, and evidently laboring under great emotion, General Pillow, surrounded by his officers, appeared in front of the troops, to see them, perhaps for the last time. In anxious expectation all eyes were turned upon him: it was a solemn moment. In a powerful, yet trembling voice, the general bade farewell to those whom he had so ably led, with whom he had so cheerfully shared the hardest fare on many occasions; to those who had followed him into the hottest fire, willingly facing death and destruction, that they might participate in the dangers he was ever ready to confront. As he stood before them, the cold winter wind blowing through his scanty white hair, his heart heaved with scorn at the malice of his enemies; but not one word of anger passed his lips. He exhorted the soldiers, as true sons of their country, to hold firmly together, and remain faithful to that cause for which they had already expended so much blood; and urged them to be prepared to fight for it again. With an ironical smile, he added, " We have not been fighting for the interests of President Davis, but for the common welfare of the whole Southern people, and for the Confederacy; we are ready to fight and die for our country, not for the private interests of a few. I am about to quit the theatre of war; but you must persevere in the path which you have selected. Wherever I may be, however, my heart and my thoughts will accompany you; and when the news of your gallant deeds reaches me, then I shall proudly exclaim: ' Well done, my own my brave fellows!' " Many an eye grew dim, and many a sunburnt, brawny hand was now stretched out to shake that of the general, who thus concluded his address: " The Government has the power to deprive me of my command, but it has not the power to deprive me of the love of my brave comrades!" When he had uttered these words, the enthusiastic cheering of the men knew no bounds. They all rushed forward, each eagerly bent on shaking hands once more with his gallant commander, and it was quite affecting to see, amongst this excited crowd, one of the wild hunters of Arkansas advance to General Pillow, and exclaim, in simple but energetic terms: " Never mind, General, though you leave us, you may be sure that, far off as we may be from you, you will never have reason to be ashamed of your brave boys."

CHAPTER XXX.

BATTLE OF SHILOH.

General Johnston, with his army, joins General Beauregard—General Grant's plan of attack—March on Shiloh—Commencement of the battle on the morning of the 6th April—Prentiss's division lays down its arms—General Johnston mortally wounded—Desperate attack of the Confederates—Brave conduct of General Grant—Grant breaks through our centre—Bravery of the German brigade—The attack of the Federal troops—The Confederates hard pressed—Want of ammunition—Beauregard compelled to fall back—Names of the generals who fell in the battle—Loss of the Confederates—Prince Polignac—Beauregard collects a new army—Charles Van Dorn and General Price come up in support.

GENERAL JOHNSTON expressed his deep sense of obligation to General Pillow for the manner in which the latter had responded to his request, and thus put a stop to any further act of insubordination amongst his troops, and he now lost no time in taking the necessary steps to form a junction with General Beauregard, on the Mississippi. Beauregard had assembled his army at Corinth, and was carefully watching the movements of the enemy on the Tennessee and the neighboring rivers, when he received the information that General Johnston was approaching with the army under his orders. The news spread like wildfire through the camp, and when that officer and his aide-de-camp rode, one fine morning, up to Beauregard's headquarters, the rejoicing was unbounded. The strength of General Johnston's army was 25,000 men, and this addition to Beauregard's force was very opportune, as the Federal Generals, Halleck and Buell, held positions at no great distance, and an attack from either of them might be expected at any moment. Johnston's columns gradually poured into the camp, where they met with a hearty welcome from Beauregard's troops, who, however, stood high in their own estimation, on account of the deeds they had performed in Arkansas, Texas, and Pensacola. Johnston's troops were in a very sorry condition; many of the men had no shoes or cloaks, and Beauregard's officers eagerly inquired if it was true that they had gone through the severe winter campaign in such a plight. "We were often much worse off than we are now," was the reply of these hardy, weather-beaten fellows. Eagerly did Beauregard's troops bring all they could spare in the shape of clothing and provisions, for they admitted that these brave men had undergone greater hardships than they themselves had. Generals Johnston and Beauregard held a private conference to communicate their views to each other, and adopt some fixed plan of action. Beauregard assumed the command of the position on the line of railway which runs from Corinth to Iuka, whilst Johnston took up a position on the line between Corinth and Bethel; and thus advantageously posted, they resolved to organize their army, all the time watching the enemy's movements.

General Grant, whose efforts had met with so much success, now wished to attack the enemy in the cotton-growing districts of the South, and, with this object in view, he concentrated all his troops on the west bank of the Tennessee, in the direction from Pittsburg toward Savannah, as he looked forward to form a junction with General Buell, who was moving in the direction from Nashville to Columbus. General Johnston, who saw with some anxiety this attempted junction of the two armies of the enemy, as it would place him in an awkward position, proposed to General Beauregard to make a combined attack upon Grant's army before Buell joined him, as the odds were two to one they would beat him.

General Beauregard, who admitted the superior strategic tactics of General Johnston, at once agreed to his plans, and it was resolved to make the proposed attack without delay, with the purpose of driving General Grant from his position, and, if possible, to take him and his army prisoners, but in any case to compel them to fall back on their transport ships, and thereby oblige them to leave all their abundant stores and ammunition in our hands. The requisite preparations were forthwith made for conveying the intended booty to Corinth. According to General Johnston's plan, Saturday morning was fixed for the attack, and 300 carts were to be ready with their drivers to carry off the captured stores at once. General Beauregard had commenced his movements already on the Thursday, but the roads were in such a bad condition that it was Saturday morning before he was ready to commence operations; consequently the general attack was postponed till the Sunday morning. If Beauregard had more carefully provided for the wants of his men, and been enabled to make the attack on the Saturday, as had been previously agreed upon, it is more than probable that on that day the Confederates would have achieved a victory, because before General Buell would have had time to come up to support Grant, the latter would, in all probability, have been routed. It is thus evident that Beauregard had delayed many preparations which ought to have been made long before.

The orders for the attack were now issued. General Hardee was to march, with his corps, and with a brigade of General Bragg, against Pittsburg, whilst the cavalry was to occupy the plain. Close on its heels was to follow General Bragg's 2d *corps d'armée*, whilst the *corps d'armée* of Generals Johnston and Polk were to advance on a much worse road, which ran in a parallel line with the other, and the whole of the reserve was to follow on a third road, under the command of General Breckinridge.

Despite the bad roads, the troops advanced cheerfully.

Every man seemed confident of victory, and before midnight on Saturday they had reached the vicinity of Shiloh, and were consequently in face of the enemy.

The morning of the 6th of April had scarcely dawned, and the first rays of light were only just fringing the undulating ground, when we beheld the enemy's army spread out before us. They had taken up a position near Shiloh, making the church their chief *point d'appui*, and occupying the road which leads from Pittsburg to Corinth, with a strong force. The whole conformation of the ground appeared as if purposely made for a battle between two large armies. A better battle-ground could scarcely be found anywhere than the one now spread before us. It was not an extensive plain, but one of those undulating, broken tracts of country upon which both armies could carry out splendid manœuvres. There was scope here for the movements of both cavalry and artillery to their hearts' desire, and the ground, in fact, offered opportunities for the full display of good generalship.

The watchful enemy had scarcely perceived the heads of our first advancing columns, when a shot from a rifled cannon sent us a morning greeting, and in a few minutes a complete change had come over the whole scene. In the stead of the peaceful stillness which only a few moments previously reigned around, the whole air now resounded with noise and tumult. Federal regiments, with flags flying and bands playing, marched into their respective positions; batteries and ammunition vans rattled forward, whilst generals, officers, and their aide-de-camps could be seen galloping to and fro like misty shadows. A similar life and activity soon displayed itself in the Confederate army, and it was a grand spectacle to behold the regiments file past one by one. Each regiment could be distinguished by its colors, appearance, and manner of marching; and these indicated to what State it belonged. The fiery, sprightly sons of Louisiana seemed almost to dance past, whilst the men of Texas and Arkansas advanced with a steady, firm step, and a self-possessed look; while the firm grasp with which they held their muskets indicated that the enemy would have hard work to do in dealing with them.

Small bodies of light cavalry, splendidly mounted, now swept past, under the command of Young, Lewis, and Connor, and the batteries of the different *corps d'armée* followed up quickly with a thundering noise. In a short time the firing commenced along the top outpost's line, and gradually increased in vigor. As yet, however, none of the batteries had been brought into play; no whole regiment had been engaged; the troops were taking up their respective positions before the conflict was to begin. Every man felt that a great battle was on the eve of being fought, and made his preparations accordingly.

At last the distribution of the troops was completed, and each corps had taken up the position allotted to it.

The *avant-garde* which was to commence the battle was annexed to General Hardee's *corps d'armée*; whilst Generals Johnston and Beauregard commanded the centre, General Bragg the right, and General Polk the left wing; and General Breckinridge took up a well-covered position, with the reserve forces under his orders. General Beauregard now ordered Hardee's columns to advance to the attack, which was directed chiefly against General Prentiss's troops, stationed between Owl and Lick Creeks.

Our men charged the enemy with fixed bayonets, and gained ground at once. General Johnston sent up Trabues's brigade in support, which decided the fight in this quarter; General Prentiss, with 5,000 men of his division, being compelled to lay down their arms, and these were sent as prisoners to the rear. This was not a bad beginning for the Confederates, and their courage rose in consequence.

General Grant, seeing that Prentiss's division was cut up, and that our men had occupied that officer's positions, immediately ordered up all the batteries he could dispose of, and opened a tremendous fire of grape upon the Confederate troops. In vain did General Johnston endeavor to keep Hardee's men together: the enemy's artillery made such havoc in their ranks that they broke and dispersed. General Beauregard then ordered his centre to advance to the attack, whilst Johnston hastened to support Hardee with one or two regiments. But scarcely had Johnston reached Hardee's lines when a rifle bullet struck him, and he fell from his horse mortally wounded.

His death caused a momentary panic amongst his troops; but resolved to avenge the loss of their beloved general, they rushed upon the foe with such energy that the Federals were driven back toward their gunboats, the commanders of which, on perceiving the critical state of affairs, opened a heavy fire on our men. General Grant found it a very difficult task to keep his centre unbroken; but despite the repeated attacks of Generals Beauregard and Polk, he held his ground.

The enemy's centre was in a very critical position, for if broken through, the whole Federal army would have been lost. General Grant made the most determined resistance to every attack we made upon him, and endeavored to fall back under the protection of the guns of his flotilla. All his troops had been actively engaged since five o'clock in the morning, and no fresh troops were available, as nearly the whole of the Federal reserve had been ordered up.

The loss of life this day was extremely severe, especially on our side; for in General Johnston we lost one of the bravest and most talented generals of the Confederate States. He was the real Commander-in-Chief—the heart and soul which gave life to the whole army. Whenever he was present, officers and men seemed to fight better, for they felt that his orders were all for the best, and placed implicit confidence in him. Through the death of Johnston, the army lost its mainstay. He was almost the only general, with the exception of Beauregard, who was not teased with orders from Richmond, and who was allowed to exercise his own judgment as regarded his plans and movements: it was quite evident he knew best how to act. By his death, the combined armies came under the sole command of Beauregard; and although the latter had many warm admirers among both officers and men, he did not, on the whole, enjoy that full confidence of the army so necessary to a commander-in-chief.

When darkness had put a stop to all further operations for the day, various instances of negligence, unpardonable on the part of a general, were discovered. The men had been fighting incessantly the whole day without tasting food, and yet nothing had been provided to satisfy their hunger; nor could the different divisions procure any more ammunition, although this was known to have been on the road since the morning; but it had not reached them at nine in the evening, while further dispositions had been taken for renewing the attack on the following morning. This damped the spirits of the men, and made them feel less confident in success.

At the very commencement of the battle, General Beauregard ought to have taken the necessary steps to prevent such mistakes; but when General Johnston fell, he was so much occupied with the duties of the sole command, which had thus unhappily devolved upon him, that he forgot to attend to what he ought to have done long before.

Whilst the troops bivouacked on the battle field, the rain poured down in torrents, so that the men had to sit in so many small pools, and vainly endeavored to keep their firearms dry. The officers occasionally consulted together, counted up their losses, and spoke despondingly of the awkward position they would be placed in if General Buell should succeed in forming a junction with General Grant. The night thus passed dismally in drenching rain, the silence being only interrupted occasionally by the stray report of a musket fired by some sentry.

At last a faint gray streak of light in the far horizon an-

10*

nounced that day was beginning to dawn. The different brigades and divisions at once commenced taking up their respective positions, and were still doing so, when the enemy's troops opened a heavy fire of musketry and artillery upon us. Without leaving us any time for consideration, General Grant now made a most determined attack upon our centre and our left wing. The attack was so energetically made, that the whole of our line began to waver. Our men became alarmed. The enemy, whom they had almost annihilated the day before —whose ranks they had almost decimated, and whom they had hoped to rout completely to-day—that beaten, defeated enemy, now reopened the battle. But the Confederate troops were not allowed much time to indulge in their reflections; the conquerors of Fort Donelson pushed them so hard, that it was all they could do to hold their ground, and General Grant, like a wounded lion, led on his men, who all seemed animated by one feeling—the desire to wipe out the stain of the previous day's defeat. The battle raged with actual ferocity in the centre and on the left wing. The Federal troops fought desperately, and did great havoc in our ranks, though our men stood their ground for a long time with great bravery. But, lo! a Mississippi regiment begins to waver. In vain do the officers exhort the men to remain firm; they gradually give way. General Grant, observing the disorder, directed a heavy fire upon the weak point, placed himself at the head of some Ohio regiments, and cut his way through our broken ranks. In spite of the efforts of General Bragg, who opened a 12-pounder battery upon him, he maintained the footing he had gained, and his men held their ground. Like corn cut down by the sickle, numbers were mowed down, but those who remained unscathed only fought with the more determination. Two brigades now advanced to General Grant's support, but at the same moment Beauregard made his appearance with the reserve cavalry and two batteries. The cavalry was ordered to charge the two advancing brigades, but before they could come to close quarters a terrible volley from the enemy brought down many from their saddles, causing great confusion in their ranks. In a few moments their unhurt comrades charged at full speed into the enemy's battalions, where a hand-to-hand fight ensued. Pistol and sabre did active work. Beauregard, finding that General Grant had lost the expected support of the two brigades, immediately attacked him in front, and compelled him, after a most fierce and sanguinary struggle, to abandon the position he had acquired at so much loss. Grant fell back in good order with the remnant of his fine German brigade—for it was they who had braved the storm that waged round them—but only to allow his men a short respite.

The battle field presented a sad spectacle, for the loss on both sides had been enormous. No preparation had been made for conveying away the vast number of wounded; in vain did these implore help from their own men—it was of no avail; all feeling of humanity had vanished, and the living walked unconcerned past the dead and the dying, bent only upon dealing more destruction.

General Beauregard, followed by his staff, now galloped along his whole line, visiting all the positions. At every point the fighting had been most severe, and the reserves had been made use of so lavishly during the battle, that now that they were expressly needed there were none at hand. Anxious and perplexed, he directed his glances around, but there was now not much time for consideration, for General Buell had succeeded in joining General Grant.

The enemy again took the offensive in great force, to try and wrestle from us the laurels which we already fancied we had won. We now learnt from some of the prisoners that the *corps d'armée* of the enemy, under Generals Nelson, M'Cook, and Crittenden, had joined General Grant's army. All the energies of the enemy's generals were now directed to one object—to force Beauregard's centre—so as to regain the positions they had occupied on the previous day.

In fine order the regiments of Ohio, Illinois, Wisconsin, and Indiana advanced to renew the battle, and, if possible, to bring it to a final issue. Our men stood this attack with unflinching courage, and succeeded in driving back the columns of the enemy, who fell back, terribly cut up, but trusting by the aid of their supports to be again able to attack us. The Confederate generals new earnestly entreated Beauregard to relieve them by reinforcements, that they might partially withdraw their exhausted troops from the fight, as most of the regiments had lost their staff officers, and had fired away all their ammunition. Beauregard urged them to hold out for one hour more with the troops they had, and he should then be able to send them reinforcements and ammunition. This was but poor comfort, as he had not the means at his disposal to keep his promise. A great portion of his reserve was already actively engaged, and the remnant, joined by a rabble of plunderers, was away pillaging the enemy's camp. Thousands of these vagabonds left their posts to make what booty they could, robbing alike friend and foe. Beauregard, whose personal daring and bravery is beyond challenge, did not possess all the necessary qualifications for a commander-in-chief. If he had striven to collect these pillagers he could have brought them up to the support of his centre and held his ground there, even if his flanks were driven in. The troops, weakened by their heavy losses, might then have formed into a closer and more compact body, without disturbing their plan of action.

All eyes were now anxiously turned toward the centre, where, for some minutes, the firing on our side had ceased. Even the bravest breathed hard when he saw the defenceless condition of our men at this point. Fresh columns of the enemy now advanced to the attack. With loud shouts and cheers these Western regiments threw themselves upon our decimated ranks, destitute of ammunition. Our men firmly awaited the attack and the volley of the enemy's columns without being able to respond to it. "Fix bayonets and forward!" was the order now given by our general. It was the only resource left. A terrible *mêlée* ensued. General Grant, seizing the opportune moment, ordered his small body of cavalry to charge our men, who were fighting with their side arms only, whilst he was driving our left and right flanks from one position to another. Our condition was a desperate one, when General Beauregard ordered the whole of our artillery to take up position near Shiloh Church, to cover our retreat. General Breckinridge was ordered, also, to gather together all the troops he could, to form them into a body of reserve to cover our retreat. About noon the order to retire was given, and the movement was commenced in very fair order. It was difficult, however, to induce the troops engaged in the centre to leave the battle field, and their own officers had positively to compel them to retreat. At last, about 3 o'clock in the afternoon, our army, after having suffered immense loss, was in full retreat, and Generals Grant and Buell lost no time in endeavoring to make it a rout. But want of cavalry, and the excellent position taken up by our guns, as also the fatigue of their own men, compelled them to be satisfied with what they had already achieved. Our troops withdrew, with much exertion, to their new positions.

Many of our poor fellows, who had been incessantly engaged for nearly twenty hours, sank on the ground, utterly beaten by fatigue, and besmeared with blood, gunpowder, and dust. The loss sustained by some of the brigades and regiments appears almost incredible. Some regiments were so decimated that the remnants had to be at once incorporated into other regiments.

Our greatest loss was, however, in general officers. First on the list stands the name of our commander, Albert Sidney Johnston: as we have already stated, he fell whilst leading his men to the attack. He was struck in the leg by a musket ball. He continued to give some instructions to his aide-de-camp,

Harris, ex-Governor of Tennessee, and when the latter returned from executing the order, he found the General sitting like a corpse on his saddle. "In Heaven's name!" exclaimed Harris, "I hope you are not wounded." "I believe I am dying," said Johnston, and almost at the same moment he fell dead from his horse. The next name on this black list is that of ex-Governor Johnston, of Kentucky, who commanded the troops of that State. He was struck by three bullets almost at the same moment, and fell to the ground. Some of his officers rushed up to help him, but he ordered them back to their men, and to leave him to die alone. His body was found subsequently, after a long search, scarcely recognizable, amongst a heap of dead and wounded. Brigadier-General Glodden was killed with his horse by a ball from a rifled gun. Major-General Cheatham received a mortal wound, after having had three horses previously shot under him. Major-General Clark was also mortally wounded. Generals Hindman, B. R. Johnston, and Bower were severely wounded, and rendered incapable of service for a long time to come. So great had been the casualties on both sides, that there was not a house within ten miles round but was full of wounded soldiers. Corinth was one great hospital, and straggling wounded men continued daily to drop in, though many poor fellows died on the road. To add to all this misery, the weather became fearfully cold, with a strong north wind blowing, which proved the death of many a poor, wounded soldier.

Our loss in men in this memorable battle amounted, according to the first rough return, to 2,400 killed, 10,000 wounded (chiefly severely), and 2,000 to 3,000 missing, making a total loss of nearly 15,000 men.

Indeed, the fearful slaughter which took place at this battle entitles it to a marked place in military records, for, fearful as was our loss, that of the enemy was as great, if not still greater. These sad results prove incontestably what enormous sacrifices a powerful people is capable of making, when it fancies it is combating for its rights and for its existence as a nation, however delusive may be that impression.

The troops on our side were chiefly from the States of Mississippi, Tennessee, Kentucky, Alabama, Louisiana, and Arkansas. Their conduct during the battle places them on the same level as that of the best European troops, and, although a portion of the reserve did neglect its duty, and, instead of helping their comrades, took to pillaging the enemy's camp, that isolated act does not in the slightest degree tarnish the blood-stained laurels earned by their gallant comrades in that fine army, which so nobly performed its duty toward its own Government that it earned even the admiration of the enemy.

It is, at the same time, but just to pay a tribute of admiration to the troops of the enemy's army, and to their generals, Grant, Buell, Sherman, Nelson, and others. It was truly no small task for the conqueror of Forts Henry and Donelson to have to sustain, with his comparatively small army, the Confederate attack; and it was a critical moment for him when the whole of Prentiss's division had, despite their bravery, to lay down their arms.

After this sanguinary two days' battle, the Federal army, under Generals Grant and Buell, after their hard-earned victory, greatly needed rest, and, consequently, they were unable to hinder Beauregard from maintaining his position at Corinth, where, being unmolested, he set to work to reorganize his army.

If this battle was not attended by any great results to the advantage of the United States, the consequences were, neverless, important, as it convinced the Confederate troops that their opponents, whether in Missouri or Virginia, or anywhere else, were foes not to be despised. Another consequence of some importance to the enemy was that they got possession of the western frontier of the States of Georgia and of Alabama, which allowed them to make raids as far as Huntsville and Decatur, and thus enabled them to parade their successes before that portion of the Southern States.

General Beauregard, having set actively to work at Corinth to reorganize his army, was most ably seconded in his efforts by his aide-de-camp, Colonel Prince de Polignac. The active part taken by this latter officer on the day of the battle, in which he displayed the bravery of a true French soldier, ought to have procured for him a special notice in Beauregard's report to President Jefferson Davis: why it was not done, can only be attributed to an aversion to render justice to a foreigner, attributed to the Southerners, who are jealous of any one else sharing their own glory.

In a short time large bodies of fresh troops joined us from the more distant Southern States. The troops under Charles Van Dorn excited especial attention. They had hastened up from Arkansas to fight for the cause of the South. Other troops from Missouri followed, under General Price, their favorite commander, and were received with great rejoicings. Thus powerfully reinforced, General Beauregard soon assembled another fine army, with the help of which he hoped, ere long, to try once more his fortune in the field.

CHAPTER XXXI.

SURRENDER OF CAPE HATTERAS.

State of affairs in Richmond—High price of provisions—General Winder—Destitution in Richmond—The blockade—Surrender of Fort Hatteras.

DURING the winter of 1862, the Government of the United States displayed the greatest activity. It had increased its fleet to such an extent as to be able to blockade all the Southern ports. Whilst the Federal troops were provided with everything which they required, and were thus enabled to withstand all the severities of the winter, our troops, on the other hand, especially the army on the Potomac, began to feel the inconvenient effects of the blockade. All those articles which the soldier so much needs for his comfort and health, gradually fell short, or were only to be had at prices so exorbitant that he could not afford to procure them. The non-combatant citizens took advantage of so favorable an opportunity to turn a penny, at the cost of the defenders of their country, and at Richmond the prices of provisions rose daily to such a height that many a father of a family looked forward with great anxiety to the future. More particularly, meat, vegetables, butter, and lard were so extremely dear that, in the hospitals, it became necessary to place the sick on half rations. The Provost-Marshal at Richmond, General Winder, issued a regulation, fixing the market prices, and imposing a heavy fine upon all who exceeded them. Matters, nevertheless, grew rather worse than better; the farmers preferred remaining at home and keeping back their produce, rather than sell it at a scanty profit; and as they had to pay fabulous prices for articles needed by themselves, such as tea, sugar, &c., the Provost-Marshal was obliged at last to withdraw his regulations, and so the farmers were again enabled to sell their provisions at their own prices. Every other article of food rose in proportion; tea and sugar became luxuries out of the reach of the majority; instead of coffee, burnt rye was used; milk rose to extravagant prices, as it was most wanted in the hospitals. No beer was allowed to be brewed, and what little remained on hand could not be obtained except by means of a medical certificate. Sickness prevailed to a great extent on the Potomac as well as in the interior of Virginia, and thousands of invalid soldiers were brought to Richmond to receive medical aid in the hospitals. Here again great misery was occasioned by the scarcity of medicines. All such stores were spoilt, and it was impossible to procure a further supply; thus hundreds died continually from the sheer want of proper remedies.

A report was spread at this time that a Federal squadron had sailed from the Northern ports for the purpose of attacking some point upon our coast, and in a few days we received the news of the fall of Fort Hatteras. This blow, although it did not fall quite unexpectedly upon us, nevertheless made a deep and painful impression upon the people of Richmond, as it proved to them that the Government of the United States was not only resolved to maintain a vigorous blockade, but was bent on gaining a footing on some part of our coast. The Government at Richmond, thereupon, bestirred itself, and Mr. Benjamin, the Secretary of War, took counsel with Generals Wise and Henningsen, as to the adoption of measures best calculated to meet the emergency.

CHAPTER XXXII.

SURRENDER OF ROANOKE ISLAND

General Wise ordered to Roanoke Island—General Henningsen's report to the Government—Neglect shown toward Wise's legion—General Wise proceeds to Richmond—Interview with the Secretary of War—Arrival of the hostile fleet—Bombardment of Fort Barton—Sinking of the Confederate steamers Curlew and Forest—Abandonment of the works—Death of Captain Wise and surrender of the forts.

As already observed in the preceding chapter, a squadron of the United States navy had succeeded in gaining a footing at Fort Hatteras, thereby securing a point from whence further offensive operations could be carried on against us. Although we were kept well informed by our agents of the plans of the Federal Government—which afforded us, in most cases, time to concert the best means for counteracting them—yet, we had the misfortune to possess a Secretary of War quite unfitted to hold so important a post. Now that North Carolina was threatened, and it became necessary to take the most active and energetic measures to oppose the enemy, Mr. Benjamin resolved to send General Wise to Roanoke Island; being glad of the opportunity of intrusting to the general a post which he well knew was, through his own neglect, in such a plight as to afford to its commandant but little scope for any display of military skill, still less for making a successful defence. Both the Secretary of War and President Davis were not sorry thus to get rid of Generals Wise and

Henningsen; dreading the influence of those officers, especially of the former, on the minds of the people. But it may be doubted whether either the Secretary of War or the President desired to give General Wise a command in which that distinguished soldier would have any chance of success; well knowing his energetic character, they were convinced that if he achieved any great success in the field he would exercise an irresistible influence over the whole army. The other generals of the Confederate army had always been supplied, on making application, with whatever number of guns, horses, and warlike stores, &c. they deemed necessary; but Wise's requisitions on such points were never heeded: on the contrary, the heads of the Government seemed bent on placing him in a dilemma, and he thus found himself under the necessity of making good the negligence of the officials from his own resources. The same course of conduct was adopted toward General Henningsen. Instead of giving him an important command, they persisted in selecting some favorite officer, however deficient he might have been in any kind of military talent, but who, in the estimation of the heads of the Government, was deemed a far more valuable man if he happened to possess personal influence in the South. Henningsen was looked upon in the light of a stranger; and it was feared that his upright, manly character might one day prove an embarrassing obstruction to the Government officials.

General Wise was, as already stated, ordered by the Secretary of War to take the command of Roanoke Island. He was, moreover, to increase his legion to the strength of 10,000 men, and to proceed to Albemarle Sound, and after taking possession of Roanoke Island, to oppose the further advance of the enemy. General Wise was assured that for more than six months Captain Selden of the engineers had been actively employed in placing the island in a fit state of defence, and that the works were so far advanced that all that remained to be done was to get the guns into position; that the island was well supplied with provisions, and that he would find in the flotilla of the Confederacy, cruising in those waters under the orders of Commander F. Lynch, a powerful auxiliary to prevent any further advance of the enemy. Wise and Henningsen were not the men to hesitate; the former set to work at once to organize the infantry, whilst Henningsen took charge of the artillery; and Colonel E—— had the cavalry placed under his orders.

General Wise and his associates set actively to work to bring the legion to the required strength of 10,000 men; recruiting was resorted to, but they had scarcely received their instructions when their difficulties commenced. Recruits were not forthcoming. In vain did General Wise solicit the Secretary of War, on the ground that the interests of North Carolina were at stake, to let him have a portion of the troops then encamped by thousands near Richmond, that he might be enabled to commence his march without delay, so as not to be exposed to the chances of a battle without being adequately prepared for such a contingency. But General Wise had to deal with a man who was determined to follow his own views. The Secretary replied to his earnest solicitation by expressing his sincere regret that he could not help him in this matter, even had it been in his power to do so; the President, who exercised great control over the War Department, having already decided that all the troops assembled at Richmond were to serve on the Potomac and Tennessee. He, therefore, entreated General Wise not to make any further delay, but to assume the command of Roanoke Island at once, as the news had been received that another hostile expedition was in preparation at Baltimore and Philadelphia under General Burnside, the object of which was the capture of Roanoke Island; that if the enemy succeeded in forcing the entrance of Albemarle Sound, and once got possession of the granaries of North Carolina, it would be a very difficult task to drive them out again. To dispel any further doubts on the part of

General Wise, the Secretary of War promised him that instructions should be sent to General Huger, at Portsmouth, to give him every assistance in his power. These various promises, none of which were ever fulfilled, induced General Wise to hasten his departure, to take command of Roanoke Island. Before starting, however, he held a sort of council of war at his headquarters to consider the condition of the legion under his orders.

At this conference, General Henningsen stated distinctly that, owing to the neglect of the Secretary of War during the campaign in Virginia, the legion was wanting in nearly everything which it required, and had thereby suffered in its organization and efficiency so much, that the fruits of a five months' campaign had been thrown away; that, even now, though we had been six weeks in camp at Richmond, nothing had been done for the equipment of the troops of the legion: the batteries were still unprovided with horses, and the muskets of the infantry scarcely fit for use. Whilst the War Department paid all due attention to the wants of other corps, by providing them with efficient arms, and throwing open to them all the resources at the disposal of the authorities, the legion had been totally neglected; and the Secretary of War had made it a point of always giving that corps the most difficult work to do. This, indeed, might certainly be considered as an honor, and would be eagerly accepted, if the legion could be satisfied that the Government appreciated the sacrifices that were required of it; but this, unfortunately, was not the case. It was only on the previous day, that the officer in command of the cavalry had informed him that as yet no saddles had been provided by the store department for the cavalry of Wise's legion, whilst a company of another body of horse, which had only just arrived at Richmond, was at once provided with them. Therefore, continued General Henningsen, he was of the opinion that before undertaking the task committed to them, they should carefully consider the serious consequences which might result to the legion, and which might in fact draw upon it the disfavor of the Government. He then proceeded to state that Captain Bolton, whom he had sent to inspect the condition of the defensive works at Roanoke Island, had sent him the following report:

"The island is in anything but a satisfactory state of defence; the works have been constructed with such an utter want of care and skill that they will scarcely be of any service. Of the twelve batteries which are put down upon the list furnished by the Secretary of War, there is only one that can be regarded as serviceable; all the others are totally useless. Moreover, the roads in Portsmouth are in such a bad condition that it will be difficult for the infantry to march along them, and for guns and wagons they are quite impracticable."

This brief and clear report could not fail to cause much anxiety to all who heard it. General Henningsen then having issued instructions to the various officers on whom the duty devolved, to exert themselves to provide for the prompt equipment and completion of the batteries, as well as that of the cavalry and infantry, left the meeting still engaged in warm debate.

Before the departure of the legion, General Wise again made requisition on the Secretary of War, but in vain. Mr. Benjamin was not the man to be overawed; he promised the general that everything that was possible should be done, and relying on this assurance, the latter was at last induced to make final preparations to proceed to his post.

The first regiment of the legion, under Colonel Richardson, commenced its march, followed by the regiments of Anderson, Tyler, and Green; next came the first and second cavalry regiments and the park of artillery, the latter under the personal command of General Henningsen. The weather was execrable, and everything held out the prospect of a very disagreeable march. The columns advanced in dogged silence, for the men were laboring under an impression that they were being sent on a desperate service, in which, cut off from all communication with the rest of the army, they would, in all probability, fall a prey to the enemy. At Petersburg a mutinous feeling became evident amongst the troops, and the officer in command found it necessary to have two of the ringleaders shot as an example to the others. This act of strict discipline had a good effect upon the men, and order was promptly restored. Notwithstanding the bad weather, the troops marched forward at a good pace, very few failing through fatigue. But on reaching Portsmouth our miseries commenced in good earnest; General Huger, who was in command at that place, treated our officers and men with a sort of lofty condescension; he seemed, indeed, to look upon the whole legion as men beneath his notice. The troops were allotted the most miserable quarters, and no complaints or representations on our part were at all heeded by him. The Secretary of War had given a solemn assurance to General Wise that he had sent instructions to the officer in command at Portsmouth to do everything he possibly could to aid the legion; this promise was shamefully broken. To add to the general annoyances we experienced, General Henningsen, who had been led to expect he could procure horses at Portsmouth for his artillery, found his hopes deceived. This rendered his artillery almost useless, and the troops had, consequently, to proceed on their march without it.

Generals Wise and Henningsen then held another conference, which led to the following results: General Wise was to take command of all the infantry, and assume the command of Roanoke Island as quickly as possible; the defensive works were to be placed under the superintendence of Captain Bolton, of the engineers, and forthwith put in a proper state; the cavalry was to take up cantonments on the shore of Albemarle Sound; whilst General Henningsen would do his utmost to procure every requisite that was needed to render his artillery efficient.

At the conclusion of this conference, the Generals separated, and at the moment of taking leave, General Wise, on shaking his worthy associate Henningsen by the hand, could not refrain from taking a foreboding view of the errand on which his friend was about to start. Smarting as he was under the effects of the broken promise of the Secretary of War, he turned round in his saddle, to bestow a look of ill-concealed scorn, in the direction of Richmond—where he had been so grossly misled—and then started off, little suspecting that when he and Henningsen should meet again it would be as fugitives without their legion.

Our cavalry now advanced under great difficulties through swampy ground to reach its intended cantonments on the shores of Albemarle Sound. Wise, meanwhile, with a heavy heart, pushed forward as quickly as he could, that no want of zeal on his part should be wanting in the service of his country. Handing over the command of his troops to the chief of his staff, he hastened forward, accompanied by two or three officers only, that he might superintend in person the arrangements for the reception of his troops, and also assume the command of the whole district. Although suffering from fever, occasioned by the continued annoyance he had recently experienced, he took no heed of his physician's advice to avoid exertion, but performed the ordinary duties allotted to him with an energy and self-denial that deserved a better reward. On reaching Elizabeth City that night, he immediately went on board a small war steamer lying off the town, and was conveyed to Roanoke Island, that he might learn from the officer in command the exact condition of the fortress. That officer's report was most unsatisfactory. According to Mr. Benjamin's representation, defensive works had been under preparation for the last six months; the truth being that little or nothing had been done. On the following morning, the general was on horseback by daybreak; and, accompanied by Captain Bolton, he made a survey of the island.

11

There can be no doubt that Roanoke is the key to the northwest portion of the State of North Carolina; it commands Albemarle Sound as well as Currituck, and is the only point which covers Norfolk. If placed in a proper state of defence, it is able to command no less than eight estuaries, four canals, and two railways; moreover, it serves to protect the richest and most important part of North Carolina; and it is obvious that a stronghold of such value ought to have been specially cared for by the Secretary of War. Should the island fall into the hands of an enterprising enemy, General Huger, in command of the troops at Portsmouth, would be inevitably obliged to surrender with his troops, as all his means of retreat would be cut off, and we should be obliged ourselves to destroy our own ships to prevent them falling into the hands of the foe. The possession of Roanoke Island would give the enemy everything he could require to carry out an extensive plan of operations, and thereby cause the greatest danger to the Confederacy; yet the Government at Richmond seemed to be completely ignorant of or indifferent to these obvious truths, and gave no attention whatever to the means for rendering this important place secure. Even General Huger seemed to be unaware of the importance of his command, and made no preparations to meet the enemy, although every man of the garrison was aware that the destination of the Federal naval and military forces under General Burnside was Roanoke Island.

General Wise set to work with the most determined energy. On the east side of Fuller Shoals, he ordered a number of large pallisades to be planted so as to stretch across from the shoals to the island, thus closing up one passage, and ordered a new post, Fort Barton, to be constructed in such a position as to command the sound. Commander Lynch placed a small flotilla at his service, and promised to keep him accurately informed by his cruisers of the enemy's movements. The news came at last that General Burnside, with the enemy's fleet, had sailed, and might be expected shortly in Pamlico Sound. General Wise, upon receipt of this intelligence, hastened back to Richmond in person, to point out to the Government the importance of firmly holding such a position as Roanoke Island, and urging the necessity for their granting the support of the 20,000 men who were lying idle at Portsmouth under the orders of General Huger. All his representations were fruitless. Mr. Benjamin desired him in the most uncourteous terms to return to his post, adding that they could not spare him any more troops, believing as they did that, under an able general, his force was quite strong enough to repulse an enemy three times his number. This unreasonable way of evading so urgent an appeal, rendered still more annoying by the ungracious tone in which it was conveyed, greatly irritated General Wise. To a few friends he confided what had taken place, and he must then have called to mind Henningsen's warning words at the Richmond conference. Gifted by nature with an iron constitution, even that gave way under all the repeated annoyances he had undergone. On reaching Elizabeth City, he was taken seriously ill, and desired to be conveyed in a litter, without delay, to Nagg's Head, a promontory opposite to Roanoke Island, that he might be near his troops. Here he was seized with a violent fever. A climax to his sorrow and suffering was now at hand. The news was brought to him the following morning that Commander Lynch had received the information, through one of his gunboats, that the enemy's squadron was in sight. Commander Lynch at the same time informed him that he would engage the enemy, so as to keep them at bay as long as possible. To appreciate the general's distress of mind, it should be remembered that the defensive works on the island were not yet half finished. The garrison of the fort consisted of the 8th and 31st regiments of the State of North Carolina, and one battalion of the 17th. As soon as General Wise received information of the approach of the enemy, he ordered up the two regiments of Anderson and Richardson, belonging to the legion, and as he was incapable of assuming the direct command of the place, he handed it over to Colonel Shaw. He despatched one of the war steamers immediately to Edenton, where General Henningsen was quartered with the artillery and cavalry, with an order for him to come over at once to Roanoke Island, to take the chief command. But before this order reached Henningsen, the island was already in the hands of the enemy.

On the 7th of February, 1862, the United States squadron of steamers and sailing vessels was reported in sight, and the Confederate flotilla, under Commander Lynch, sought shelter under the guns of the forts on the island. Lynch drew up his little fighting squadron in line of battle at the entrance of the harbor to meet the enemy. It was a dull, foggy day. A small steamer sent out to watch the movements of the Federal ships, now came back at full speed, pursued by one of the enemy's gunboats. A 48-pound shot from Barton's battery, athwart the gunboat's deck, warned the commander that he had better not advance any farther. After firing a few shots at the fort, which did no damage, the gunboat turned back and rejoined the Federal fleet. Great activity was now displayed in Barton's battery, and more guns were brought into position. About noon the fog partially cleared off, and the Federal fleet appeared in view. Their ships at once opened fire, which was briskly returned by the fort. Ere long, however, two of Commander Lynch's vessels, the *Curlew* and *Forest*, were sunk by the enemy's guns, which disaster induced him to sail away with his remaining vessels, and leave Roanoke Island to its fate. During the night the Confederates worked hard to improve their defences, and to bring more guns into position, under the superintendence of Major Schermerhorn and Commanders Kinney and Selden. It was impossible to convey any information either to Nagg's Head or to General Henningsen, as the enemy's cruisers cut off all means of communication. At daybreak next morning the enemy reopened fire, which was quickly responded to by our batteries. Colonel Shaw, upon whom the command had devolved, soon became convinced that the defence was hopeless. He, therefore, ordered the guns to be spiked, and with his troops withdrew to the north side of the island. The enemy continued to pour shot and shell into Fort Barton, which, in less than two hours, became a total ruin. Colonel Shaw, in spite of the entreaties of his officers, resolved to surrender. The news that Captain Wise, son of the general, had been killed, confirmed him in this resolution, and he sent one of his aide-de-camps to stipulate for the terms of capitulation. The fort was, however, surrendered unconditionally on the 8th February. General Wise's grief on receiving the news of the surrender of the fort and also of the death of his son can be more easily conceived than described. I was now charged with despatches to Richmond, to announce the surrender of Roanoke Island at headquarters.

CHAPTER XXXIII.

GENERAL WISE.

Anxiety at Richmond, consequent on the surrender of Roanoke Island—General Wise claims the body of his son—Great grief of the father—He sends to Congress a formal accusation against the Secretary of War and General Huger—A Committee appointed by Congress adopts his views—Want of confidence in the Government—Burnside releases the prisoners of war.

GREAT excitement prevailed at Richmond respecting the fate of Roanoke Island. All sorts of rumors were in circulation. Every one knew well enough that the island had been surrendered, but the most contradictory statements respecting the defence passed from mouth to mouth, or appeared in the newspapers. It was reported, for instance, that a great battle had taken place; that the engagement commenced by our small squadron under Commander Lynch, who, after he had succeeded in sinking half the enemy's fleet, was compelled at last to yield to superior numbers; and that, in order to prevent his own ships falling into the enemy's hands, he had blown himself up in the air; that the enemy, provoked at this determined resistance, had stormed Roanoke Island and put half our men to the sword. The more absurd these statements were, the more eagerly were they believed; and, as the greater portion of Wise's legion consisted of men from Richmond and its vicinity, the excitement in the town was the more intense. Notwithstanding my assurance that Colonel Shaw, to avoid bloodshed, had capitulated—that our loss consisted of only eight killed and thirty-one wounded—no one would believe me. All thought it far more probable that the slaughter had been immense, that no man was left to tell the tale, and that Richmond would have to go into general mourning.

President Jefferson Davis and Mr. Benjamin, his Secretary of War, held long conferences together; the subject of which was, most probably, General Wise and his legion.

I received an order from General Wise to join him at Portsmouth, as he wished me to apply for the body of his son, and also to take a temporary command. Burnside immediately complied with General Wise's request, and issued the necessary orders to give up the body of the captain to the brave old general. In a small inlet of the bay, on board a Federal war steamer, the coffin containing the body was brought to us. The officers and men spoke to us in the most friendly terms, and informed us that every attention had been paid to Captain Wise until he breathed his last. I shook hands with the officer who had landed, thanking him in the general's name. He took a courteous leave of me, and his boat was soon gliding along toward his steamer with measured strokes. I stood for a few moments on the shore, watching his progress, and then returned in a mournful mood in charge of the body of poor Captain Wise. On reaching Portsmouth all the church bells tolled, and a procession was formed by the numerous friends of the deceased. At the porch of the church we made a halt, awaiting the arrival of General Wise. With bowed head and faltering step, the old general approached, leaning on the arm of another of his sons, the Rev. — Wise, and accompanied also by his son-in-law, Dr. Lyons. Evincing great emotion, he went up to the coffin, and ordered the lid to be raised, that he might once more behold the features of his lamented son. The brother and brother-in-law of the departed could no longer suppress their grief, and burst into tears. The old general took the dead man's hand in his own, and exclaimed, in a tone of anguish which startled all present: "You have died for me; you have died for your father!" And large tears rolled down his cheeks. "He died for me! he died for me!" he repeated in broken accents, and then fell insensible to the ground.

I never could have supposed this man to be capable of showing so much feeling. I remembered seeing him, some years previously, in his capacity as Governor of the State of Virginia, sign the death warrants of John Brown and Cook with a firm hand, though his own daughter, on her knees before him, with tears in her eyes, besought him to pardon them; when Cook's brother-in-law, formerly Governor of Indiana, who had come all the way to Richmond to intercede for him, pleaded also in vain. I remember it well. Wise took out his cigar case, and turning to me, "Do you smoke, Colonel?" he said; "these are good Havanas." He lit one of them, and then addressing the suppliants, said, in a stern voice—"This man has forfeited his life to the law, and the law must have its course." And now, to see that that heart of stone could melt, to see that giant mind prostrated by all that it had undergone, made a powerful impression upon me. More dead than alive, the stricken sire was taken away from the coffin of his son, and removed in a carriage to Richmond.

The affair of Roanoke Island created the most indescribable sensation, not only in the city of Richmond but through the whole South. The people began to feel that something must be wrong at headquarters, and a strong feeling of animosity grew up against the President, and his confidential advisers. For two days the effigy of a black coffin with a rope upon the lid might be seen conspicuously displayed near the residence of the President, bearing a very ominous inscription. Despite all the efforts of the police, the perpetrators of this scurrility could not be discovered. It was decided in the Senate that a special committee should be formed to inquire into all the circumstances connected with the attack and defence of Roanoke Island. It was thought that this was due to the reputation of the army. Meantime the state of health of General Wise was so precarious that the news of his death was almost hourly expected. But his strong frame enabled him gradually to recover, and he was soon well enough to make an official report on all that had occurred. He assembled his staff at his bedside and dictated a formal protest against the conduct of the President, of Mr. Benjamin, and of General Huger. This protest was couched in moderate but firm language, but contained such unanswerable proofs of the failings of the Government that even the obstinate Secretary of War must have been astounded when he read it.

On the 3d of March, General Wise forwarded a formal accusation to the Congress. He stated that he had willingly accepted the command of Roanoke Island, but that after satisfying himself by a personal inspection of the defenceless state it was in, he reported to that effect to the Secretary of War, pointing out to him the consequences that must be expected to result, as the island was the key to the whole coast; and that shortly afterward he informed the Government of the approach of a hostile squadron consisting of twenty-four ships, quite capable of destroying all the batteries on the island within twelve hours, with the distinct avowal that the garrison was not in sufficient strength to withstand the enemy. This report, as we have previously shown, had been treated with contempt, no notice having been taken of it, and his personal appeal to the Secretary of War had met with no better success, although at that interview he took great pains to demonstrate the necessity for having reinforcements as well as supplies of ammunition without delay. That, in short, all his efforts to effect his object had been fruitless; while an effectual check was given to any further remonstrance on his part by the following peremptory order, brought to him by an aide-de-camp from the Secretary of War:

11*

"OFFICE OF SECRETARY OF WAR,
"*January* 22d, 1862.

"General Wise is ordered to proceed at once to his post at Roanoke Island.

"JUDAH P. BENJAMIN,
"Secretary of War."

General Wise concluded by stating, that in pursuance of this order he left, although fully convinced he had been sacrificed. The result we have already shown.

Such was the purport of the accusation which was laid before the Congress, and that body immediately ordered the matter to be referred to a special Committee of Inquiry. The result was that the Secretary of War was made responsible for the defeat of the Confederate troops at Roanoke Island, as it appeared that defeat might have been avoided if the representations of Generals Wise and Henningsen had been attended to.

"If blame attaches to any one (said the report of the committee), in this matter, it ought to fall upon the Secretary of War and General Huger." The committee further proposed that they should both be dismissed, and that a vote of thanks should be passed to Generals Wise and Henningsen for their conduct.

President Jefferson Davis and Mr. Benjamin had little expected such a result, and it even startled the public mind not a little. Confidence in the measures of the Government was already on the wane. The President, nevertheless, promoted Mr. Benjamin to the post of Secretary of State of his Cabinet, and this had the effect of still more weakening the trust of the people in the Government.

Fourteen days after the capitulation of Roanoke Island, General Burnside released all the prisoners of war on their taking an oath not to serve against the United States.

CHAPTER XXXIV.

THE BATTLE OF NEWBERN.

My mission to Raleigh, North Carolina—Generals Clark and Martin—General Branch and Colonel Spreil—My inspection of the cavalry at Newbern—A trapper's adventures—Burnside's attack of Newbern—Conduct of the cavalry—Railway bridge destroyed—Retreat on Raleigh—Dismissal of Generals Branch and Gattlin.

As soon as the men of our legion had arrived at Richmond, I received orders to proceed to Raleigh, the seat of the Government of North Carolina, to concert measures with Governor Clark for the fortification of the coast, as the new Secretary of War was of opinion that General Burnside, after the easy conquest of Roanoke Island, would lose no time in attacking Beaufort and Newbern, with the view of acquiring possession of the whole of the North Carolina line of coast.

I found General Clark an upright soldier-like man. After listening to all the details connected with the surrender of Roanoke Island he sent for the officer in command of the troops in North Carolina. That officer, a gallant veteran with only one arm—having lost the other at the battle of Matamoras, in Mexico—soon after made his appearance, when the Governor requested us to make a general inspection of the coast. After I had taken my leave of the Governor, General Martin, the officer above alluded to, took me with him to his headquarters that we might concert together further proceedings. Here I was introduced to his aide-de-camp, a Scotchman, who had only recently joined the Confederate army. We formed a very cheerful party, and freely discussed the general state of affairs in America. I expressed the hope that my new acquaintance would live to see peace restored on that continent—a hope that was never fulfilled, for he fell at Baton Rouge. After inspecting the coast defences, General Martin directed me to proceed to the two most important points of defence along the coast, with orders to send him a report of their condition. I proceeded forthwith to Goldsborough, which commands four lines of railways. Here I was introduced to General Gattlin, whose manners I found anything but pleasing; he spoke, too, of the enemy with contempt. He had a considerable force under his orders, but the state of his troops showed a great want of discipline. From Goldsborough I proceeded to Newbern, at the railway station of which place I was met by the commanding officers of the cavalry force quartered there, and I then proceeded to pay my respects to General Branch, the chief officer in command.

On the following day I accompanied the general and his aide-de-camp on a visit of inspection to the forts which defended Newbern. Colonel Spreil, the aide-de-camp, belonged to the 2d cavalry regiment, and led the way at a rattling pace over the fine railway bridge which here spans the river Neuse, and we reached the forts just as the men were going through their drill. Fort Thompson, which, according to the general's idea, was a masterpiece as a defensive work, mounted fifteen 64-pounders, two of which were rifled. The officer in command of the battery was not up to his work, but felt convinced that if the enemy's fleet should make its appearance, its commander would very soon manage to establish his headquarters at Newbern. Fort Ellis was not completed, but nevertheless, it mounted nine guns, also 64-pounders. The works were carried on here just as if no danger was apprehended. The commander of the place was an easy-going sort of man, smoking his pipe by his fireside, and apparently caring as little about his general and staff as he did about Burnside and his fleet. This man's coolness and unconcern were quite astounding. " If my comrades," said he, " should really attempt to defend the place, I will stand by them ; should they run away, I am not far from the bridge, so I may as well smoke my pipe quietly, and not bother myself by anticipating the course of events."

We then proceeded to Fort Thompson, where we found the commandant practising his men at the guns. My astonishment, I must own, was aroused at the precision the artillerymen consistently displayed in *not* hitting their mark ; and I came to the conclusion that if General Burnside had only the slightest notion of how matteers stood, he would at once make sail for Newbern, and take the place without risking the loss of a man.

Exhausted by our long ride, I requested General Branch to accompany me to the cavalry encampment, where I had been invited to dine. General Branch offered his arm to the colonel's wife, and the other officers followed. As long as dinner lasted, which, by the by, was a very good one, all went on smoothly ; but as soon as the champagne went round, every man present was eager to make a speech. Americans, I have observed, are all fond of displaying their oratorical powers on festive occasions. After a speech of some half an hour's duration, General Branch proposed a toast in honor of the Confederacy, which was responded to in a speech scarcely inferior in length, by the colonel of the 2d regiment of cavalry, in the course of which he dilated in glowing terms on the matchless gallantry of his troops—their prowess being such as to throw the deeds of the Greeks and Romans into the shade ; according to him the whole corps was ready to die, if needful, to the last man. I need not add that this speech was received with tumultuous applause. " Gentlemen," concluded the gallant colonel, rising from his seat, " let us make

Newbern a second Sebastopol—before the walls of which the enemy must perish!" Cheers resounded on all sides! "Yes! Newbern shall be a second Sebastopol!" General Branch then rose and made another speech, and stated that his guest, Colonel Estvàn, had, with 10,000 men, defended Sebastopol against all the combined forces of England and France! The noise increased. Colonel Spreil was again on his legs, and said that with 10,000 of his own brave fellows he would have taken Sebastopol in fourteen days, and not have left one stone upon another.

I was now called upon to make a speech in reply. "My friends," said I, " how would you go to work if General Branch, with 10,000 of his best men, undertook the defence of Sebastopol, and Colonel Spreil, with 10,000 of his cavalry attacked it? What would be the result?" They stared with astonishment at these words, and I sat down, curious to see how they would solve their own problem. Another subject was then broached, but I soon perceived that I had lost their favor. At last the general rose to depart, and we returned to Newbern with our small staff.

On the following day I visited the cavalry encampment, to inspect the two regiments there. I found them a fine body of men, but as regarded their weapons, there was much room for improvement; a great portion of the troopers were armed with heavy carbines with bayonets, in addition to a sword and revolver.

When on horseback, fully accoutred, one of these men had the appearance of a movable arsenal; probably the colonel did not deem himself safe unless his men were thus armed to the teeth. The horses, too, were in a very bad condition; while the manœuvring was indifferent, and the men seemed to have no idea of sword exercise, each man using his weapon as best suited his own notions. So I returned to Raleigh anything but satisfied with the result of my inspection. Before waiting upon the Governor, I solicited an interview with

General Martin, and was received by him with a bland smile. "Well, Colonel," said he, "what do you think of the troops?" "If," I replied, "they can fight as well as they talk, we need not be under the slightest anxiety for the safety of our coasts." "You are right," he replied; "all that they can do is to talk, and that I fear will be our ruin. If General Burnside only knew how to turn his recent advantage to good account, he would be in the possession of our whole line of coast within a fortnight. Look here," he continued, as he spread a map on the table, "if Newbern and Beaufort are taken, Burnside will push on to Goldsborough and Weldon by a flank movement, which will place our main roads of traffic and railways in his hands, and our army will be split in two. His fleet will attack Wilmington, and our forts, Caswell, Smithville, and Fisher, under Commander Iverson, will have to surrender. All these gentlemen, with the exception of Commander Iverson, who formerly served in the United States army, have no idea of the importance of the posts which they hold, and, believe me, it is a most difficult task to make them aware of their duties. Often whole companies will leave a battle field with their commanders, not from cowardice, but simply because they fancy they have had enough fighting for the day, and that others should have their turn also. When you return to Richmond, Colonel, I wish you would seriously represent to the Government the necessity that exists for sending out new commanders to all the forts along the coast, as well as some able engineer officers; the cavalry might be very well spared from Newbern, and that force replaced by some efficient battalions of infantry. We also stand in need of a few thousand stand of arms. If this is not done, I look upon Newbern as lost, and Goldsborough, Weldon, and Wilmington, also. Having frankly given you my opinion, I recommend you now to pay your respects to Governor Clark."

After taking a cordial leave of the general, I proceeded to pay the Governor a visit. He happened to be out, but I accepted the invitation of his secretary to take a stroll with him outside the town. As we went along, this amiable old gentleman also opened his mind to me. "This unfortunate war," he said, "can never have a happy termination; all revolutions end badly, and I fear this will be the case with ours. The people generally have never been consulted by the leaders of the movement, and I suspect that many amongst them are simply working upon the minds of the people for their own ends. I grieve, when I think how many loyal Unionists have been compelled to pretend to show a feeling of sympathy for a Government which, hitherto, has only brought misery upon them."

About two miles outside the town, we met a tall, imposing looking man, dressed in leathern clothes, with moccasons on his feet. Two revolvers and a bowie knife were stuck in his belt, together with a tomahawk, while on his shoulder he carried a rifle of unusual length. His hair and beard seemed quite unacquainted with the use of a comb, and altogether, his appearance was remarkable. This prairie trapper passed by us with a polite "good evening." As we turned round to look after him, with some curiosity, he suddenly stopped, leaned upon his rifle, and stared hard at my companion, whose countenance suddenly betrayed great emotion. "Father! father!" exclaimed the trapper, as he rushed into my friend's arms and met his embrace. Fourteen years previously he had left his home to seek his fortune in the far West, and since then no tidings had been heard of him. After the father had presented to me in due form the son whom he had supposed dead long ago, the latter related his adventures to us.

He had been to Oregon, where he tried his hand as a gold digger and hunter. When he heard of the civil war between the North and South, he resolved to return home; but having no money, he performed the journey of 8,000 miles on foot, from Oregon to North Carolina, over mountains, and through forests and prairies; having, on his venturous journey, encountered wild beasts and hostile tribes; and at last, on reaching the frontier of Missouri, he was made prisoner by a detachment of dragoons under Colonel Sturgis, but who, on hearing his story, allowed him to proceed home unmolested, influenced, no doubt, by the reflection, that as the Almighty had, in so wonderful a manner, watched over the safety of this man in his perilous journey homeward, it was not for man to stop him in the fulfilment of his object. The news of the return of this long-absent wanderer from the remote region of Oregon on foot, spread like wildfire through the town, and the whole population crowded round him to hear his adventures. He did not remain long in his father's house. A commission as captain in a regiment of infantry was granted him, and the poor fellow was shot in action shortly afterward, and thus his ardent wish to die for his country was accomplished.

On my return to Richmond, I delivered my despatches, but was soon summoned back to Raleigh. On my arrival there, I was informed that General Burnside had already collected his fleet, with the apparent intention of attacking Newbern. I started accordingly at once for General Branch's camp, to see what steps he had taken for the defence of the place. At Goldsborough the most extraordinary rumors were in circulation. Thus General Burnside was said to have attacked Beaufort, and, as had been reported after the surrender of Roanoke Island, had put the garrison to the sword, after a valiant defence. As I proceeded on my way, I found the excitement had increased. At Kingston I left the railway, and procured horses, and rode on as fast as I could, accompanied only by an aide-de-camp.

As I approached Newbern, the distant roar of cannon became more and more distinct. Suddenly a number of horsemen galloped past me in full flight, and amongst them I fancied I could discern the gallant colonel with whom I had dined not long ago. He gave me a hurried nod and passed on. On reaching Newbern I did my best to rally the men, and so far succeeded, that they sunk one of the enemy's gunboats, and blew up the forts, that they might not fall into hostile hands, and thereby impede the movements of our troops. A 24-pound gun just then burst, and the fragments fell amongst my men, who forthwith took to their heels. Newbern I found looking bad enough.

General Branch had secured a railway carriage for himself, and started off inland. Troops without their officers passed me in confusion, and throwing away their arms, rushed across the bridge. They all told wonderful stories of the feats performed by their respective regiments. According to their account they had all fought like so many devils, but the force of the enemy not being less than 100,000 men, they had no chance against them. The fact is, General Branch had run away, and all discipline was at an end. I crossed the bridge and endeavored to restore some kind of order amongst the troops, but in vain. The 19th regiment of infantry, under Colonel Burgwine, now came up; I asked him to throw out his men as skirmishers, in order to protect the baggage, and to allow time for the withdrawal of the guns. The colonel, who was a brave soldier, acquiesced in my request, and ordered his men to halt. A few other companies joined, and they kept up so well-sustained a fire that the enemy's advancing troops, which, on the flight of our own, had pushed too far forward, were compelled to fall back, fancying that we had received reinforcements. This was a great point gained, as it enabled us to save our valuable baggage. The Federal troops now delivered so deadly a fire that our troops were driven from their positions, and we had to cross the bridge, to which we set fire immediately after, in order to prevent its falling into the hands of the enemy. In a few moments dense columns of smoke denoted that this work of destruction was in progress.

Whilst this noble bridge, once the pride of the people of

North Carolina, was thus becoming a prey to the flames, the enemy actually stopped firing to witness the grand and awful spectacle. The flames rapidly increased, the timbers crackled, and the whole structure finally fell with a tremendous crash into the river below; and then, for a brief interval, all was still again. The enemy presently reopened fire, and drove the Confederate troops from their position in front of the town. Inside all was confusion. The inhabitants endeavored to save themselves and their chattels, and every kind of vehicle serviceable for such a purpose was eagerly laid hold of. In vain did we endeavor to persuade the scared citizens that General Burnside was an honorable enemy, a man of humane disposition, and that there was no reason for this precipitate flight; it was all in vain. As the last train started the enemy's shot reached the station, but fortunately did no damage. The Confederate troops rallied at Kingston. General Branch found it no easy task to reëstablish his reputation for bravery. General Burnside, apparently satisfied with the advantages he had so easily gained, turned his attention more to the civil administration of the place than to military measures. Had he been aware of the disorganized state our army was in, he might have then given it a death blow. Had he taken advantage of the moral defeat which we had sustained, he could have easily driven us out of both Kingston and Goldsborough, and have caused our local government at Raleigh to decamp; he might have threatened Weldon and Wilmington, and no doubt many inhabitants of North Carolina would have greeted his arrival among them very cordially. As it happened, however, Burnside, who had us really in his power, allowed us to escape with only a fright. The confusion which prevailed at Newbern spread to Raleigh, for as soon as General Gattlin, who was at Goldsborough, heard of Branch's retreat, he became so alarmed that he was incapable of doing anything. General Branch's repeated orders to join him with all the troops he could gather together met with no attention; his officers shielded themselves behind the general's responsibility, and would not take orders from any one else. The managers of the banks at Raleigh packed up their cash and fled toward Charlotte, as it was feared the enemy might soon occupy the former place. But as General Burnside desisted from any further onward movement, the Confederate troops were allowed time to reorganize.

On these events becoming known at Richmond, the Secretary of War ordered Generals Branch and Gattlin to resign their commissions. The command was then given to General Anderson; and the Confederate Government also ordered all the disposable troops on the Potomac, under General Ransom, to proceed to the support of the army in North Carolina. Indeed, the Secretary of War exerted himself to the utmost to make good the losses suffered by the Confederate forces in that quarter through the misconduct and incompetence of their commanders.

CHAPTER XXXV.

THE "MERRIMAC" AND THE "MONITOR."

Activity in the dockyards at Portsmouth—Mysterious naval preparations—The *Merrimac* completed—The Confederate squadron steams out of harbor—Speech of Captain Buchanan to the crew of the *Merrimac*—Position of the enemy's squadron—The *Merrimac* first attacks the *Congress*, and then sinks the *Cumberland*—Renewed attack on the *Congress;* surrender and destruction of that ship—Captain Buchanan wounded—Arrival of the *Monitor*—Action between the *Monitor* and the *Merrimac*—The *Merrimac* returns to Norfolk.

THE Confederate troops had left their positions on the Potomac and at Manassas, and were quickly retreating on all sides toward Richmond, in order to make that capital the basis of their operations. Only Jackson's corps and Ewell's division had been ordered to take up positions in the Shenandoah Valley, for the purpose of repelling any movements which the enemy might undertake in that direction. In the interval every means was devised to convert the town of Richmond into a second Sebastopol. The James River had to be put in such a state of defence as to protect the capital from an attack by the enemy's fleet. To this end the inspectors and superintendents of the dockyards at Portsmouth displayed the greatest activity. The naval establishments, which had all been repaired and rebuilt since their demolition, were, consequently, all set busily to work, and an extraordinary number of hands were engaged in hastening all kinds of warlike preparations. The dockyards and the arsenals were also put in a state of defence, and large slabs of sheet iron from Anderson's foundery were brought to Portsmouth for the casing of ironclads. The people were, as usual, very inquisitive, but the Government kept its secrets effectually; so much so, that the public only acquired information in a general kind of way, and of such a character as it suited the Government to spread. Everybody talked of *the* ship that was being constructed in the dockyard, and which was to be cased over with iron of such a thickness as to be impenetrable to even the heaviest shot. This was, however, not fully believed in; it was rather construed as a boastful rumor purposely spread by the naval authorities, by way of accounting in somewise for the large sums which had been lavished without any apparent result.

A few days before the *Merrimac* put to sea there was a rumor current that she had sunk in the basin of the dockyard, and no little discontent was manifested by a portion of the public, which went so far as to cause a demand to be made upon the Government for the removal of Mallory, the incompetent Secretary of the Navy, as he was held to be.

In the meanwhile Commodore Tatnall and Captain Buchanan daily made regular inspections throughout the dockyards. At length, on the 12th May, 1862, the riddle was solved, much to the satisfaction of the impatient citizens; and the Confederate fleet, consisting of the ironclad *Merrimac*, mounting ten heavy 68-pounders; the corvette *Patrick Henry*, with twelve guns (24 and 32-pounders); the steamer *Jamestown*, mounting two guns, and the gunboats *Leager*, *Beaufort*, and *Raleigh*, with one gun each, started for Hampton Roads. Thousands of spectators had assembled to witness the animating spectacle of a naval engagement of so novel a kind, and it was indeed an interesting sight to see the little Confederate armada steaming out.

This small squadron was commanded by Captain Buchanan, who had hoisted his flag on board the *Merrimac*; and before starting that officer harangued his officers and crew in the following terms:

"We are now about to see the faces of our enemies; this honor has for a long time been withheld from us, and granted only to the land forces. This day, however, we shall have that gratification. You shall see your enemies; and I promise you that it will not be long before you are engaged with them. Remember that you fight for your rights and for your country. You see the enemy's ships yonder. You must destroy them. I do not say, Will you do it? for I know you will!"

This curt address was not lost on the men; they received it with loud cheers, and even those who, up to that moment, may have felt some scruples in serving on board such an iron prison as the *Merrimac*, plucked up in spirit. The iron monster now steamed away into the bay, but looked withal so dark, ominous, mysterious, and uncouth a structure, that it seemed to move along unnaturally on the waters. No human being, indeed, was to be seen on this moving fortress, as it towered gloomily over the little flotilla of gunboats, which sought the protection of its formidable armament. The thousands who had gathered together on the shores, to watch the progress of the Confederate fleet, looked on with beating hearts, and eyes anxiously strained.

The formidable ships of the Federal navy were anchored out in the quiet bay, within easy distance, their pennants waving gently in the breeze. The *Cumberland*, a splendid frigate, mounting forty guns, was in advance, and to the right the frigate *Congress*, whilst a little further back the stately *Minnesota* rode at anchor, surrounded by several small steamers, and in the distant horizon appeared the numerous masts of merchant vessels.

The enemy now began hurriedly to signal from their mastheads, which certified plainly enough to our crews that their approach was not unexpected. Presently a tremendous fire was opened from the ports of the *Minnesota*, on which ship was hoisted a flag, as a signal for the commencement of the engagement. All the enemy's small craft now scrambled under the protection of her guns like chickens under the wings of their parent bird, seeking shelter in the direction of Fort Monroe.

Great activity was now observable on board the enemy's two frigates. Their ports opened, and their formidable guns showed their angry mouths as if in defiance of the approaching foe. As soon as our vessels had got within range, all the gunboats kept some distance astern, and the *Merrimac* passed on steadily by herself. As soon as she got alongside of the *Congress*, she fired a broadside into her, which was immediately replied to by that frigate, and by all the land batteries as well, but with literally no effect, for the shot glided harmlessly off the *Merrimac's* iron sides like so many hailstones. Thus unhurt, she steamed toward the *Cumberland* without taking the slightest notice of the fire directed upon her by the unfortunate ship which she had doomed to destruction. When within forty yards of the *Cumberland* the crew of the *Merrimac* could distinctly hear the orders that were given on board that frigate, and the remarks made by her crew, "What the devil is this, coming? What can she be about?"

The commander of the *Merrimac* now raked the *Cumberland's* decks with an enormous cylinder shell, and this fearful missile dealt tremendous havoc amongst her crew. The *Merrimac* then swept round in a half circle, running her pointed beak straight into the sides of the *Cumberland*. The captain of that frigate, meanwhile, directed a heavy fire upon the *Merrimac* from every gun which could be brought to bear upon her at such close quarters; the shots, however, glanced harmlessly off the deck and sides of this sea monster, which continued its course, and the *Merrimac's* sharp point was soon buried in the frigate's stalwart hull. A stunning crash is heard, and the next minute the magnificent frigate is seen reeling about like a drunken man. Her brave captain, unwilling to yield, continues his fire in spite of the desperate condition of his ship. Gradually the frigate settles down deeper and deeper in the water, and the waves are seen pouring in at the portholes; once more she rises and vomits forth fire on her assailant, and then, finally heeling over, the fine ship sinks to rise no more, carrying a large number of her ill-fated crew along with her. She went down noiselessly— her brave crew emulating her in this respect by meeting their fate without uttering a cry. For a few moments after she sank, the waters were disturbed where she had but so lately been riding in all the pride of conscious strength, and then settled calmly over her.

The destruction of this splendid ship, with so many of her crew, in broad daylight and the calmest weather, in the midst of this beautiful bay, must have caused a panic among the remainder of the enemy's squadron. Nevertheless, the *Congress* kept her ground, and prepared to defend the honor of her flag against the redoubtable ironclad. The *Merrimac* now steered straight for that frigate; but her career was presently checked by her getting into shoal water. Her captain, judging that it would be impracticable for him to get any closer to the *Congress*, then opened a heavy fire upon that ship. Ere long the *Merrimac's* projectiles pierced through the frigate's wooden walls, and caused such destruction on board that her commander was obliged to strike his flag and surrender. Captain Buchanan then ceased firing, and signalled the gunboat *Beaufort*, ordering Lieutenant Parker, her commander, to go on board the *Congress* and receive her flag, and to bring away all the officers and crew. Captain Smith and Lieutenant Prendergast of the *Congress*, in reply to this latter summons, requested permission to remain on board their ship, in order to take care of the wounded, which was readily granted by Captain Buchanan. At this juncture, however, the land batteries most injudiciously again opened fire upon the gunboat *Beaufort*, and although no casualty ensued therefrom, Captain Buchanan was so incensed that he ordered red-hot shot to be

12

fired into the *Congress* to effect her total destruction. Just about this time, however, he was struck on the foot by a Minié bullet, and was obliged to hand over the command to his first lieutenant, Jones, to whom he gave stringent orders to sink the unfortunate *Congress*. The lieutenant executed this command to the letter, and in spite of all the efforts of the enemy's frigate *Minnesota*, and of the *Roanoke* and *Lawrence*, to assist their stricken consort, the *Congress* was utterly destroyed.

Meanwhile a feeling of prodigious excitement pervaded the crowd of spectators on shore. Two of the enemy's formidable frigates had already been destroyed by our iron scourge, and the next day no doubt she would effect the demolition of the enemy's remaining ships. Our sanguine people already indulged in pleasant anticipations of a reopened intercourse with Europe. So certain, indeed, did many feel at the realization of their hopes, that they at once set about taking measures for the opening of the port preparatory to various mercantile speculations. They complacently dilated, too, upon the consequences that might be expected to ensue from the triumphal progress of the *Merrimac* to Washington; not doubting that she would destroy everything in her way thither. Probably but few were composed enough to sleep that night. Thousands, indeed, encamped on the shores of the bay, eagerly awaiting the dawn of day and the recommencement of the naval battle.

The day broke at last, and discovered an enormous assemblage of people awaiting the coming event in eager expectation. The enemy's frigates *Roanoke* and *Lawrence* had sought protection under the guns of Fort Monroe, but the colossal frigate *Minnesota* still lay quietly at anchor in the bay. Alongside of her, however, was to be seen a curious little craft of no particular form, resembling more a capsized whaler than anything else. By and by, the *Merrimac* steamed out into the bay toward her antagonist, amidst the vociferous cheers of the thousands collected on the shores.

Captain Buchanan had sent his gunboats *Jamestown* and *Yorktown* ahead, to reconnoitre the strange-looking little craft. They approached her with the utmost caution, and as they gradually drew near, she fired two shots at them from the enormous guns that now peeped from the turret on her deck, by way of welcome or warning; they received the compliment in the latter sense, and hastily retreated. The *Merrimac* now put on full steam, and bore down on her little enemy with the object of running her beak into her so as to sink her by sheer weight. She had already got to within thirty yards' distance, and was preparing for the fatal thrust, when the *Monitor* twisted suddenly round, like a fish, and at the same moment discharged one of her heavy guns point blank at the *Merrimac*, to let her know that she had now to encounter a foe as formidable as herself. The *Merrimac* then slowly ranged alongside her diminutive antagonist, and both opened fire with ordnance of a more destructive character than had ever before been employed in naval encounters : 100 and 120-pounder Armstrong, and other equally powerful guns, discharging their fire at a distance of 150 yards. But it was to little purpose; the balls glancing off equally from the iron sides of both ships.

This useless cannonade continued for more than two hours, when another attempt was made by the *Merrimac* to run down her enemy; but the *Monitor* again skilfully avoided the intended shock, and managed, moreover, to send a shell through one of the portholes of her antagonist, spreading death and destruction among the crew. The *Merrimac* now continued her fire with redoubled fury; but it was steadily replied to; and the commander of the *Merrimac*, seeing the impossibility of seriously damaging his opponent, at last veered round, and steamed away toward Norfolk, leaving the *Monitor* in possession of the waters which had been the scene of this unparalleled conflict.

The multitude assembled on the shores, eagerly watching

the progress of the fight, could not comprehend how it was that the *Merrimac* failed to destroy the insignificant-looking craft that had dared to attack her. But, when they ascertained the real state of the case, and that the little enemy was also one of those wonderful ironclads, capable of disputing the entrance of the port with the *Merrimac*, they were exceedingly wroth, and denounced in no measured terms, not only the *Merrimac*, but the Naval Secretary, by whose directions she had been constructed, for not having built at the same time a couple of such ships, in order to insure the opening of the harbor.

It happened, however, that the movements of M'Clellan's army were assuming such an aspect as speedily to divert the attention of these politicians to other and no less important matters.

CHAPTER XXXVI.

DESTRUCTION OF THE "MERRIMAC."

M'Clellan's ill-concealed plan of operations in the Peninsula—Preparations on both sides—M'Clellan not supported by the Government—He assembles his troops at Fortress Monroe—Alarm at Richmond—General Huger ordered to destroy the fortifications at Portsmouth—Federal troops take possession of Portsmouth—The *Merrimac* destined for New York—Arrival of the enemy's ships—The *Merrimac* ordered to be blown up.

It was no longer a secret to the Confederate chief that it was General M'Clellan's intention to transfer his operations to the Peninsula. Large forces were, accordingly, ordered to proceed there forthwith, and instructions sent at the same time to General Magruder to place Yorktown, as well as Williamsburg, in such a state of defence that, if threatened, both should be able to stand a siege. General Magruder, who had for a long time held a command on the Peninsula, lost no time, accordingly, in carrying out these instructions, and he soon fortified Yorktown so strongly, that it was in a condition to stand the siege of a large army.

General M'Clellan, who had been greatly annoyed at the defeat of the Federal army at Manassas, must have been much mortified to find that all the secret plans he thought he had so carefully prepared should be, as they now were, revealed through some underhand agency. No sooner was his intended scheme of operations known at Washington, than it was communicated by means of active espionage to the Government at Richmond, where the necessary steps were forthwith taken to counteract it. As our generals were thus possessed long beforehand of the knowledge of M'Clellan's intentions, they were enabled to prepare for every contingency. Our voluntary abandonment of Manassas must have caused no small astonishment to the enemy. If the secret of M'Clellan's comprehensive plan of operations had not oozed out, and if the Federal Government had given him all the support in their power needed to carry out that plan, and had placed all the disposable troops at his command, its success would have been brilliant, and this fratricidal war might, probably, have been long since terminated.

But, as I have already said, the authorities at Washington acted with very little foresight, and they still continued to display the same want of common sense that led to the disasters at Bull Run and Manassas. By this mismanagement on their part, M'Clellan was deprived of the triumphs which he fancied he had effectually secured. Now that the general's plan was known to a great extent, he had no further reason for concealing it, and he proceeded at once to superintend the embarcation of his troops with all his habitual zeal and energy. As he was prevented from making use of the direct communication between James river and Richmond, owing to its being blockaded by the *Merrimac*, he promptly collected a fleet at Alexandria, and by its aid succeeded in conveying his troops to Fortress Monroe, with the intention of advancing from that point upon Richmond by land. The Federal Government acted as if it really wished to throw every possible obstacle in the way of the execution of a plan which was already beset with difficulties. Thus it deprived the general of M'Dowell's corps, and condemned the latter to inactivity; a measure which at a subsequent period became the cause of a very serious misfortune to the arms of the Federal Government.

At last, General M'Clellan, having succeeded in assembling

his army under the walls of Fortress Monroe, resolved to push on by the shortest road with the greater portion of his force to Yorktown—leaving the fleet to convey the remainder of his troops up the York river—in order to cut off any attempt at retreat on the part of the Confederates.

The news of M'Clellan's operations in the Peninsula caused the greatest consternation throughout the South. The confusion which prevailed, at Richmond especially, but indeed all through the Peninsula, was extreme; and although the Confederate Government had for weeks past been informed of M'Clellan's plans, the news of his landing at Fortress Monroe fell upon them like a thunderbolt, and the most contradictory orders were thereupon issued. The dread that then prevailed at Richmond must be ascribed chiefly to the conduct of President Jefferson Davis and his wife, who, as soon as intelligence of the advance of the enemy had reached them, not only took every precaution to place their family in safety, but despatched to North Carolina all the valuable property at Richmond which had been placed at the President's disposal; such as plate, pictures, works of art, jewels, &c. Such a course of proceeding caused much unnecessary alarm to the good citizens of Richmond, and no little irritation. So complete was the removal of the President's effects, that it was said that Mrs. Jefferson Davis actually ordered all the curtains to be taken down, and the carpets taken up, that they might be packed up with the rest of the furniture of the presidential residence for removal to North Carolina. This was not considered a becoming example of the firmness and magnanimity expected from the elected head of the Confederacy for the purpose of encouraging the citizens. The effect was, as may be supposed, to bring about a general removal from the town. Great confusion also prevailed at the various public offices; the Government property was removed to North Carolina, and all the bank-note presses to Columbus. The Secretaries of War and the Navy, Randolph and Mallory, proceeded to

Norfolk and Portsmouth; not, as might have been supposed, to take measures for saving what could be preserved at those important naval stations, but to destroy everything. A humiliating day for the cause of the Confederacy was now at hand. General Huger was intrusted with the disgraceful task of destroying the valuable docks and Government stores at Portsmouth. Although there were no less than 30,000 excellent troops in and around Norfolk, the order he received was fully carried out, and thus the docks and building yards became a prey to the flames. General Huger proved by his zeal in performing this work that he was well suited for it. Property to the value of many millions, much of which might have been saved, was destroyed in the most reckless manner. Such precipitation, indeed, was displayed in the process of general demolition, that the fact of the *Merrimac's* lying in the bay was quite overlooked. As soon as the Secretary of War had ordered Huger to burn the dockyard at Portsmouth, the chief of the naval department lost no time in sending orders to Captain Tatnall, who commanded the *Merrimac*, to send all the smaller vessels to Richmond, and then to sail with the *Merrimac* toward New York, to destroy all vessels laden with corn he should meet with, and after having performed this service to blow up the *Merrimac*—his instructions appearing to imply also that he was to share the same fate!

It will be seen from this that the Confederate ministers knew how to issue orders on a grand scale; but it was a much easier task to burn trading vessels than to oppose a foe like M'Clellan. The Confederate troops conveyed all their guns to Suffolk and Petersburg. The flames from the burning dockyards at Portsmouth made General Wool, in command of the Federal troops at Fortress Monroe, aware of the retreat of our forces, and he did not hesitate to take immediate possession of that port so pusillanimously abandoned, which might have held out for months against an army of 30,000 men.

The example lately shown by the commanders and crews

of the Federal frigates *Cumberland* and *Congress*, in the gallant but hopeless defence of their ships when opposed to the *Merrimac*, ought surely to have inspired the Confederate authorities with sufficient resolution to make some attempt to retain their hold of such valuable naval stations as Portsmouth and Norfolk.

Thus Norfolk and Portsmouth were abandoned or demolished by the Confederate troops, while outside in the bay lay the victorious *Merrimac*, little aware of the sad fate that awaited her. Captain Tatnall, her commander, being quite at a loss how to obey the orders he had received, was anxiously pacing up and down the deck of his ship. To attempt to destroy the shipping at New York was practicable enough, but to blow himself up in the air to please Mr. Mallory was rather too much to be expected of him! He thought it advisable, under the circumstances, to hold a sort of council of war in his cabin, when he put the following questions to his officers:

1. "Are the officers of the *Merrimac* ready to take her to New York, and there to fulfil the orders that have been sent to me?"

Reply: "Yes."

2. "Is the *Merrimac* so constructed that she can stand the fire of all the batteries of Fortress Monroe?"

Reply: "No!"

After a long debate it was finally resolved to run up the James River to assist in its defence. Captain Tatnall accordingly set to work, and during the night everything that could be spared was thrown overboard; but as she rose some eight feet in the water in consequence, she could no longer be properly called an ironclad, for her hull below the water line was unprotected, and she was, therefore, no match for the *Monitor*. The hostile fleet shortly made its appearance in the bay, and Captain Tatnall, perceiving the hopeless position he was in, ordered the boats to be lowered, sent his crew of 340 men on shore, and ordered the *Merrimac* to be set on fire from stem to stern. The work of destruction was more speedily completed than could have been imagined. Dense volumes of smoke rushed out of the portholes. Gun after gun exploded, and in a short time that famous vessel, a striking instance of man's constructive power, so recently the conqueror of two formidable frigates, was wrapped in one mass of vivid flame. Ere long a fearful explosion announced that the flames had reached the powder magazine, and so terminated the career of the *Merrimac*.

CHAPTER XXXVII.

SIEGE OF YORKTOWN.

M'Clellan advances on Yorktown, and commences the siege—Abandonment of that city—Magruder's retreat—M'Clellan advances against Williamsburg—Attack and repulse of General Hooker—He is supported by Kearny and Heintzelman—Activity of Magruder—M'Clellan sends reinforcements—Hancock's successful attacks—Desperate exertions of General Magruder—M'Clellan comes up and drives back the Confederates—Consternation at Williamsburg—Magruder holds out—General Johnston takes the chief command—Retreat on Richmond—A cavalry combat—Retreat of the Confederates.

GENERAL M'CLELLAN, in spite of the bad condition of the roads, continued his advance on Yorktown, resolutely overcoming every obstacle on the way, and thereby inspiring his troops with full confidence in their commander. On approaching that place, however, he found that the Confederate General Magruder had, by using the utmost exertion, placed that city in an excellent state of defence, and that consequently it would be necessary for him to lay formal siege to it. The requisite siege works were then commenced under great difficulties, and the heavy guns brought up. It is only those well acquainted with the topography of the country who can fully estimate the difficulties which the Federal troops had to overcome.

After a month's hard labor the batteries were so near completion that the guns could be mounted. During all this time the Federal troops had to sustain a continual fire, and to bear the brunt of occasional *sorties* from the garrison. Magruder, moreover, had assembled a force at Yorktown strong enough to enable him, if necessary, to take the open field and give battle to the enemy. Whilst thus actively at work and animated by a feeling of confidence, Magruder received an order from the Secretary of War to evacuate Yorktown as quietly as possible—leaving all his guns in position—and to fall back upon the second line of defence at Williamsburg. This unexpected order gave, as may be supposed, the greatest annoyance to Magruder, who, most reluctantly, issued directions for the retirement of his troops. To conceal this movement from the enemy he ordered all the guns to open a heavy fire upon the besiegers, and at the same time sent two or three regiments to make a demonstration by way of a feint. As soon as it grew dark, Cullen's brigade commenced the retreat as noiselessly as possible, on the road toward Williamsburg. On the following morning two other brigades followed in the same manner. By the 3d of May the greater portion of the troops had left Yorktown, only three regiments of infantry remaining behind. The whole of the cavalry and two batteries of horse artillery occupied the farthest outworks. During the night all the men were called in, and, under the personal command of General Magruder, proceeded on their march toward Williamsburg, the cavalry being ordered to remain in the vicinity of Yorktown to watch the enemy's movements. Our retreat was effected with so much secresy, order, and silence, that even the outlying pickets of the enemy were not aware of it.

As soon as the news of the evacuation of Yorktown reached General M'Clellan's headquarters, he ordered the cavalry under General Stoneman to follow in pursuit; in pursuance of which a detachment under the orders of a daring young officer, whom we afterward learned was the Duc de Chartres, rapidly attacked our rear, doing us considerable mischief. After a few of these cavalry skirmishes, the Confederates finally succeeded in reaching the lines at Williamsburg.

From the quantity of military stores left behind us at Yorktown, the enemy's general must have been no little amazed that so strong a force should have abandoned a place so well supplied with war *matériel*, and which, moreover, was so well fortified as to be capable of sustaining a long siege.

Without los of time, M'Clellan resumed active operations, and advanced with his whole army. General Hooker led the van, and as soon as he reached our first intrenchments, he proceeded to attack Williamsburg. The attack was so determined that Colonel Miller, of the Confederate army, was unable to hold his position, and his troops began to waver. General Hooker continued the attack with renewed vigor, and a fierce fight ensued, in which the Confederates had the worst of; it but Colonel Cobb coming up to Miller's support, threw himself upon Hooker's division, and brought him to a standstill Anderson's brigade shortly afterward made its appearance, and fell upon Hooker's right flank; thus, this officer, although his troops behaved well, was compelled to give up his vantage ground and fall back. The numerical superiority of the Confederates told seriously against Hooker, who was compelled to retire with a loss of 1,700 men and some guns. The roads were in such a dreadful state, that the artillery and ammunition vans could scarcely move along. General Hooker, who is an able soldier, did his best to save his fine division, but Cobb was not inclined to let him off easily, and compelled him to retreat, fighting step by step.

Hooker's position became every minute more critical and desperate. His daring had imprudently led him into an engagement which he might have avoided, but he was too high spirited and too much excited now to acknowledge it. It was only when he found out the mistake he had made that he had not to deal with Cobb's brigade alone, but with a whole *corps d'armée*, that he sent to General M'Clellan for support.

The general acceded to his urgent request, and immediately ordered up Kearny's division to his aid. He could not have sent a better man. Kearny was of that chivalrous character so often to be met with in the French army. He had lost an arm in the Mexican war, and he afterward joined the French army as a volunteer aide-de-camp in the Italian campaign, greatly distinguishing himself at Solferino and Magenta. Kearny brought up his men at the double quick to support Hooker, although the execrable state of the roads somewhat retarded him, but he eventually reached the hard-pressed division. It was a fine sight to see Kearny lead on his men, eager for the fight as they were. He seemed to be ubiquitous; now leading on his centre, now ordering up a battery; in another moment charging at the head of his troops; his striking, manly form was prominent, wherever the fight was thickest, setting a noble example to his soldiers. The opposing troops were soon intermingled in a regular *mêlée*, and both sides fought desperately. Owing to the state of the ground, our cavalry was not serviceable, much to the regret of its officers; it was also very difficult for the artillery to manœuvre. The struggle, which had commenced at the verge of a wood, was gradually drawn into the forest itself, and here, under the crackling branches of venerable trees, amidst the roar of the artillery, many desperate hand-to-hand encounters took place, such as have seldom been witnessed in other wars. There was something so wild and terrible in the aspect of this strife, that those who survived that day's fight look back upon it with a shudder.

General Magruder, meanwhile, continued to order up fresh troops, and in a few hours he had so mauled Hooker's division, that it was reduced to little more than a fragment; Heintzelman and Kearny also suffered heavy losses. The goddess of victory already held the balance in our favor, when General M'Clellan pushed forward some fresh brigades along a dam, with a view of taking possession of the works on our left flank, hoping thereby to redeem the fortunes of the day. General Magruder, who had betimes discovered the enemy's intention, forthwith brought up the reserve, which consisted of General Pickett's body guard, in support of the works in question. In a twinkling they galloped across the plain which separated them from the works, and reached them just as the Federal troops, under General Hancock, were advancing to storm the post. General Pickett, joined by a regiment stationed there, now furiously attacked the Federals, and a most desperate struggle ensued. "Bull Run! Bull Run!" shouted our men, as a sort of battle cry. The Federals replied by pouring a fearful volley into our ranks. The carnage was terrific, compelling our men to fall back, when General Hancock followed in close pursuit. General Magruder then ordered up the 2d and 9th cavalry regiments to charge the enemy. But this was of no avail; the ground had been so soaked with rain that the horses sank up to their knees. Suddenly a shout of a thousand voices broke upon the ear like the rushing of a mighty wind from the wood. What did this portend? There was little time left for us to speculate. Charge after charge was made upon our men, and the news then spread that General M'Clellan, with the main body of his army, had arrived on the field of battle. This explained the loud cheers from the wood. Our men could no longer stand their ground. M'Clellan, in person, led on his troops into the midst of the fire. Magruder, now finding that the battle was lost, ordered a retreat to be sounded, and directed Hill's division, which had just come up, to cover the movement. All the wounded, and a great portion of the baggage, were left in the enemy's hands. The shades of night put an end to the fight; a heavy rain, too, began to fall, and these circumstances fortunately prevented the enemy from completely overwhelming us. Tired and worn out, our troops returned to Williamsburg, where the excitement had become intense.

It was now resolved to abandon Williamsburg, and to fall back on Richmond, much against the will of General Magruder, who had seen the fortifications of the town growing gradually under his own inspection, and he had great confidence in their strength. But the dread of the energetic M'Clellan prevailed at this juncture.

General Johnston having now arrived, he was intrusted by the Confederate Government with the chief command of the army. He at once ordered the retreat to commence, although Magruder insisted that he could still hold Williamsburg against the enemy. But the Federal General Keyes had already taken up a position between Williamsburg and Richmond, a manœuvre which allowed us no time to hesitate, as he not only menaced the retreating troops from Williamsburg, but threatened the safety of Richmond itself. General Magruder consequently made the necessary dispositions to rejoin the main body of the army at Richmond. Hill's division was ordered to hold Williamsburg until the retreating army had at least twelve miles' start, and, with the cavalry and Cobb's legion, to cover the retreat. When the sun rose blood red on the following morning the streets of Williamsburg were deserted by the troops, with the exception of a few patrols of cavalry with drawn swords and revolvers in hand. Some anxious-looking citizens or wounded soldiers might occasionally be seen, but every house and shop was closed. Our cavalry, charged with the duty of covering the retreat, drew up in excellent order, in double line, to await the enemy; and in a few moments pistol shots announced the approach of the foe. Small bodies of Federal cavalry dashed into the town, but on reaching the outskirts they found our troopers drawn up, ready for action, and immediately galloped back. In a short time the advancing tramp of a large body of horse became distinctly audible. We drew our swords, looked to our revolvers, and prepared for the expected fight. The very horses seemed to be aware of what was coming, and pawed and neighed and chafed continually. A squadron of lancers first made its appearance, and the remainder of the enemy's cavalry soon followed. The word of command was now issued on both sides, and the hostile squadrons met in deadly combat. For a long time victory remained undecided. The clashing of swords and the report of revolvers, intermixed with words of command, was all that was heard. Our men now gained a decided advantage, when a column of the enemy's infantry darted out of the wood in order to cut off our retreat. General Hill ordered a cavalry regiment of Cobb's legion to charge them and drive them back into the woods. The commander of the regiment, Young, carried out this order in admirable style, and by a brilliant charge drove back the infantry into the thicket. He had scarcely achieved this, when another column of the enemy's infantry made its appearance on the other side, and poured a volley of bullets into our victorious ranks. Surrounded on all sides, General Hill now ordered a retreat. The trumpets sounded, and our men, turning round, cut their way back through the enemy, with some further loss.

General M'Clellan, satisfied with the day's results, ordered no pursuit to be made, as his troops stood in need of rest, and, besides, the poor, wounded fellows on both sides, who lay in numbers on the roadside, had to be attended to. His humane conduct on this occasion not only earned for him the respect of his own troops, but the esteem of our officers, which they did not hesitate loudly to express. M'Clellan had achieved a great success. He had driven our troops out of two of their strongest fortified positions, and by the sanguinary battle at Williamsburg had considerably shaken the confidence of our men.

CHAPTER XXXVIII.

BATTLE OF FAIR OAKS.

Disorganized state of the Confederate forces—The army reinforced by General Lee—Selfish conduct attributed to Government officials and others—Mutual recriminations—Movements of the Federals against Richmond—Pestilence spreads amongst the Confederate troops—General Johnston determines to attack the Federal army—Battle of Fair Oaks described—Defeat of the Confederate forces.

On our troops reaching Richmond after their retreat, they were there joined by reinforcements organized for the purpose by General Lee, which needful aid inspired them with renewed hope and courage. The poor fellows were, however, so worn out by forced marches and by the constant pursuit of the enemy, as well as from inefficient arrangements for their comfort, that they looked more like spectres than living men. The roads, the means of transport—in short, everything they had to depend on in such an emergency, were in such a wretched condition that even the stoutest hearts despaired of a happy termination to the toilsome sufferings and privations brought about by this unfortunate war.

It was surely enough to dispirit them at such a moment to have good ground for believing that some of the chief men at the helm were more intent on the attainment of their own ambitious ends than on attending to the sufferings and pressing wants of the army. Nor were the representatives of the people free from a similar imputation; many amongst these legislators were, at all events, not above huckstering about the price of their not very irksome labor. I do not intend, however, that all should be included in this censure: there were, undoubtedly, to be found in that body men of sound patriotic views—men who were eager to do their best to promote the welfare of the common cause. But these certainly constituted a minority, and their influence was altogether insufficient to check the growing tendency to self-aggrandizement at the seat of government.

On the arrival of our disorganized and dispirited army at Richmond, General Lee, who had made himself well acquainted with its condition, immediately set about remedying the evils resulting from its recent defeat. I was directed to occupy, with my regiment, the farthest outpost, and there to keep a good lookout upon the advancing enemy, with strict orders to remain on the defensive, and carefully to avoid all unnecessary collision with our foe. I had scarcely returned from visiting my outlying pickets, when a flag of truce from the Federal forces was announced. I rode down the road, and met a young officer who had come, on the part of General M'Clellan, to request that we would send medical men to look after our numerous wounded, as his own medical staff was insufficient to undertake the duty. This humane act proves incontestably the commiseration felt by M'Clellan for the wounded of his enemy, and prompted me to despatch forthwith one of my officers to General Johnston's headquarters, with my urgent recommendation that General M'Clellan's suggestions should be acted upon, and that a sufficient number of surgeons should be promptly ordered to proceed to Williamsburg on this duty. The humanity displayed by the general commanding the enemy's forces created a feeling of warm admiration among our troops, great numbers of whom had near relatives among the wounded we had been compelled to leave behind in the dense woods and sickly swamps, and who were out of the reach of any succor from us.

In noticing this conduct of General M'Clellan I cannot refrain from remarking that both our officials and our newspapers had all along been holding forth about the cruelty with which the enemy treated the prisoners in their hands : charges entitled, most likely, to about as much credit as those attributing to some of our officers the atrocity of throwing torpedoes into the wells when we evacuated the towns.

It has seemed strange to some amongst the numerous enemies of M'Clellan in the United States, that I and others serving with the Confederate army should entertain so great a respect for him, and be so candid as to freely express it. That esteem, as far as I am concerned, rests on the knowledge I have had many opportunities of acquiring of his straightforward, soldierly conduct, and especially of his humane endeavors to protect the enemy's property, and his care for the welfare of the wounded and other prisoners who fell into his hands.

To return, however, to my narrative. A number of medical officers were, in pursuance of my recommendation, sent off to Williamsburg, under an escort of the enemy's troops.

M'Clellan, having about this time proceeded with his forces up the York River, in order to join General Keyes' troops, that had disembarked at West Point, with the object of forming plans and commencing the necessary operations for the siege of Richmond, we had ample time to reorganize our scattered forces, and to bring up fresh troops from other Southern States. The States of North and South Carolina were cleared of almost all their forces, for now all eyes were directed to Richmond, at which place it was believed the drama would be played out.

The enemy, however, as well as ourselves needed rest, for his forces had greatly suffered from bad weather and its concomitant sickness. Meanwhile, M'Clellan continued his works for the siege of Richmond, taking his preliminary measures with great circumspection. North and South were now fair.

ly face to face, watching each other's movements—the one aggressively, the other defensively. By degrees the warm weather made its appearance, and the fields and roads were in so favorable a state as to enable large bodies of troops to manœuvre again. The end of May came on, and the two armies still occupied their respective positions on the James River, the monotony of general inaction being relieved only by occasional outpost skirmishes. In the mean while however, disease spread among our forces to a most alarming extent: virulent, obstinate fevers, caused by the miasma of the neighboring swamps, prevailed to a great extent, and the ravages that ensued became so great as to cause much anxiety to General Johnston. The deaths, indeed, were so numerous, that sufficient persons could not be procured at Richmond to undertake the task of burying the bodies, which lay exposed in the churchyards by hundreds, spreading pestilence around. The medical faculty anticipated fearful consequences from this state of things, and General Johnston contemplated gloomily the inroads disease was hourly making in his brave army, which almost seemed as if it were doomed to sink altogether into an inglorious grave. In this dire emergency he resolved at all costs to attack his intrenched opponents. The various *corps d'armée* chosen for this purpose were therefore promptly drawn together, and on the afternoon of the 31st of May, during a violent storm, General Johnston attacked the enemy's troops, then occupying both sides of the Chickahominy. General Hill commenced a furious attack on the enemy's left wing, which being in a well intrenched position, was enabled to make a good defence, and all Hill's efforts to storm the position were in vain. Anderson, with his division and two batteries, rushed to his support, and a most desperate struggle ensued, the enemy defending his position with great resolution; and the ground was ere long covered with the dead and dying. Anderson so placed his batteries as to establish a cross fire, and under the protection of these guns again led his men to the assault. A determined fight now commenced on the parapets of the enemy's works, whilst the fire from the two batteries frustrated any attempt on his part to bring up reinforcements. The federal troops defended themselves obstinately, disputing every foot of ground with their assailants, and as yet the Confederates had no advantage. The commander of the Federal troops strenuously urged his men to hold their ground, and they responded to his appeal by standing by their guns till numbers of them were cut to pieces. At this moment their leader was struck down by a bullet, and at this sight their stubborn resistance began to falter, and they gradually fell back. Thus the Confederate troops by degrees got a firm footing on the obstinately contested position. Another impetuous rush was made by the Confederates, and the enemy was driven headlong from his works and sought safety in flight. Johnston now ordered our cavalry to take up the pursuit, and General Wickman, at the head of his squadron, swept the plain —his eager troopers, like a flock of ravenous hawks, dealing death and destruction to all they encountered.

An indescribable panic seized the enemy, and they gave way along their whole line. Generals Keyes and Naglee in vain tried to rally the fugitives. It seemed as if no human power could stop them in their disorderly flight.

At this moment, however, General Heintzelman rapidly brought up his division to stem the pursuit of the Confederate troops, and planted himself like a rock between the pursued and their pursuers. His men, Irish and Germans, fought and died like heroes in this work of salvation. All Hill's and Anderson's attempts to repulse them were futile; the Germans and Irish kept their ground, and succeeded in covering the flight of their vanquished comrades. They steadily opposed every fierce onset of our elated troops, and stood like a wall between them and their own defeated forces, in order that some of the fugitives might be enabled to reform their ranks, and thus in their turn try to assist those who had come to their rescue. In this way a line of battle was once more formed and the struggle was again maintained with desperation. General Anderson, seeing that it was hopeless to make an impression on those firm columns, now ordered forward Pickett's brigade to the attack, so as to cut off the enemy's retreat. Before this order could be executed, however, the troops were met by the enemy's brigade commanded by General Sumner, who fell on them with the bayonet, whilst a battery which Sumner had ordered up played upon them at the same time, causing great havoc. Pickett's brigade now turned and hastily retired: this necessarily led to the retreat of the divisions of Anderson and Hill. Johnston vainly put himself at the head of his best troops in order to reopen the action; all his efforts were useless: the victorious enemy pressed on with loud cheers. The generals halted to make a last effort; but it was of no avail. Sumner rushed on our troops, who had lost all self-possession, and drove them back to Fair Oaks, until night put an end to the struggle.

CHAPTER XXXIX.

BATTLE OF SEVEN PINES.

Efforts of General Johnston and others to reorganize our troops—Touching interview between the General and his son, Colonel Johnston—Plans for the coming battle—My cavalry regiment attached to Longstreet's division—State of the camp at night—Preparations for action—Approach of the enemy's columns—Commencement of the battle—Heavy cannonade—Our successful cavalry encounter—Desperate contest at the centre—General Johnston's repeated attacks—Resolute stand of the enemy, and heroism of the German troops—General Lee's attack eventually repulsed—General Johnston makes a final effort at the head of his troops, and is grievously wounded—The Confederates gain the victory—Fearful losses caused by the battle of Seven Pines—Sufferings of the wounded.

The Confederate troops were, as may be expected after the loss of so obstinate a battle, and the untoward circumstances that invariably accompany a hasty retreat, thoroughly exhausted—many among them falling to the ground in utter helplessness; they were gradually brought in and placed in the houses nearest the field of battle.

Generals Johnston, Lee, and Longstreet, however, exerted themselves to the utmost to arouse their sinking spirits, and promptly ordered that all necessary measures should be taken to procure the means of transport for those who were seriously wounded. Besides which, they had to determine what positions should be occupied by our troops on the ensuing day—another day of battle. Tired and hungry, many of our poor fellows strolled about wearily and moodily. No lively song or passing jest—no joyous laugh denoted that they felt confident of success in the anticipated battle of the morrow. They obeyed the orders of their officers sullenly, and almost reluctantly. But a change was at hand. Fresh troops from Richmond now came up; five regiments from South Carolina and Alabama; whilst the batteries of the Washington artillery rattled heavily past under their gallant commander. Walton next followed, enveloped in clouds of dust; regiments of cavalry from North Carolina, Tennessee, and Kentucky, their bright swords glistening as they reflect the light of the watchfires that lie on the road. The arrival of comrades to share in the perils their fellow soldiers have to encounter has always a happy effect upon the spirits of any troops. The newcomers were accordingly greeted with joyous shouts of welcome, and every scrap of provisions that had not been consumed was gladly produced and shared with the newly arrived forces. The events of the recent battle were eagerly listened to by them, related as they were by the men who had taken part in this obstinate and protracted conflict. Hopes of better luck on the morrow were now loudly expressed, and promises of mutual support eagerly went round. The camp became quite animated—the men's courage was renovated; defeat was no longer deemed possible, and even fatigue seemed to be for the moment forgotten. More serious business was meantime in preparation at the headquarters of the general-in-chief. Seated near a campfire, General Johnston was thoughtfully occupied in studying a map that lay before him, a knot of officers standing in a group close by their chief. The critical state of affairs was fully understood by all present, and every eye was anxiously turned upon our beloved commander. Presently the general asked for his son, Colonel Johnston, who was one of the aide-de-camps of President Jefferson Davis. As soon as the colonel seated himself by his father's side, the latter tore a leaf of paper out of his pocketbook, and, after writing on it a few lines, he handed it to his son, with the words: "Give that to your mother." He also wrote a few words upon another leaf; but this he folded and sealed, and then handing it to his son, said, "Deliver this to President Davis. You can now go," he added, bidding him adieu, cordially, "and let me see you to-morrow." When just about to mount his horse the colonel hastened back to say a few more parting words to his father, who had now risen to watch his departure. The general folded his son in his arms with ill-concealed emotion, and then repeated in a cheering tone his directions that he would be sure to come to see him on the morrow. "Yes, yes, father," replied Colonel Johnston, in a voice hoarse with emotion, as he tore himself away. He then mounted his horse, and in a few moments was lost sight of in the darkness of the night. For some time after his son's departure the old general stood with outstretched arms, as motionless as a statue, staring fixedly at vacancy. Not a word had been uttered by the generals and other officers present at this affecting interview. At length their chief turned round, abruptly exclaiming, "Now, gentlemen, to business." The scene, simple as it may seem in description, was in reality most impressive. Could the general have had some kind of foreboding of what was to befall him on the following day?

We now all proceeded to the tent of the commander-in-chief, where maps and plans were strewed on large tables. In a few distinct and emphatic words, Johnston gave his instructions to each general in turn, urging one and all, in manly words, to uphold the honor of the posts respectively assigned to them. He particularly urged that those regiments which had suffered so severely from the late sanguinary battle should be looked after and well cared for, and that they should be spared as much as possible. "To you, General Holmes," said he, addressing that officer, "I intrust the reserve. As regards the necessity for employing it, that I leave to your own judgment, well knowing you will do your duty as a brave and trusty officer of the Confederate army. And now, good night, gentlemen; we all stand in need of rest to prepare ourselves for the heavy work in store for us to-morrow."

Generals and staff officers now separated—gliding off silently, like so many shadows of the night, to their respective quarters.

All was now still as death in the camp, the silence being broken only by the occasional challenge of a sentry, or by the stray report of a musket. Later in the night, I was directed to join General Longstreet with my regiment, and to place myself under his orders. We were, on our part, therefore, obliged to forego the hoped-for rest, and to make our way to the extreme right wing, where Anderson's troops were posted. We reached the appointed place about midnight, when we found the whole division already on the move. All needless baggage was sent off to Richmond, whilst the soldiers struck their tents and put out their watchfires. Anderson explained that he had made most careful preparations for executing the task allotted to him for the following day.

As soon as I had reached the division to which I was now attached, I ordered my men to feed their horses, and to examine their arms and accoutrements, that they might be in proper order for immediate service. We then encamped upon the damp ground, all of us impatiently awaiting the dawn of day. It was a beautiful night; a mild but refreshing breeze blew over the encampment, and no one could have supposed that on so small a patch of ground lay encamped two hostile armies, numbering together 100,000 men, mutually animated by a feeling of mortal hatred, and who only awaited the first golden streaks of the rising sun to begin the hideous work of slaying each other. Before all the preparations were quite completed the word of command was given to advance, and the infantry began to move in dense masses over the fields, while my troopers sprang into their saddles. By this time noisy sounds, in which was mingled the hum of many human voices, succeeded the stillness of the night. Aide-de-camps, orderlies, officers of every description, rode along the front of the troops. Suddenly a large body of horsemen was seen advancing. It was General Johnston and his staff, who had come to inspect the different columns already drawn up in position. In a few pithy words the General admonished the officers to do their duty.

For a few moments all was quiet, but this short lull was soon disturbed by a musketry fire, which increased in intensity every minute. The prologue of the battle had commenced. An officer from the outposts came galloping up with the news that the enemy was already advancing in dense columns, and that our pickets were obliged to fall back before the heavy fire to which they were exposed. Cole's legion was immediately sent up in support of our foremost troops. The roar of cannon now became audible in the centre and on our left flank, denoting that the battle had commenced in good earnest, whereupon the batteries on both sides took up the fire with spirit. In a few minutes the earth seemed to shake, while the air vibrated sensibly from the incessant firing of great guns. Our foot soldiers advanced at the quick step; all thoughts not connected with the deadly work in hand had vanished from the minds of the men—they were intent solely on slaughter and destruction, so eager were they in their desperate resolve of taking this day a bloody revenge for their late defeat. The cavalry, in compact array, impatiently chafed for the arrival of the order for them to take part in the battle. The first wounded men were now brought to the rear: poor fellows, many of them had already the shadow of death marked upon their countenances, and as they were carried past they called upon us to avenge them. My men were getting frantically impatient, uttering imprecations between their long moustaches and beards at being so long kept idle. At last the wished-for order came: "Cavalry, prepare to charge." General Holmes then led our two cavalry regiments somewhat to the left, to an open field, where we drew up in readiness for action. On our right, one of our batteries was keeping up so well sustained a fire that the dense clouds of smoke hanging around concealed everything from our view. We had scarcely got into order and prepared for the onset when the trumpet blasts of the enemy's cavalry reached our ears, and in a few minutes, from behind a small hillock, the enemy's dragoons and hussars came into view. "Charge!" and in a few moments after this inspiring word was uttered we were upon the enemy, using our swords, revolvers, and lances with deadly effect; and in this fierce encounter many a brave fellow soon bit the dust. We drove back the enemy's cavalry, but whilst in pursuit, a heavy fire from a body of the enemy's infantry assailed our flank, compelling us to wheel round and fall back to our former position with a few captured horses as trophies. Meantime the battle was raging with fury in the centre. General Johnston, having ascertained that owing to the preceding heavy rains the bridges over the Chicahominy in the enemy's rear had been swept away, resolved forthwith to turn this circumstance to good account. Gathering together all the troops that could be spared, he made repeated attacks upon the enemy's centre. The hasty manner, however, in which these attacks were made, was unfavorable to their success, and General Lee repeatedly urged him, but in vain, to be more sparing with his reserve. Our foes were, in fact, in a very critical position, having behind them a stream so swollen by the rains as to bar their only means of communication with their forces on the opposite bank; while in their front they were exposed to the vehement attacks of an exasperated foe, fighting almost under the walls of their capital—before the gates of the very sanctuary of the Confederacy.

Column after column was pushed forward by General Johnston into the thickest of the fight, and the return of each of the shattered remnants proved the stubborn resistance of the foe. Some German regiments from Michigan performed prodigies of valor on this occasion. Most of their officers were killed, and their ranks were fearfully cut up; but nothing could prevail against the stern resolution of their defence. Death stared them in the face wherever they looked, but their courage never flagged. It was a sad episode in this bloody fight, when these brave German soldiers from the far West were seen to fall man after man. Such devotion proves clearly that they cherished the land of their adoption with cordial affection. General Johnston still persevered in his attacks with unabated vigor, ordering up regiment after regiment, with a stern resolve to succeed, by reiterated blows, in eventually beating the enemy. General Lee at length brought up some fresh brigades, with the whole of the reserve, and with these troops dashed forward at a rush, courteously saluting General Johnston with his sword as he passed, whilst the troops gave the commander-in-chief a cheer; but it was not one of those hearty, confident cheers that imply a certainty of success; it was rather the solemn war-cry of men in a state of desperation, and which baffles description. The havoc now dealt amongst our men was fearful to contemplate. They kept falling incessantly on every side, their places being promptly supplied by their comrades. General Johnston sat on his horse all through this scene of carnage, perfectly calm and collected, issuing his orders to his aide-de-camps, who flew right and left to see them executed. The battle had now lasted for many hours, and yet the scales of victory still hung on the balance.

General Lee had now to fall back with shattered troops, the blood streaming from many of his officers, and his surviving men powerless from sheer fatigue. At this juncture General Johnston, putting spurs to his noble charger, galloped up with his staff to where Longstreet, Magruder, and Hill had collected their men in something like order. In a hoarse voice he ordered them to form in a compact mass, and then, addressing a few emphatic words to the troops, said he would lead them in person against the enemy. In vain did Longstreet and the other generals endeavor to dissuade him from such a step; they would themselves, said they, with musket in hand, lead the men on if he wished it, but they urged that he ought not to expose himself to such a risk. "What a loss to Richmond it would be—what a loss to the cause of the Confederacy, if he were to fall!"

To this remonstrance Johnston replied, he was quite aware that every man, down to the smallest drummer boy, had this day done his duty, and that he was resolved also to perform his. Calmly, but firmly, he ordered the officers to their various posts, and then in person took the active command of the attacking columns. It soon spread through the ranks that General Johnston was going to lead the troops in person, and a cheer resounded along the lines. The three divisions of Longstreet, Hill, and Magruder advanced in fine order, with flags flying, and drums beating, and as they pressed forward, even the wounded gave them a cheer. It was clear that these men were determined to conquer or to die with their beloved commander. Fearlessly the enemy awaited the shock. In a few moments a renewed conflict took place, and the battle raged with redoubled fury on the same ground that had already witnessed such desperate fighting—such fearful carnage. A few brigades of the enemy came up in support of their comrades, who appeared unable to withstand Johnston's furious attack; the battle had now reached its height. In the midst of his men, who were falling around him on all sides, Johnston seemed bullet proof. But suddenly he placed his hand to his side; he turned deadly pale, and blood was seen to flow down his clothes; he was grievously wounded, and presently fell from his horse. In a moment his officers were around him, and endeavored to carry him from the field. The report that Johnston had been killed spreading through the ranks, our men, like so many incarnate fiends, fell upon the enemy, who had, during this hard-fought day, so re solutely confronted them. So extraordinary, however, was the effect of the cry now raised on all sides, of "Johnston is killed," that the enemy's troops could no longer withstand the terrific onslaught of our maddened men. Their ranks wavered, and they precipitately fled from the bloody field.

The victory of Seven Pines was dearly bought. Our commander, General Johnston, was not mortally wounded, but the injury he received was most serious. The losses inflicted on both armies by this conflict were indeed fearful in extent. Killed and wounded were lying by thousands on the battle field, and the cries of the latter for help were heart-rending in the extreme. Our men, however, were so excited by the contest, that they seemed bereft of the feelings of humanity, and were solely intent upon recruiting their exhausted frames with food and rest. General Lee, on whom the command devolved after Johnston's fall, exerted himself to the utmost to provide for the wounded, and took measures to have them gradually conveyed either to Richmond or to the houses that lay near to the field of battle.

CHAPTER XL.

INVESTMENT OF RICHMOND.

State of the hostile armies after the late battle—M'Clellan not properly supported by his Government—Official blindness—Disposition of the Federal forces—Alarm at Richmond—General Lee's great activity—The Federal army appears before Richmond—Destitution in the city—Effective defensive measures—Comparative inactivity of the Federal generals—The Confederates assume the offensive—Stuart's dashing raid—Desperate cavalry fight—Exciting single combat—Success of Stuart's raid—M'Clellan remains on the defensive—General Lee prepares for the attack.

THE most important duty that obviously lay before General Lee, on assuming the supreme command of the Confederate forces, was to reëstablish order and discipline among the troops, and bring them back to their former state, with a view to the complete reorganization of the army.

The day succeeding the battle of Seven Pines the beaten and mortified Federal troops took up their new positions, and the pickets and patrols, who were generally on the alert, now remained quietly at their posts, without attempting to disturb us by desultory firing. Rest was indeed indispensable to both armies after their late extraordinary exertions. General M'Clellan's army had greatly suffered, but perhaps not so much as ours. His officers were enabled, by their coolness and skilful conduct, to spare the lives of their men, whilst on our part great losses were often occasioned by the blind adoption of ill-considered measures.

The commanders of both armies turned their first attention to the wounded, and then endeavored to fill up the fearful gaps in their ranks by means of reinforcements. General M'Clellan was, however, only enabled to obtain scanty aid of this kind, as his Government regarded with no little jealousy the prospect of the successful career of this young general. They could not be blind to the fact that in spite of the difficulties of the country through which he had made his way, he had, by his bold flank marches and successful actions, succeeded in pushing his way to the walls of Richmond. That M'Clellan had instilled a spirit of confidence into his army, was a fact patent to the world. But his Government, instead of sending all their disposable troops to the Peninsula, in order to gain possession of Richmond by a decisive blow, split up their forces, leaving General M'Dowell inactive at Fredericksburg, General Burnside at Newbern, and from 20,000 to 25,000 men before Charleston.

But one object should have occupied the minds of the Union Government: the capture of Richmond. The moment was opportune. New Orleans, the richest and most important centre of commerce of the South, had fallen into the hands of General Butler, after a combined attack by the Federal fleet and land forces. Memphis, the second most important town on the Mississippi, was in the hands of the Union; the dreaded *Merrimac* had ceased to exist. The York and James rivers, with their deep channels, were open to the Federal ships, and the efficient army under M'Clellan was so near Richmond as to be within hail of the inhabitants of that city. All amongst them who could do so were leaving the place. It only required the employment of powerful means to destroy the fortifications that protected the town. All political animosity should have ceased at this juncture, and but one idea should have prevailed at Washington, that of using every possible exertion to avert the impending disasters. Every man, whatever his party, whether Democrat or Republican, should have thrown aside factious feeling, and united with his fellow citizens in upholding the cause of his country. Lincoln no doubt meant well, and endeavored to do his duty thoroughly; but he was, unfortunately, surrounded by a party, who, governed by selfish motives, did not scruple to bring their once happy, but now afflicted country to the very verge of ruin. M'Clellan was made to suffer from this factious conduct, which not only grieved him sensibly as a patriot, but greatly obstructed his operations as a military commander, and in fact threatened to endanger the eventual safety of his army.

The nearer the Federal forces approached Richmond the greater became the tumult and disorder there. The conduct of the Confederate Government on this occasion, instead of allaying, served to increase the confusion; for instead of making a decisive effort with the forces then at Richmond, they ordered all the public officials to pack up their effects and hand them over to the charge of the ordnance department, and directed the magazines to be cleared and their contents carried away farther South. President Davis himself showed the white feather, for he hurried off with his wife and family to North Carolina, and, as may be supposed, this did not serve to allay the alarm of the people. In short, dismay and confusion reached their highest pitch. General Winder's secret police lost all power of acting. The civic authorities of Richmond were anxious to do something, but were too bewildered to grapple with the mischief. A small number of desperate fellows from Baltimore took advantage of these circumstances, and, at a public meeting which they convened, actually passed a resolution for burning down Richmond, the moment the enemy should attack the town. The sick and wounded were conveyed into the interior; many public buildings, as well as private houses, were made ready to be set fire to, and the distracted city was apparently on the eve of a great catastrophe.

General Lee actively exerted himself in placing the fortifications in better order, and in constructing new works at various points. Nor was this active energy on his part superfluous; for the defences of Fort James were not far advanced when the Federal ships appeared within six miles of them. It was indeed only when the enemy was close upon us, that many measures were adopted which ought to have been taken weeks before. General Lee was busy in all ways night and day, exerting himself on behalf of his many sick and wounded, and was intent not only on increasing the numerical strength of the army, but did his best to inspire it with fresh ardor.

Meanwhile, General M'Clellan advanced slowly and cautiously, but with determination, and one morning his troops were descried encamped in a crescent-like order around Richmond. M'Clellan and the chief of his staff, General Marcy, commenced their operations by encircling Richmond with a belt of intrenchments, which were calculated not only to protect their men, but were made with a view of effectually investing the place. The hostile armies worked away steadily at their respective fortifications within gunshot of each other, and the advanced sentries were so near as to be able to converse together. They indeed not unfrequently exchanged such gifts as tobacco and brandy on the sly, keeping up quite a friendly intercourse.

In the mean time great distress prevailed in Richmond. The commonest necessaries of life rose to prices which but few could afford to pay, and there was such a scarcity of medicines that thousands of poor fellows went to their graves for the want of them. The inhabitants of Richmond will never forget that sad epoch. The soldiers themselves were in want of the commonest articles of food. These horrors did not, however, damp General Lee's energy. After having put Richmond in a respectable state of defence he ordered Generals "Stonewall" Jackson, Ewell, and Stuart from the Shenandoah Valley to Richmond, and gave orders to Generals

Beauregard and Smith to send up all the troops they could possibly spare. The hospitals were all cleared, and arrangements made for the reception of 10,000 wounded. Artillery and ammunition wagons rattled through the streets of Richmond, while orderlies and aide-de-camps might be seen galloping about in all directions; troops, too, were hourly arriving. They came in a sorry plight, it is true; but ragged and emaciated as they were, they nevertheless marched in with their bands playing and colors flying, and with every appearance of being determined to make a stout fight for their independence.

All these occurrences could not have been unknown to Generals M'Dowell, Fremont, and Banks. Information must have reached them, not only through their own spies, but from deserters, that General Lee was concentrating all his forces round Richmond, for the purpose of striking a determined blow at M'Clellan's army. These officers ought, therefore, to have used all their influence with their Government to be allowed to join M'Clellan, so that the fall of Richmond might be insured. But nothing was done. M'Clellan was allowed to expend his energies unaided before the gates of the beleaguered city, and so the Confederates were allowed to concentrate their troops at Richmond without opposition.

When our preparations were at last so far completed that we were enabled to take the offensive, General Lee ordered Colonel Stuart, with two regiments of cavalry and a 12-pounder battery of horse artillery, to make a general reconnoissance of the enemy's lines, but to keep a special lookout upon General M'Dowell's movements, as it was known that his outposts were within twenty miles of Richmond. For this purpose, the 9th and 15th regiments of cavalry were selected—tried soldiers, who had served in every part of the country; and, under the command of the gallant Colonel Stuart, they proceeded along the turnpike road, in the direction of Hanover Court House. The advanced guard made itself acquainted with the ground through the medium of the farmers in the neighborhood. The reserve was intrusted to the charge of Baron Barke, a Prussian officer who had recently joined the Confederate army, and was acting as aide-de-camp. The cavalry rode quietly along the enemy's road. It was beautiful summer weather, mild and clear, and in every way suited to a cavalry expedition. The main body was enabled to ride on in perfect security, so perfect was the confidence felt in the circumspection of Captain Norton, the officer commanding the vanguard. So we lit our short pipes, and sang snatches of songs as we moved along; many a nigger looking over the fences, and wondering where we were going. Every half hour a report was regularly sent in by Captain Norton, who had managed matters so well, that the farmers, apprized of our raid, kept us informed of all the enemy's movements, either by preconcerted signals, by word of mouth, or in writing. It was truly a bold undertaking to make this raid between M'Clellan and M'Dowell, for if the latter had only taken a little precaution, so daring a feat could have been checked at once. But General M'Dowell seemed to have been mentally blind just then. It is true that he had sent out patrols and skirmishers, within twenty miles of Richmond, but this had been so carelessly managed, that the precaution was wholly futile. So long as any kind of information was forwarded to headquarters, it was deemed sufficient, and all was believed to be right.

"Our outposts are actually within twenty miles of Richmond!" were words that had a magical effect on those who heard them; in truth, the word *Richmond* had a wonderful effect upon the Federal troops, and General M'Dowell always made it a point of dating his despatches to Washington, from the nearest possible point to the former city. Instead of devoting all his energy to the prosecution of measures that would serve to give effectual aid to M'Clellan, and especially to protect his right wing, he rather avoided coming at all in contact with the troops of that general. He seemed quite satisfied that a handful of his troops should be really in front of Richmond. It was natural that M'Clellan, aware of M'Dowell's presence near Hanover Court House, should place sufficient confidence in his skill as a general, as to trust to him to cover his right wing; for owing to the immense extent of his own lines, his chief attention was directed to his centre, that he might be able to repulse any attack upon that point. We believed that our cavalry expedition had but very little to fear from M'Dowell, and our surmise in this respect proved to be correct. Scarcely had our foremost troopers come within sight of M'Dowell's videttes, when the latter hastily fell back upon Fredericksburg. As soon as we became aware of this somewhat overcaution of the enemy, great exultation was felt by our men, who now became convinced of the successful issue of our expedition. Cheerily did we push forward along the fine road to Hanover Court House, when suddenly one of our foremost troopers came galloping back at full speed, bringing the news from Captain Norton, that the advanced outposts of General M'Clellan's right wing were visible.

Colonel Stuart despatched orders to Captain Norton to halt, and sent six squadrons in the direction where he presumed the enemy's cavalry to be posted in order to attack them. He then directed Captain Norton to make a flank movement, and, if he should find the enemy had been defeated, to follow in pursuit. For the first time, a squadron of our newly formed lancers was to take part in this attack. Although the men had only just gone through a few weeks' exercise with the lance, it was judged desirable to see what kind of service they would render, in order to determine whether it would be advisable to increase the number of that arm. The squadrons were ordered to proceed at a slow trot, on each side of the road, the leading squadron being directed, as soon as they came upon the enemy's outposts, to fall upon them rapidly, and drive them back in disorder. We had already ridden some distance when we saw our leading squadron dash forward at full speed, amidst a fire of musketry and revolvers. The enemy's bullets whistled around us also, but fortunately did us no harm. Scarcely, however, had we reached the verge of the wood when we saw our troopers hurriedly galloping back, hotly pursued by the 5th regiment of the United States dragoons. There was thus no time to be lost now, and with a ringing cheer we dashed forward to support our comrades. On perceiving our advance the enemy wheeled round and galloped off. We had ridden about two thousand yards when we suddenly came upon the encampment of another squadron of the enemy's dragoons. These poor fellows had barely time to get into their saddles and to draw their swords; but their leader (Major Williams, if I remember rightly) performed his duty on this emergency like a good soldier, encouraging his men as best he could, but every second brought us closer, and we were soon in the midst of them. After a short encounter the Federal dragoons took to flight in the greatest disorder. We were in full pursuit of them when a strong cavalry force, consisting of the enemy's dragoons and lancers, under Colonel Rush, came up to the rescue. We collected and reformed our troopers, who, in the eagerness of pursuit, had become dispersed, and in a few moments the hostile squadrons were engaged in a deadly conflict. Colonel Rush and Major Williams led on their men in good style, and showed us that we had experienced cavalry officers to deal with. One squadron was left behind as a reserve, while the whole of the remainder charged. The opposing cavalry masses met with a shock which shook the ground beneath the horses' feet. In this fierce encounter, upon which a cool, refreshing breeze from the wood played as if in mockery, swords clashed, horses neighed and plunged, and trumpets sounded.

But, alas, for the issue of the struggle! our men get the worst of it; our rough, well-seasoned fellows from the prairies of Missouri and Texas turn tail! The enemy's swords flash all the quicker, and our flight becomes general. In vain is our reserve squadron brought up; it is also carried away in the flight. At this critical moment for us a thundering cheer is heard from a new quarter; Captain Norton and his men make their appearance through an opening in the wood, and dash with impetuosity upon the exulting foe. The giant form of Norton, brandishing his Mexican sabre, is plainly seen at the head of his men, and in a moment the scene changes; our scared troopers reform and fall back to renew the fight. Colonel Stuart with the main body of the brigade then came up, and it was the enemy's turn to take to flight, our troops pursuing them in hot haste. Colonel Stuart after this ordered men and horses to halt, for the purpose of a little needful rest.

Meantime an episode in the fight occurred, in the shape of a duel between one of the enemy's dragoons and one of our Texans, on a small field close by. The dragoon evidently scorned to join in the flight of his comrades, and displayed such skill in the management of his horse and in the use of his sword, that it was quite a pleasure to watch him. In vain did the Texan make lunge after lunge at him, and try all sorts of expedients to overcome his antagonist. The dragoon sat as firm as a rock in his saddle, wielding his sword like a brand of lightning. By the manner in which he handled his horse and weapon I judged at a glance that he was an old German trooper, and I could not help watching the exciting combat with very great interest. The Texan still continued to wheel round his opponent on his fleet barb, eagerly seeking to find an opportunity for dealing a home thrust, whilst the dragoon, with a cool, steady eye, followed all the movements of his impetuous antagonist. At last they close in earnest. A blow, a parry, and a thrust follow close on each other. The Texan had slashed the dragoon's shoulder, so that the blood began to flow, which aroused a cheer from the Texans looking on, but, at the same moment, the former received a back stroke which cut through the sleeve and flesh of his left arm. The Texan now backed his horse like lightning, and his fellow troopers rushed forward to look at his wound; but without paying any heed to his hurt he again dashed at his opponent and made a lunge at his breast. The dragoon parried it with great dexterity, and at the same time let fly a *quarte* which caused a slashing wound in the Texan's back. The latter spurred on his horse to a little distance, and before I could take means to prevent the cowardly act, he took out a pistol and deliberately shot the brave dragoon, who fell dead from his saddle. The bullet had entered just below the region of the heart.

Much moved at his fate, I ordered a grave to be dug to receive the remains of the brave German trooper. We buried him in his regimentals, with his trusty sword on his breast, and his pistols by his side. This sad act having been performed, I sent for the Texan, and after reprimanding him severely for his cowardly conduct, I ordered him to seek service in some other corps, telling him that I could not think of allowing a fellow of his stamp to remain in my regiment. The Texan scowled at me with his wild catlike eyes, and muttering a curse, mounted his horse and rode away.

Touched as I was by the death of the brave dragoon, it was quite a relief to my feelings when the trumpets gave the signal to mount. We now started at a good trot toward the Pamunky river, where, according to the reports of our scouts, we might expect to find plenty of booty without encountering much hindrance from hostile forces, inasmuch as M'Clellan was under the impression that M'Dowell was posted here. M'Clellan could hardly have imagined that the latter, as soon as he was informed of our advance, had withdrawn his outposts, and had abandoned the field to us.

We reached the Pamunky river without difficulty, driving back the few troops left in charge of the stores. As soon as this was accomplished, a portion of our men were set to work to destroy the storehouses and the vessels on the river, which were soon in a blaze; whilst another detachment was employed in driving in the numerous horses and mules that were grazing here. By nightfall the work of destruction was completed, and we advanced toward the York River Railway to break up that line. Sending the artillery and captured stores forward, we continued our march, after a short rest, along the enemy's lines, they not having the slightest notion of our proximity to them. About ten o'clock at night we reached the York River Railway, and our men were just about to begin the work of tearing up the rails, when we suddenly heard, in the stillness of the night, the sound of an approaching train. Colonel Stuart ordered his men, who were armed with double-barrelled rifles, to draw up at both sides of the railway, and to send a volley into the train as it came up. This was done; but, happily, as I afterward learned, with no effect. The engine driver put on increased speed, and the train glided onward, and was soon out of sight. In a short time we distinctly heard the sound of approaching cavalry, and our vedettes came hurrying back with the information that large bodies of the enemy's troops were advancing in our direction. There was no time to lose now in crossing the Chickahominy. This operation we succeeded in performing, after a smart ride; and we had just reached the opposite bank, when the advancing enemy came in view.

On reaching Richmond, our troopers met with an enthusiastic reception; and the information which we brought to General Lee was of the utmost importance, as it confirmed the report that had already gained belief, of General M'Dowell's inactivity. General Lee accordingly came to the safe conclusion that he might now concentrate his whole force against M'Clellan, who was totally ignorant of the critical position in which he was placed. With commendable prudence, however, he had commenced moving his front a little more to the north of Richmond, and concentrated his forces so as to occupy a more defensive position until the expected reinforcements of Generals Burnside and Pope should reach him. Cautious and skilful as was this step on the part of M'Clellan, General Lee was not the man to lose so golden an opportunity of defeating the enemy as soon as he should, by the arrival of reinforcements, be enabled to make the attempt. With what success he achieved his object will be seen in the succeeding " War Picture."

CHAPTER XLI.

THE SEVEN DAYS' BATTLE BEFORE RICHMOND: JUNE 25TH TO JULY 1ST, 1862.

I.—A COUNCIL OF WAR.

General Robert E. Lee, our General-in-Chief—His active preparations for the impending struggle—Holds a council of war: officers present—Relative position of the hostile armies.

II.—FIRST DAY: COMMENCEMENT OF OPERATIONS.

"Stonewall" Jackson's flank march to Hanover Court House—Drives back M'Dowell's troops—M'Clellan's counter manœuvre—Jackson's orders to General Branch ill executed, rendering Hill's attack on M'Call's division at Mechanicsville indecisive.

III.—SECOND DAY: BATTLE OF GAINES'S MILL.

Heavy Confederate cannonade—Retreat of the enemy from Mechanicsville—Passage of the Chickahominy—Arrival of troops under Longstreet and Hill—M'Dowell's inactivity—Battle of Gaines's Mill—Severe and obstinate fighting. bravery of the Irish brigade—Hideous aspect of the battle field—Sufferings of the wounded aggravated by neglect—Inadequate preparations at Richmond for their care.

IV.—THIRD AND FOURTH DAYS: BATTLE OF PEACH ORCHARD.

Defeat of the Federals by "Stonewall" Jackson—Their severe losses—M'Clellan's retreat compared with that of Radetzky in Lombardy, in 1848—Arrival of Jeff. Davis on the field of battle—Cool reception given to him—The enemy's strong intrenchments—Orderly retreat of the Federal army.

V.—FIFTH DAY: BATTLE NEAR WHITE OAK SWAMP.

Strength of the Federal position—The Confederates compelled to retire—Murderous fire of the Federal troops—Wilcox's brigade nearly cut to pieces—General Lee's anxiety as to the issue of the contest.

VI.—SIXTH DAY: BATTLE AT FRAZER'S FARM

Destructive artillery fire—M'Clellan receives reinforcements—Alarm of the Confederate officials at Richmond—The fighting resumed—Heroism of General Hill and his troops—Desperate nature of the struggle: no quarter—Anecdote of Major Peyton and his son—Critical position of the Confederates—Tardy arrival of reinforcements under Magruder.

VII.—SEVENTH DAY: BATTLE OF MALVERN HILL.

Magruder opens the battle before daybreak, and drives the enemy to Malvern Hill—Fearful effect of the fire of 268-pounders from the Federal ships—M'Clellan holds his ground firmly until midnight, and succeeds in withdrawing his shattered forces to James river—Reflections on his character and talents as a commander.

I.

A COUNCIL OF WAR.

NOTHING had escaped the keen perception of General Lee, and he consequently made his preparations for the execution of his plans so effectually as to insure success, provided the troops did their duty thoroughly. Once more, accompanied only by his aide-de-camps, he visited the most distant outposts; again he inspected each separate brigade, each fortified post—in short every position, before he proceeded to put his comprehensive measures in force.

All the available troops from the interior of the country had been collected together; and besides the significance of this fact, everything indicated that preparations were making for a desperate struggle.

On the 25th of June, another great council of war was held, at which nearly every man of note in the Confederate army was present. There stood the general-in-chief, Lee, calm and dignified, greeting with a friendly smile his colleagues as they approached him, and for each of whom he had already cut out his work. With a keen glance he surveyed the countenance of each officer separately, as if he wished to impress the features of all upon his memory; with the feeling that he expected much from these men, whom, perhaps, he should never behold together again. By his side stood conspicuously the portly figure of Colonel Baldwin; on his left, the eye of the spectator rested upon the thoughtful face of "Stonewall" Jackson, the idol of his men, who was twitching the hilt of his sword in a nervous manner, as if the room was too narrow to hold him, and as if he longed to be in the open air again at the head of his columns. A little on one side were the two Hills; in front of them stood the veteran General Wise, with his eager, animated look. Further to the right was a separate group, consisting of Generals Huger, Longstreet, Anderson, Whiting, Ripley, Branch, and Magruder. As soon as all the officers invited to the council had arrived, General Lee explained his plan of operations; pointing out to each the special duty he had to perform. The scheme was admirably conceived; with well combined action, a brilliant success seemed certain. As soon as the sitting was over, all the officers shook hands, and each of them left for his own post in order to proceed to active work.

If we consider the relative position of the two armies, the advantage was unquestionably on the side of the Confederates; for General M'Clellan's army, posted upon both banks of the Chickahominy, was too much extended, and had moreover great difficulties to contend with in manœuvring, owing to the numerous ravines which intersect the ground. M'Clellan's front line was more than twenty miles in extent, forming a semicircle, which extended from James river to Ashland and Richmond; while another portion of his army had crossed the Chickahominy from Meadow Bridge to Bottom Bridge, and occupied the banks of the river, which had been fortified; so that, notwithstanding its immense extent, his army possessed a good line of defence to fall back upon.

II.

COMMENCEMENT OF OPERATIONS.

SCARCELY had dawn broken on the 26th of June, when "Stonewall" Jackson's numerous forces began moving in a direction parallel with the railway line. After a forced march, they reached Ashland, in the vicinity of which were General M'Dowell's outposts, about which, however, Jackson gave himself no further trouble than to send a few detachments of cavalry to drive them back upon Fredericksburg. After Jackson had allowed his troops the rest they needed, he rapidly continued his march upon Hanover Court House, upon gaining which point, he drove back the enemy's troops. As soon as M'Clellan was informed of Jackson's movements, and was made aware of the dangerous position this manœuvre had placed him in, he adopted the best measures in his power to prevent Jackson's further advance upon his line of communications. He forthwith ordered one of his most active officers, General Fitz John Porter, to take with him two divisions, as well as the reserve of the regulars, and with this force to hold their ground against the threatened attacks of Jackson and of General Hill.

General Jackson's *corps d'armée*, strengthened by the addition of Whiting's division, now consisted of about 30,000 men, and he was therewith in a position to carry out operations on a large scale. As soon as he had crossed the Chickahominy, he sent two brigades, under the command of General Branch, to operate between the two rivers, Pamunky and Chickahominy, with instructions to advance as rapidly as possible, and to endeavor strenuously to overcome all obstacles, so as to give full scope for the free action of the attacking army of the Confederates at Mechanicsville—Jackson himself purposing to advance toward Coal Harbor.

It happened, unluckily, that General Branch, as had occurred on a former occasion, proved timid and undecided. As long as he acted directly under General Jackson's command, he obeyed his instructions to the letter, and his courage never drooped; but when out of his sight, he became nervous and unresolved how to act. This was one of his unfortunate days—he hesitated: delaying his onward march from hour to hour, instead of advancing boldly as Jackson had distinctly ordered him.

In the mean time, General Hill (I.) vigorously attacked the Federal division under General M'Call, in front of Mechanicsville. But notwithstanding all his efforts, M'Call held his ground; General Hill then sent his aide-de-camp to order up Branch's brigade, but in this he was foiled, for the latter did not make his appearance upon the battle field until night had put an end to the combat.

III.

SECOND DAY. BATTLE OF GAINES'S MILL.

By daybreak on the 27th June, our artillery opened a very heavy fire upon the enemy's front, with such effect, that when they observed General Branch's brigade advancing to attack their right wing, they relinquished their position before Mechanicsville, and fell back, fighting, upon their second line of defence. Just at the moment we had effected the passage of the Chickahominy, General Longstreet's splendid *corps d'armée*, consisting of well-proved troops from the army of the Potomac, came up, as did also the division of General Hill (II.). The order was now given for the whole force to advance. The divisions of Hill (II.), Anderson, and Whiting, forming the centre, advanced upon Coal Harbor, whilst Jackson, Hill (I.), and Longstreet, forming the left wing, marched along the banks of the Chickahominy; and Magruder, who commanded the right wing, was ordered to remain on the defensive, in consequence of the swampy state of the ground. General Wise assumed the command of Fort Darling, on the James River. All these formidable operations, in connection with the two former engagements, must have opened the eyes of General M'Clellan as to our intention of quitting our uncomfortable position at Richmond, so that we might be enabled to act with greater scope. He ought, therefore, to have immediately ordered M'Dowell's *corps d'armée*, which had been lying inactive for four months before Fredericksburg, to make a demonstration on the Richmond road. Had he done so, the operation would have prevented General Jackson's flank march.

But General M'Clellan had been deceived in his estimate of M'Dowell's generalship, for, notwithstanding all the information he had received of our combined manœuvre, the latter remained unpardonably inactive and indifferent in his own safe position, thereby exposing M'Clellan's army, which had suffered severely from sickness as well as from desertion, to our overpowering attacks.

When General Lee was fully assured of M'Dowell's inertness, he immediately ordered a general and simultaneous attack on the whole of M'Clellan's lines. As soon as the news was announced of General Jackson's arrival at Coal Harbor, the Commander-in-Chief, accompanied by his staff, proceeded to Gaines's Mill, and ordered the divisions of Anderson, Hill (I.), Longstreet, and Pickett to commence the attack. Before our columns were in movement, the roar of cannon on our left wing informed us that Jackson had commenced operations in that quarter. This belief caused the greatest enthusiasm amongst our troops.

M'Clellan's position on this day was a most peculiar one. With one portion of his army he had crossed the Chickahominy, southward, and faced General Magruder's force, whilst the main body of his army was posted more to the rear and closer to the railway, at which point he was firmly resolved to give battle. His arrangements displayed much skill and circumspection. The different troops took up their respective positions with remakable precison, firmly awaiting our onset. This was the first time that the two hostile armies stood opposite to each other on an almost equal footing as regards numbers. The Federals had, however the advantage of a better covered position, whilst our troops were fully exposed to their fire. The attack was opened by the columns of Hill (I.), Anderson, and Pickett. With a loud cheer these troops advanced amidst a tremendous fire from the enemy. Hundreds fell from the bullets of the foe; but this did not daunt our men; they advanced till they came face to face, eye to eye, bayonet to bayonet, and then a terrible conflict ensued. A Federal brigade, commanded by Meagher, and consisting chiefly of Irishmen, offered the most heroic resistance. After a severe struggle our men gave way, and retired in great disorder. At this critical moment, foaming at the mouth with rage, and without his hat, General Cobb hastened up, sword in hand, with his legion, followed by the 19th North Carolina, and 14th Virginia regiments, and renewed the attack. But the efforts of these troops were in vain: the brave Irishmen held their ground with a determination which excited the admiration even of our own officers. The remnant of Cobb's broken legion then fell back. The 19th regiment had lost six ensigns, and most of the superior officers were struck down. Generals Hill (I.) and Anderson again brought up their men to the attack, and the fight was renewed with greater fury than before, some of the regiments exceeding all their former deeds.

Our soldiers displayed a stoical disregard of death that placed them on an equal footing with veteran troops, for despite the sanguinary harvest which death this day reaped in our ranks, no kind of disorder ensued, and it should be remembered that this fearless resolution was evinced not only by the more experienced portion of our troops, but by many regiments that had never been under fire before. It is, however, due to our opponents to admit that they sustained the shock of our incessant attacks with undaunted bravery. Although some of their brigades had been fighting from four o'clock till eight P. M., they had continued to stand firm, and it was only when they found, at the last named-hour, Jackson was about to attack them in the rear that they abandoned their positions. Although their loss must have been very severe they retired in good order, with drums beating and colors flying, taking their slightly wounded men and their baggage along with them; and when hotly pressed in pursuit by Davis and Wickham's cavalry regiments, they faced round and repulsed them.

Night now threw her sable veil over the field of slaughter; it seemed, indeed, as if nature was anxious to conceal from the eyes of the living the harrowing spectacle of death's doings. Gradually, all had become still, save the faint echo of a distant cannonade on our left flank; but that too presently subsided. The majority of our soldiers, overcome by the exertions of so obstinate a contest, sank down helplessly upon the ground, to catch a little fitful rest. Although I was also so fatigued that I could scarcely keep my seat on horseback, nevertheless, accompanied by one of my aide-de-camps, I rode to that part of the battle field where the struggle had been fiercest. The havoc of war that was here noticeable, even in the gloom of night, was fearful to contemplate. Whole ranks of the enemy's dead lay extended on the ground they had occupied at the outset of the battle. The number of wounded too, was proportionately great, while their groans and cries for help were audible on all sides, and were truly heartrending. In bygone days I had been on many a battle field in Italy and Hungary; but I confess that I never witnessed so hideous a picture of human slaughter and horrible suffering.

The preparations for removing the wounded were on too small a scale, and the men detached for this service not sufficiently numerous for their melancholy work; and as may be supposed, the surgeons had more on their hands than they were able to accomplish. By dint of considerable trouble, and with the aid of some humane officers, I succeeded eventually in getting matters into a little better order. Luckily, I came upon some of the ambulances left behind by the enemy, and gladly made use of them to convey the wounded to Richmond. Whilst we were performing this sad task, many a poor fellow breathed his last, rendering all our efforts to succor him unavailing. By midnight I had the first train of conveyances ready, viz., sixty vehicles of various kinds, containing 200 men, all severely wounded, and with great labor I got this train of carriages into town. At the first hospital I came to I was refused admittance. "All right," was the curt but fruitless reply to my request for admission; "pass on to the next hospital." At the next hospital I met with the same reply. A friend then told me that if I would wait a little he could help me, as he would turn a large building he used for storing up tobacco into a hospital. I had therefore, no alternative but to wait an hour and a half with my load of dying men in the street. I did my best to alleviate their sufferings by procuring them water, tea, and other refreshments; but the late hour of the night and the confusion in the town greatly impeded my efforts.

At last the temporary hospital was ready, and a sad hole it was for such a purpose: an open warehouse, unprovided with doors or windows, and with merely a few planks to serve for beds for the dying soldiers. On this memorable day our brave fellows had to endure everything: hunger, thirst, and heat, besides facing death in its most fearful forms; and now, wounded at the very threshold of the dwellings of their own friends, whose rights and property they had been fighting for, we beheld them left to die uncared for in an open shed!

And yet this city numbered as many as 40,000 inhabitants; it contained, moreover, many churches, admirably adapted for hospitals on such emergencies, and was well provided with clergy. Yet no church door was opened, no minister of religion came forward to soothe the last moments of the dying soldier. With mixed feelings of sadness and indignation, I gave the order to place the wounded men inside the wretched building, and, having bestowed a parting look on the ill-cared-for sufferers, I mounted my horse snd hastened back to rejoin my regiment.

IV.

THIRD AND FOURTH DAYS. BATTLE OF PEACH ORCHARD.

GENERAL JACKSON had executed his flank march without much interruption on the part of the enemy; and as soon as he reached the post assigned to him he led his columns to the attack. Though much tired after their fatiguing march, these "*Sansculottes*" attacked the enemy with indomitable spirit, overpowering all resistance. Like a whirlwind General Stuart swept all before him with his cavalry; while Jackson's men seemed to be frantic; throwing away their muskets and drawing their bowie knives, they fell with savage fury upon their victims. The carnage which ensued was terrible, and, although the enemy attempted, in their desperation, to make a stand, they were completely overthrown. Their flight became a rout, the men throwing away their muskets and running for their lives.

For a moment it was supposed that the defeat of M'Clellan's army was complete; two of the enemy's generals of brigade had already been abandoned by their men, when, at this most critical moment for the Federal army, General Heintzelman made his appearance with his division, and renewed the combat. With equal bravery and skill he succeeded at first in warding off our attacks, and thus enabled the defeated brigades to reform, but it was of no avail: the flight of the Federal troops ere long became general.

General Heintzelman was compelled, in his turn, to give ground, and to fall back on the Chickahominy, leaving all the wounded, baggage, stores, &c., of the Federal forces in our hands. General Jackson might well exclaim, "Enough for to-day." No other general of the Confederate army had achieved the task allotted to him with so much celerity and success.

In this battle the Federals lost 2 brigadier-generals, 115 staff and other officers, and 3,000 men, as well as their baggage. In a strategical point of view the success of Jackson was of far greater importance, as General M'Clellan was thereby completely cut off from his line of retreat. Consequently, when Jackson's success became known at our headquarters, a firm conviction was entertained that the whole of M'Clellan's army was lost. The exultation this gave rise to was extraordinary. On joining my regiment early in the morning, I found my brave troopers indulging in the greatest excitement, as each and all of them were anxious to take part in the hoped-for capture of M'Clellan and his army in the coming battle. I could not avoid shrugging my shoulders when the officers of the regiment explained their views to me. I well remembered what occurred in Italy in 1848, at the time of Radetzky's retreat. It was a parallel case. The Italians had then prepared in their imagination comfortable quarters for the brave old Austrian and his army, and the Podesta of Milan felt so confident of victory and its attendant consequences, that he proceeded to the vanguard of the Italian army, in order that he might receive with due ceremony the conquered hero. But by that very time the latter had overcome every difficulty in his path, and had quietly retreated to his strongholds of Mantua and Verona.

I had scarcely rejoined my regiment when I received the order to advance with the whole line. I looked sadly at our once fine division. Many of the regiments were terribly cut up. Some, whose full complement, like that of my own, was 1,100 men, could not muster more than 300 or 400 efficient men; nay, the 7th Georgia and 21st North Carolina regiments could only muster 180 men each. The number of officers placed *hors de combat* was proportionally great. Indeed so palpable was this that I had not the courage to inquire after many a missing friend, not doubting that he had met with a soldier's death on the field of battle.

Just as our division had begun to move, Jefferson Davis made his appearance, accompanied by Colonels Davis, Johnston, and Smith, of the cavalry, and by the Secretary of War, Randolph, with members of his Military Cabinet. The conqueror of Buena Vista did not, however, meet with an enthusiastic reception, as with a cold eye and rigid bearing he rode along the front of the regiments, addressing, occasionally, a word of recognition to some personal acquaintance.

As soon as our division had succeeded in wending its way through the chaos of dismounted guns, tumbrels, dead and wounded men, and reached the open ground which allowed room for action, we were astonished to find in the enemy's positions, of which we now took possession, that nothing had been left but a few broken weapons and some baggage. They had taken everything else away with them in their retreat; the number of dead bodies alone denoted how fierce the struggle had been. The defences were of immense strength, and of much greater solidity than we had imagined. We received orders to proceed as quickly as possible; to watch the enemy's movements, and follow on his heels; and we had scarcely passed the White House when our attention was attracted by a dense column of smoke, about a mile and a half to the right of the railway, apparently rising from the forest. Approaching cautiously in that direction, we discovered a huge burning pyramid. The Federal general had ordered everything that could not be taken away to be piled up and burnt. Property to the amount of millions of dollars was thus consigned to the flames, that it might not fall into the hands of the victors. Our men rushed to the burning pile in order to save all they could from the flames.

Hundreds of casks of preserved meats, coffee, sugar, rice, wine, including even champagne, and similar delicacies, with which the Federal army was amply provided, and of which we Southerners scarcely knew the names, were here piled up for destruction. But the enemy had done their work so skilfully that our poor fellows managed to get but little out of the fire. Fortunately, however, the whole place was strewed with serviceable cloth cloaks, which proved most useful to our ill-clad troops. Everything denoted that M'Clellan had retreated in good order, and that he did not dream of capitulating to his enemy. From some of the stragglers of his army we learnt that he had crossed the Chickahominy with his whole force, abandoning his former plan of retreat, and had taken the direction of James River, probably with a view to keep up a communication with his flotilla. I accordingly despatched one of my officers with this information to General Lee. Shortly after I received an order to halt; and just then the fine divisions of Hill (I.) and Longstreet came up at the double quick, in order to give the *coup de grace* to the supposed flying enemy.

V.

FIFTH DAY. BATTLE NEAR WHITE OAK SWAMP.

About five miles from Darbytown, on the Newmarket road, we came in view of the hostile army, which had taken up an admirable position. The plain here is grown over with thickets of fir trees, and the ground is so very uneven and ill-adapted for cavalry movements that we were compelled to remain inactive.

General M'Clellan had taken up a position which had Frazer's farm for its centre. He ordered this point to be defended with 19 pieces of heavy ordnance, drew his best troops together there, and calmly and firmly awaited our attack.

It was of vital importance to us to drive away the enemy from the vicinity of our capital, no matter at what sacrifice: there was no alternative. But M'Clellan was well aware of the critical position in which he also was placed. Through the folly of M'Dowell, and through the dilatory conduct of the Federal Secretary of War, Stanton, he had been fairly left in the lurch. Many other generals would, perhaps, under such circumstances, have courted death in the turmoil of battle. But, notwithstanding the immense losses he had sustained during the battles of the last four days, M'Clellan, like a good soldier, resolved to try again the chances of war at the sword's point.

The spirits of our men, excited by the recent fighting, had become almost ungovernable. No sooner was the enemy in sight than they fell upon them furiously. But the Federals were undismayed, and received the attack as deliberately as if they were on parade; while the batteries in their centre, opening a terrific fire upon our advancing troops, caused havoc and confusion in our ranks. General Lee, seeing this, ordered up all the troops he could spare to their support. M'Clellan, however, kept up such an incessant fire upon every column as it came up to take part in the attack, that whole files of our men were mowed down by showers of grape. The scene that then ensued is almost indescribable. For nearly seven hours did the battle thus fiercely rage, within a very small compass, without either party gaining an inch of ground. All our reserves were engaged. Wilcox's brigade was almost cut to pieces; the men fell on all sides, and cries for water to quench the thirst of the wounded painfully resounded in every quarter; but there were no springs on these arid plains to assuage their thirsty cravings.

General Lee, looking somewhat disconcerted, rode along the lines of the shattered regiments, and with a hoarse voice ordered up Magruder's and Wise's brigades; and we then commenced burying our dead. In a few words he directed General Longstreet what position he was to occupy on the morrow, and a moment afterward galloped off with his aide-de-camps to visit the other brigades.

VI.

SIXTH DAY. BATTLE AT FRAZER'S FARM.

Dawn had scarcely broken on the horizon when the thunder of the cannon again shook the earth. A battery which General Anderson had brought up during the night, and stationed much closer to the enemy's lines, was discovered by the Federals, and was terribly mauled by their rifled cannon: every shot told, and the splinters flew about in all directions. In a short time five guns out of the twelve of this battery were dismounted, yet the officer in command unflinchingly held his ground. Meanwhile our columns had formed, although the men were weakened through insufficient food. Wearied, too, as they were by the exertions of the previous days, they almost staggered as they marched, but, nevertheless, were not disposed to shirk the stern work that now remained for them to do. When the increasing light rendered objects more discernible, I took a glance at the enemy's formation, and noticed with no little anxiety that, from the greater massiveness of his columns, M'Clellan must have received reinforcements in sufficient strength to enable him to withdraw his wearied men from the front, and to bring fresh troops to bear against our wornout soldiers.

General Lee, now quite convinced of the critical state of affairs, gave orders to "Stonewall" Jackson to keep his corps in readiness to cover the retreat of the army, should that contingency arise. Instructions were sent to Richmond, moreover, that proper measures should be taken for the prompt removal, if needful, of all State property from the town. Orders were then given to the divisions of Hill (H.), Longstreet, Anderson, Cobb, and Whitticombe to advance to the attack.

One of the most desperate actions now commenced which

has perhaps ever been fought. The loss we suffered on this occasion is fearful to think of. Perceiving the havoc his artillery was making among our men, M'Clellan brought up considerable forces from his reserve, and with these troops poured volley after volley of musketry into our ranks. Step by step his troops gained ground, till at length some of our companies threw down their muskets and fled. M'Clellan, taking advantage of the favorable moment, ordered his cavalry to move on our flank. Anderson then, rapidly placing himself at the head of three of our horse regiments, bore down furiously upon the enemy's squadrons. The charge was a brilliant one. With a defiant hurrah our troopers dashed upon their opponents, and such was the dismay produced among them, that, without allowing us time to try the temper of our blades, the hostile cavalry turned tail and fled ignominiously. But it was impossible to follow up our success in face of the enemy's rifled cannon, and we, in our turn, had to fall back out of the reach of the murderous fire poured into us. The enemy, taking courage from the disorder thus occasioned in our ranks, advanced to attack us, shouting as they approached, "On to Richmond!" These vaunting words rang along the whole of the enemy's line, and when they became audible to us, many hardy soldiers who had successfully fought our foes in far-off Missouri and in the plains of Arkansas, felt their hearts swell with indignation. After six days' hard fighting—after incessant bloodshed—after all our harassing toils and privations—all now seemed lost! A feeling of depression, almost amounting to a panic, now took possession of the minds of many. For a moment these symptoms were so alarming that a general flight appeared imminent. In vain did the officers of the staff endeavor to rally the failing spirit of the troops. This was a perilous moment for the Confederacy.

In this desperate state of affairs, while the enemy continued advancing to the reiterated shout of "On to Richmond!"

General Hill brought up some regiments he had managed to collect for the purpose, and, seizing the flag of the 4th North Carolina regiment, which he had once commanded, exclaimed: "If you will not follow me, I will seek death alone!" In answer to this powerful appeal, several officers rushed forward to shield their beloved general with their own bodies, while the men of the regiment vehemently shouted, "Hill, lead on your North Carolina boys!" Cavalry officers, too, were seen to dismount and to take the vacant places of infantry officers who had fallen. Hill now rushed intrepidly to the attack, followed by his men, in whose breasts he had rekindled a courage amounting to exultation. The enemy was startled at seeing columns that but a few moments before had been in full flight thus reappear in fierce array to renew the attack. Hill fell like a wounded lion upon his pursuers, and the conflict was then waged chiefly with cold steel, for there was no time left for loading and firing. The animosity with which the men on both sides fought was almost diabolic; quarter was not thought of, the bowie knife and the bayonet did the sanguinary work. The son sinks dying at his father's feet— the father heeds not his dying child. Yon savagely excited soldier cares not that his brother has been killed within a few paces of him; nor do the most intimate friends, in this scene of unrestrained butchery, heed the last groan of their cherished comrades; all the bonds of human nature are broken; one hideous craving alone seeks gratification—revenge on the foe!

It was here that the son of Major Peyton, a lad fifteen years of age, called to his father to help him, as a bullet had smashed both his legs. "I will help you," replied the major, "when we have beaten the enemy. I have other sons to lead in the path of glory!" Then shouting "Forward!" he himself fell only a few yards further mortally wounded. Many deeds of heroic bravery were performed on both sides. Indeed, it would be difficult to point to any page in military history where that virtue was more fully displayed than in this memorable battle. So intense was the animosity that animated the contending foes, that even many a wounded man lying helpless on the ground would strive with a last effort to plunge his knife into the breast of some fallen enemy near him.

General Hill's success enabled the other generals to rally and reform some of their scattered troops, and, in a short time, by such means, the battle was renewed along the whole line, and continued to rage until far in the night. It was essential to our chances of success that we should maintain the fight until reinforcements could reach us, and we felt assured that the enemy's troops were quite as much exhausted as our own.

By eleven o'clock at night, the divisions of Magruder, Wise, and Holmes arrived, and took up a position in our front. Had these generals performed their duties with activity and care, a vast deal of bloodshed might have been spared, and the enemy would have been driven back upon his reserves as early as the forenoon. But, unfortunately, these three divisions arrived just seventeen hours too late. The generals were not quite certain as to their proper line of march, and, consequently, their columns kept crossing and recrossing each other, thus causing the loss of much precious time. Nevertheless, late as this succor was in reaching us, the shattered remnant of our army owed its eventual safety to its interposition.

As soon as the three divisions in question had gone, to the front, the regiments which had been engaged were withdrawn, and every effort was used to reorganize them, and to recruit the exhausted strength of the men during the night by the much-needed supplies of food. Fortunately, there was just then no lack of such stores. Proper measures were taken, also, to remove the wounded and to bury the dead.

VII.

SEVENTH DAY. BATTLE OF MALVERN HILL.

ON the 1st of July, as early as two o'clock in the morning, when the stars were still twinkling in the heavens, General Magruder renewed the fight. In a very short time the cannonade opened along the whole line, and so desperate was the sustained attack of our forces, that by the time noon had arrived M'Clellan was driven from all his positions, abandoning his wounded, his baggage, and many guns. Magruder followed closely in pursuit, but with caution, as he had to clear the surrounding thickets of the artillery and riflemen that were concealed under their cover.

At half past four in the afternoon, our troops reached the well-known farm belonging to D. Carter, called Malvern Hill. Here General M'Clellan had resolved to make a stand, and had accordingly drawn up his troops in order of battle. General Magruder lost no time in attacking them. Our columns, in splendid order, soon cleared the ground which separated them from the enemy, and advanced to attack them in their intrenched position. But a hail of bullets created fearful gaps in our ranks, and our troops had to retire for shelter behind the trees. Generals Smith, Anderson, and Holmes again led them on, when suddenly guns of an enormous calibre opened fire upon us with terrible effect. This cannonade proceeded from the ships, moored at a distance of no less than two and a half miles from the field of battle. Our men now attacked the works on Malvern Hill with desperate courage. But M'Clellan resolutely held his ground, and it was not until midnight that he was compelled to give way before the persevering and heroic efforts of our troops.

This battle of the seventh day will ever be remembered

as the Battle of Malvern Hill, and will hold an enduring place in the annals of the South.

In none of the previous battles before Richmond had the fighting been confined to so small a space as in this action; and in addition to the effects of this concentrated strife, the fire of monster guns from the enemy's ships must be taken into account, as an aggravation of its horrors; it was a fearful sight to see these 268 lb. shells crash through the wood and explode. This was the first time in the history of war that such enormous shells were used. I repeat, that the Battle of Malvern Hill will ever be a great and proud memorial for that people, who here displayed their indomitable spirit and fixed determination to conquer or die for their liberty and national independence.

It was at Malvern Hill, moreover, that the enemy's leader, General M'Clellan, displayed his talents in the most advantageous light. Notwithstanding his enormous losses, our desperate attempts to annihilate the Federal host failed to accomplish that much-cherished object of our whole army; and for that unfulfilled wish torrents of blood were prodigally shed.

I may venture to say that, if M'Clellan had received the support that had been promised him, he might have given a crushing blow to the Confederacy. But it was only after his army had been routed that Burnside made his appearance with his corps. What might not the result have been, if that general had arrived a fortnight sooner, and if M'Dowell had not been virtually isolated from M'Clellan?

As General M'Clellan withdrew his shattered forces through swamps, forests, and all sorts of difficult ground, he could well exclaim, like Francis I, after the battle of Pavia, "All is lost except honor!" Still undaunted, he retreated to James River, to find protection under the guns of his flotilla.

The tribute of admiration we here venture to pay to General M'Clellan is conscientiously bestowed. There are few, if any, generals in the Federal army that can bear comparison with him. Abandoned at the most critical moment by M'Dowell; left to his fate by the Secretary of War, Stanton, from party pique; cut off from his line of retreat, he adopted a basis of operations on a plan of his own, that puzzled the comprehension of less able men, and in its execution he defended every inch of ground with bravery and skill. His last halt at Malvern Hill is a proof of his military talent, and he is entitled to as much credit for his able combinations as for the determined stand he there made. But his troops had, at the close of these fierce conflicts, become much demoralized by the effects of the previous six days' fighting, and had lost heart; whilst many of his generals, having failed to comprehend adequately the ideas of their commander-in-chief, gave him little or no support.

CONCLUDING OBSERVATIONS.

If the question be raised how it has happened that the success which the Federal Government reasonably looked forward to obtain, in the struggle for the maintenance of the Union, turned chiefly in favor of the South, the only safe conclusion we can come to is, that it must be ascribed to a want of unity amongst the Federal generals.

If that Government had only possessed a few such men as Sterling Price, of Missouri, the Leonidas of the Confederate army; if the leading members of that Government could have been content to sacrifice their own ambition and vanity to a patriotic regard for the real interests of their cause, affairs might have taken a very different turn. The honor awarded by a nation to its sons is not based on the rank or titles they may hold, but is a consequence of the acts which they perform. All the distinctions which mere vanity strives to obtain are utterly barren; it is only the memory of disinterested, undaunted patriots that endures in the hearts of their countrymen. What the Washington Government had to contend against, was both a want of unity, and a general craving for personal notoriety.

Such was the nature of the cancer that ought to have been cut out before it was so deeply rooted as to become incurable. Why did Fortune, it may be asked, smile so often upon the arms of the Confederates? Because, we reply, with a few exceptions, their generals acted harmoniously together, and were well supported by their Government and press; whilst the Federal Government, on the contrary, had to contend with three distinct political parties, each of which endeavored to impede the action of the other; and this practical source of disunion caused the troops, as well as the people, occasionally to lose confidence in their leaders, political and military, and necessarily rendered the task of the latter much more difficult than it would otherwise have been. In fact, it is beyond question that the Federal Government, with its inexhaustible resources, with its powerful fleet and army, might long since have annihilated the seceding party in the Southern States, whom they regarded in the light of rebels, if its generals had but energetically concentrated their operations.

The United States Government should only have had two points in view in directing their offensive operations: the first and cardinal point being Richmond, which ought to have been taken at any cost, for, if once in their power, the deathblow to the Confederacy would have been given. Whatever people may say about moving the seat of Government further south, it matters not; with the fall of Richmond, the Confederacy would have succumbed likewise, for Richmond was not only the abiding place of the most rabid Southern fire-eaters, but of the thousand overawed partisans of the Union, who would have plucked up courage to judge and act for themselves, had the pressure upon them been removed. The Confederate Government—which, it must be remembered, had not been really acknowledged, for President Davis was elected merely by a small body of partisans—would then have fallen to the ground.

The Confederate Government is perfectly well aware of this, and this is why they exert every nerve to make a stand at Richmond. All the resources indispensable to carry on the war are concentrated in and around that city. Virginia is a rich and productive State, quite capable of providing for the wants of a large army: iron and coal mines, rich pastures, corn land, and all sorts of cattle, are to be found plentifully within it. Richmond, besides being the seat of the Confederate Government, is rich in arsenals, arm founderies, manufactories of different kinds, and great baking establishments for the army. If driven from Richmond, the Confederate Government might possibly make a stand for a fortnight in North Carolina, but would then be compelled to decamp hastily to the other side of the Mississippi.

When General M'Clellan took post before Richmond, he was perfectly well aware of the momentous task he had before him. . Knowing the enemy's strength, he never treated them with contempt; but he well knew the vast importance of unity and self-confidence. It was not his fault that he was beaten before Richmond; his failure must be attributed to the blindness of his Government, who looked upon the foe as one easily to be vanquished. When M'Clellan had placed an iron collar round the throat of that foe, which he intended to draw gradually tighter, and had obtained a footing so close to Richmond that he could send his cannon balls into the very centre of the city, the Government at Washington ought to have concentrated all its thoughts and energies to the one great object of sending M'Clellan as many troops as would enable him to assume and maintain the offensive.

The second point which the Union Government should have kept in view is the command of the Mississippi. The Federal Government ought, at any price, to have taken possession of that great road of communication, no matter what amount of troops it would have been necessary to employ for that purpose. If it could have obtained the possession of this great watercourse, it could at once have cut off a portion of the Confederate States from all communication with those places on which they depended for supplies, and compelled them, through sheer necessity, to return to the Union. With various stations for her ships on the Mississippi, and an army of 200,000 men in the field, the United States could hold its own against all comers. The Government at Washington should not have attached so much importance to its flanks; for on the one side they were protected by their powerful fleet, on the other by a brave and numerous people ready to step forward in the defence of their Government as soon as they were satisfied that the latter was in earnest. If it had collected together all the troops scattered over the different parts of its vast territories; if it put at their head a leader provided with the means of conducting the large army we have designated—a leader who had gained the love of his soldiers—there can be no question that he could have achieved the greatest results. One decisive blow— one great victory—would have sufficed to induce the soldiers to follow him willingly unto death, wherever he chose to lead them; and that, too, without the allurement of bounty, or of any promised reward, but simply for the honor of fighting for the national cause.

The various acts of cruelty that have been occasionally perpetrated during this war may be accounted for by the fact of the armies being composed of heterogeneous elements. There was no true soldier-like spirit, no clear conception of the laws of military honor amongst these great masses, such as are to be met with in the armies of more civilized nations. The troops comprised a singular mixture of semi-savages, civilized men, patriots, and hot-headed partisans, with some few chivalrous adventurers.

This lamentable war would long since have been terminated if the Union Government had actively and resolutely bestowed, at the commencement of the contest, serious attention on its more important issues, and have then readily made those sacrifices which it is now driven to. The whole affair was treated with too much levity: indeed, it appeared almost as if a wish prevailed amongst many to provoke a war. Over-confidence in their resources, national vanity, party spirit, and private interests all served to kindle the spark which has grown up into a mighty conflagration, that has let loose the hellhounds of war to ravage this unfortunate land. When will a controlling hand be stretched forth to restore peace between the fratricidal opponents? When will the mild angel of peace descend with the olive branch to restore tranquillity and order in the dwellings of man, and to implant love within hearts that are now filled with deadly hatred and revenge?

Who can tell?

Ere long, let us hope and pray, for who does not sincerely desire it? But it needs the combined efforts of strong will, powerful intellect, and untiring energy, as well as of undaunted courage, to recover and reunite the loosened elements of former content, prosperity, and liberty. Anticipating, as I fervently do, so desirable a consummation, I trust that thousands will join me in heartily wishing that the American Republic, once the pride of the world, may arise strong and powerful from this disastrous struggle; that the blood which has been shed in torrents during this war may serve to fertilize the soil of liberty, and that a new Union may arise, greater, stronger, and more free than its predecessor!

BIOGRAPHICAL SKETCHES

OF

Generals of the Confederate Army.

P. G. TOUSSAINT BEAUREGARD.

GENERAL BEAUREGARD, who is of French extraction, was born in the year 1818, in the State of Louisiana, and is the son of a wealthy planter there. After being educated at the Military Academy at West Point, he served with distinction in the Mexican war, and received the rank of captain after the battles of Contreras and Churubusco; for his conduct at the battle of Chapultepec he was promoted to the rank of major. On leaving active service he was promised the post of Superintendent of the Academy at West Point; but owing, as it is reported, to political intrigues, the appointment was cancelled. On the eve of the outbreak of the War of Secession, he was intrusted with the command of the troops called out by the State of South Carolina to act against Fort Sumter. The surrender of that stronghold, as well as General Beauregard's subsequent achievememts, are to be found narrated in the text of this work. Beauregard is a short, thin man, with a dark complexion, and a most lively temperament. Although the expression of his countenance can hardly be called prepossessing, his manners are nevertheless most courteous and urbane, denoting a man of good breeding and education. After the great battle of Manassas, praises and honors were showered upon him by the whole Confederacy, but the Southern authorities have subsequently treated him with coldness and neglect.

THE LATE
ALBERT SIDNEY JOHNSTON.

The late General A. S. Johnston was born in the State of Kentucky in the year 1803. After going through the usual course of education at the military school of West Point, he joined an infantry regiment in 1826. Appointed adjutant to General Scott, he served throughout a campaign against the Indians, but soon afterward left the army and emigrated to Texas. He entered the Texan army as a private soldier, but General Rusk soon made him adjutant-general of his command. He soon rose to be senior brigadier-general of the Texan army, and was promoted to succeed General Houston, which led to a duel between them, wherein Johnston was wounded. In 1837 he took the command-in-chief in Texas, and in 1839 acted as Secretary of War of the New Republic. When the annexation of Texas to the Union ended in the Mexican War, he went to Mexico at the request of General Taylor, and was elected colonel of a volunteer regiment, the 1st Texan Rifles, and specially distinguished himself at the battle of Monterey. He afterward took part in the war against the Mormons. For his distinguished services he was promoted to the rank of brigadier-general in 1857, and to the post of Military Governor of Utah. At the outbreak of the civil war, General A. S. Johnston joined the Southern Confederacy, and was killed at the battle of Shiloh, near Corinth. His loss was deeply regretted by the whole Confederacy, but especially by the troops, who were devotedly attached to him. He was of noble and commanding presence, courteous and affable in his address, of a generous and kindly disposition, and was universally esteemed and beloved.

ROBERT EDMUND LEE.

GENERAL LEE was born in Virginia in the year 1808. He is a collateral descendant of Washington, and is the owner of Whitehouse, a splendid property which formerly belonged to that great man. He was educated at West Point, and commanded a corps of engineers in the Mexican campaign, during which he was severely wounded at the battle of Chapultepec, and was twice brevetted for distinguished gallantry. In 1852 he was appointed Superintendent of the Military Academy, and in 1855 was made lieutenant-colonel of the 2d Cavalry. Meanwhile, Lee was sent with M'Clellan, then a captain, to the Crimea, to watch the operations of the siege of Sebastopol. When the Civil War in America broke out, he was at San Antonio, Texas, in command of his regiment, but joined the Confederacy, and was intrusted with the chief command of the Confederate troops in Virginia, and subsequently was appointed Commander-in-Chief of the whole Confederate army.

THOMAS JEFFERSON JACKSON.

GENERAL T. J. JACKSON (usually styled "Stonewall" Jackson) was born at Clarksburg, in the county of Lewis, Virginia, in the year 1825, of very respectable parents, who both died when he was quite young, leaving him unprovided for. An uncle on his mother's side then took charge of him, and gave him the best education he could afford. His studious habits and good conduct procured for him the office of constable for his county, when he was but sixteen years of age. In 1842, a young man in his district was offered a cadetship at West Point, but not having much inclination for a military career, he declined it. Jackson endeavored to get the vacant appointment, though strongly dissuaded from trying for it by his friends, who feared he might not succeed in passing his first examination. Jackson himself was aware that he was scarcely competent to undergo this ordeal; but not disheartened, he energetically set to work to qualify himself, and, provided with a letter of introduction from Mr. Hayes, a member of Congress, he made the venture. Jackson succeeded in gaining admission to the Academy, and in 1846, having received his appointment as second lieutenant, he was ordered to join General Taylor's army on the Rio Grande. After the battle of Buena Vista, Jackson was transferred to General Scott's army, then engaged in besieging Vera Cruz. He was promoted to the rank of first lieutenant for his bravery, and was present in nearly every affair in which the troops of General Scott were engaged; and, for his dashing conduct, was soon promoted to the rank of major. In this campaign, his health suffered so severely that he was obliged to retire from active service. He then accepted the offer of a professorship in the Military College at Lexington, in Virginia, which appointment he held until that State seceded from the Union. It has been alleged that Jackson is a fatalist, like Napoleon and some other great generals; this imputation, however, has been denied by his intimate associates; but all parties concur in representing him as a highly moral, straightforward man, deeply imbued with religious faith. As a commander he is very strict in the maintenance of discipline, but is, nevertheless, almost worshipped by his men. Many of his brilliant exploits, especially his conduct on that memorable occasion on which the name of "Stonewall" was bestowed upon him, are to be found related in previous portions of this work. His appearance is not prepossessing. He is about six feet in height, and awkward in his movements, and has a small but well-formed head, gray eyes, a straight nose, and light brown hair. He is taciturn rather than communicative, and his tone in conversation usually serious; but on occasions he can be cheerful and animated. Friends and foes all concur in ranking "Stonewall" Jackson as the most distinguished officer, if not, indeed, the ablest general of the Confederate army.

NOTE.—Just as these concluding sheets were passing through the press, the unwelcome news reached England of the death of the subject of the above brief sketch, from the effects of wounds received at the sanguinary battle of Chancellorsville.

"He had often dared the extremest dangers of the battle field, and his hairbreadth escapes were recounted with wonder by his men, who had almost come to regard him as endowed with a charmed life. In him the Confederate army has lost a beloved and trusty leader, whose very name was a tower of strength. By common consent, General Jackson was pre-eminently the hero of the war. He had no personal enemies, and no political antecedents lent a sinister aspect to his fame. The motives which actuated him in espousing the cause for which he so zealously contended, were pure and lofty. Indeed, we have been assured that it was not without a severe struggle, and, at last, an earnest conviction that he was doing his duty, that he drew his sword on the side of the Confederacy. From the people of the South his memory will receive the solemn, affectionate, unstinted homage which a nation pays to its chief martyr, while in this country, the admiration felt for his brilliant achievements, and the respect to which he entitled himself by his private virtues, have caused his death to be regarded with an intensity of regret, rarely bestowed on any but our own countrymen. He was, moreover, so pious and God-fearing a man, that it is said he never engaged in any unusual enterprise without first making it the subject of special prayer."

General Jackson was twice married.

The *Times* thus eloquently adverts to the death of the hero:

"The Confederate laurels worn on the field of Chancellorsville, must be twined with the cypress. Probably no disaster of the war will have carried such grief to Southern hearts as the death of General Jackson, who has succumbed to the wounds received on the eve of the great battle of the 3d of May. Even on this side of the ocean, the gallant soldier's fate will everywhere be heard of with pity and sympathy. Not only as a brave man fighting for his country's independence, but as a most consummate general, 'Stonewall' Jackson will carry with him to his early grave, the regrets of all who can admire greatness and genius. From the earliest days of the war, he has been conspicuous for the most remarkable military qualities. That mixture of daring and judgment which is the mark of 'heaven-born' generals, distinguished him beyond any man of his time. Although the young Confederacy has been illustrated by a number of eminent soldiers, yet the applause and devotion of his countrymen, confirmed by the judgment of European nations, have given the first place to General Jackson. The military feats he accomplished moved the minds of people with an astonishment which it is only given to the highest genius to produce. The blows he struck at the enemy were as terrible and decisive as those of Bonaparte himself. The march by which he surprised the army of Pope last year would be enough in itself to give him a high place in military history. But perhaps the crowning glory of his life was the great battle in which he fell. When the Federal commander, by crossing the river twelve miles above his camp, and pressing on, as he thought, to the rear of the Confederates, had placed them between two bodies of his army, he was so confident of success as to boast that the enemy was the property of the army of the Potomac. It was reserved to Jackson by a swift and secret march to fall upon his right wing, crush it, and, by an attack unsurpassed in fierceness and pertinacity, to drive his very superior forces back into a position from which he could not extricate himself except by flight across the river.

"He fell by a cruel chance, having received his mortal wounds in the confusion of a *mêlée* from the fire of his own troops, 'all of whom would have died for him.' On the evening of the 2d of May, his men, mistaking him and his *cortége* for some of the enemy's cavalry, fired with fatal effect, killing and wounding several of the party, and the lamented general himself received three wounds in the arm and hand. Amputation of the arm was necessary, and from the effects of this the Southern hero sank, after considerable suffering, at the end of a week.

"By the death of General Jackson the South has lost a great and controlling mind—one of those born leaders of men who can infuse their own spirit into all around them. Such a commander is the soul and strength of a cause when it asserts itself in arms. The combination of sincerity and enthusiasm with the professional skill that amounted to a genius for war is rare indeed. Power cannot evoke, nor can the wealth of empires create it. The adherence of such men to a cause or principle makes the difference between success and failure to the side they select. Had his last victory been more complete it would not have compensated the South for the loss of General Jackson, whose fall has thrown such a dark shadow over the memory of the day. That fall was untimely, for he was still young in years, and the work to which he devoted his life is unfinished. He might have done his cause more service, but he had achieved a full measure of fame; and rarely has so brief a period established such an unquestioned military reputation."

STERLING PRICE.

General Price was born in Edward county, Virginia, in the year 1810. He migrated to Missouri in 1830, where he settled as a farmer in Charlton county. In 1844 he was elected a member of Congress, and, as such, took his seat in the House of Representatives at Washington. When the events in Texas led to the war between the United States and Mexico, Price resigned his seat as a member of Congress, and took the command of a Missouri volunteer regiment, receiving the rank of colonel. Returning to Missouri on the termination of the Mexican war, he was, some time after, elected Governor of that State (in 1852). When Abraham Lincoln had been elected to the presidency of the United States, and the civil war broke out, the border States soon followed the example set them by Carolina and other Southern States in seceding from the Union. General Price, adopting the cause of the Confederacy, was intrusted with the command of a body of volunteers, and rendered such service to the cause by his skill and activity that he has entitled himself to be regarded as an able officer and gallant soldier.

C. FREDERICK HENNINGSEN.

Amongst the many military men of talent with which the present age abounds, there are none perhaps whose career furnishes more varied interest than the subject of this brief sketch. In whatever field of action we behold him, whether in the wilds of Tartary, in Circassia, in the Basque Provinces, in Hungary, at the sanguinary siege of Comorn, or in the pathless mountains of Nicaragua, we ever find him manifesting the same high military qualities and the same scrupulous love of honor. General Henningsen was born in London in the year 1816. When scarcely sixteen years of age the civil war in Spain, consequent on the death of Ferdinand VII, had just broken out, and attracted the general attention of Europe. Henningsen, prompted by an energetic spirit, joined the Carlist chief, Zumalacarreguy, as a volunteer, in the Basque Provinces. He soon rose to the rank of captain in that general's body guard, and was made a knight of the order of St. Ferdinand. On his return to England he published a "History of the War in Spain," a work which earned for him the favorable opinion of both the Duke of Wellington and Marshal Soult. When scarcely twenty years of age he returned to Spain with the rank of lieutenant-colonel, and, after the battle of Villar de los Navarros, was entrusted with the command of the cavalry. As a reward for his gallantry before Madrid he received the rank of a full colonel, and the order of Isabella. He next served with the Russian army in the campaign against the Circassians, and wrote a work on the Caucasus, which was published by the Russian Government as an official document. He next published a work entitled, "The Revolutions of Russia," which was well spoken of at the time. He subsequently went to Hungary, and was intrusted with the command of Comorn. When the struggle there was over, Henningsen turned his attention to the improvement of firearms, and superintended the construction of the first Minié rifles introduced into America. But he continued to devote himself to literary pursuits, and published the following works: "A Twelvemonth's Campaign under Zumalacarreguy;" "The White Slave," a novel; "Eastern Europe Sixty Years ago," a Russian novel. But of all his writings, "Analogies and Contrasts" met with the greatest success. When the war in Nicaragua assumed a serious aspect, the want of a good leader was felt. Some of President Walker's friends proposed Henningsen, who had then taken up his residence at New York. An offer was thereupon made to him, and, on accepting it, he embarked for Nicaragua. At the termination of the war there he proceeded to Georgia, of which State he became a naturalized citizen, and when the war of secession broke out he accepted the post of second in command of Wise's legion, in the service of the Confederates. The dilatory conduct of the Government, however, has hitherto not afforded him an opportunity for the display of his military talents. General Henningsen is tall, and quite the soldier in appearance; he speaks eight different languages with the same fluency as he does his mother tongue, and is incontestably a most accomplished and well-informed military man.

JOSEPH ECCLESTON JOHNSTON.*

This officer, who is a native of Virginia, entered the Military Academy in 1825, passed thence to the 4th Artillery, and retired in 1837; but, on the breaking out of the Florida war shortly afterward, he entered the Topographical Engineers and served during that contest. In 1846, as lieutenant-colonel of the Voltigeurs, he served during the Mexican war, having been present at all the engagements between Vera Cruz and the capital, was twice wounded and twice brevetted. In 1860 he left the line and became quartermaster-general to the United States army, with the rank of brigadier-general. He is very simple and unassuming in his bearing, but his countenance is expressive of great resolution and capacity. General Joseph Johnston, who took service in the Confederate army at the outbreak of the Civil War, was very severely wounded at the battle of Seven Pines.

* The substance of the above and of the four subsequent sketches is derived, by permission of the proprietors, from the columns of *Once a Week*.

EDMUND KIRBY SMITH.

KIRBY SMITH, who is from the State of Florida, was a cadet in 1841, and served through the Mexican war, at first as a lieutenant of the 5th Infantry—wherein were two other officers of the same name, both of distinguished bravery, and both slain in action—and afterward in the 7th Infantry, and was twice brevetted for gallantry. He was for a time mathematical professor of the Military Academy; and in 1861 was a captain in the 2d Cavalry. This able officer joined the Confederate forces soon after the commencement of the war of secession, and it was his timely arrival with the strong division under his command, at the close of the battle of Manassas, that decided the victory of the Confederate army.

BRAXTON BRAGG.

GENERAL BRAGG is a native of North Carolina. He became a cadet of the Military Academy in 1833, and was known by name at least throughout the Republic for his heroic conduct during the Mexican war, especially by his gallant defence, when a lieutenant of the 3d Artillery, of Fort Brown—a little earthwork hastily thrown up by General Taylor on the bank of the Rio Grande, opposite the city of Matamoras; and also by his subsequent conduct at Buena Vista, when his battery, supported only by the 1st Mississippi Rifles, charged and routed the Mexican army, after the volunteer infantry had fled *en masse*. He received four brevets during that war. In 1854 he was only a captain, and retired from the service some years since. On the breaking out of the Civil War he was intrusted with an important command, and received the rank of a general.

15*

JAMES LONGSTREET.

This distinguished officer, one of the ablest generals of the Confederate army, was born in South Carolina. He became a cadet in 1838, and was attached successively to the 4th and 8th Infantry, was present at Monterey, and all the battles in the Valley of Mexico; was wounded at Chapultepec, and twice brevetted. In 1858 he passed from the line into the paymaster's department, and belonged to it at the commencement of the present struggle in 1861. The very active part taken by General Longstreet in the great battles and other military operations of the Cival War, will be found narrated in the previous pages of this work.

BIOGRAPHICAL SKETCHES

OF

Generals of the Federal Forces.

G. B. M'CLELLAN.

GENERAL GEORGE B. M'CLELLAN was born at Philadelphia in the year 1826, and is the descendant of an old Scotch family, the lairds of Kirkcudbright. He received his military education at the academy of West Point, which he quitted in 1846, after a course of careful study, and with a certificate of exemplary conduct, and with the rank of second lieutenant of engineers. He served in the Mexican war, and distinguished himself at the battles of Contreras, Churubusco, Molino del Rey, and Chapultepec. For his gallant conduct in the latter engagement, he received the brevet rank of captain, and had the command given to him of a company of sappers and miners. At the conclusion of the war he returned to West Point, and remained there on duty with his company until 1851. About this time he introduced the bayonet exercise into the American army, and prepared a military manual, which is now used as a text book in that service. In the spring of 1852 he served under Major Marcy, in the expedition for exploring the Red river, and soon after joined the staff of General Persifer Smith, a senior engineer, and was engaged in surveying the rivers and harbors of that State. In 1853 he superintended the western division of the survey of the North Pacific Railroad route; returning in 1854, he received a commission in the cavalry, and was soon after appointed a member of the commission sent by the United States Government to the seat of war in the Crimea, to watch the progress of the siege of Sebastopol; having for his associates, Colonel R. E. Lee, the present Commander-in-Chief of the Confederate forces, and Major Mordecai. The result of his observations was a critical report on the "Organization of European Armies, and the Operations of War."

At the conclusion of the war, M'Clellan returned to America, and after two years' service resigned his commission, and became Vice-President and Engineer of the Illinois Central Railroad, which post he held for three years. On the civil war breaking out, the command was given to him of the militia in the State of Ohio, with the rank of major-general. He soon greatly distinguished himself by his victory at Rich Mountain. After the disaster at Manassas, he was placed at the head of the Army of the Potomac, and on the retirement of General Scott, was appointed to fill his post as Commander-in-Chief. M'Clellan may truly be said to possess most of the qualifications required to constitute a good general. The pages of this work will be found to bear full and impartial testimony to the bravery, sagacity, and calm judgment displayed by him on many occasions—especially when in command of the Army of the Potomac—and also to his successful efforts in organizing the Federal army.

FRANCIS SIGEL.

This officer, who holds a deservedly high place amongst the generals of the Federal army, was born at Sinsheim, in the Grand Duchy of Baden, in 1824, and was educated in the military academy at Carlsruhe, the capital of that duchy. In the political outbreak in Germany in 1848, he joined the revolutionary party, and eventually emigrated to America, selecting the State of Missouri as his new home. When the tide of civil war threatened the security of Missouri, he appealed to all the German settlers in that State to rally round him in defence of their homesteads. All those men who had formerly served under him in Germany hastened to join his flag; a mark of confidence of which he had much reason to feel proud. The great skill and ability with which he led his legion in their progress through the prairies of Missouri, was so highly appreciated, that the rank of major-general was bestowed upon him.

AMBROSE EVERETT BURNSIDE.

GENERAL BURNSIDE, of the State of Indiana, was born in the year 1824, and was educated at West Point. In 1847 he received the appointment of lieutenant of artillery in the United States army, and served in the Mexican campaign. In 1852 he quitted the army and was appointed a railway engineer. When the Civil War broke out the command was given to him of the 1st regiment of volunteers of the State of Rhode Island. In 1861, in consequence of the great activity and military skill which he displayed, he was promoted to the rank of a brigadier-general, and was subsequently, also, intrusted with the command of the military and naval expedition directed against the coast of North Carolina.

DON CARLOS BUELL.

GENERAL BUELL, who is a native of the State of Ohio, was an infantry cadet in 1837, and served with much credit in the Mexican war, during which he was twice promoted for the bravery he displayed. After the battle of Churubusco, in which he was severely wounded, he received the rank of major. On the termination of the Mexican war he was appointed adjutant-general, but quitted the service in 1851. General Buell espoused the cause of the Union, on the secession of the Southern States; he is a distinguished officer, brave and energetic, and his kind-hearted conduct toward the prisoners who fell into his hands has won for him golden opinions even among the Confederate soldiers.

HENRY WAGER HALLECK.

GENERAL HALLECK was educated at West Point, as an engineer, and at one time was a professor in that military school. Before the Civil War broke out he was known as the author of various military works, and also as a rising barrister at San Francisco, in California, in which State he had previously served with distinction during the Mexican war, that led to its annexation to the United States, and he was promoted to the rank of captain. He left the service in 1854, and subsequently became Secretary of State for the province of California, under the military government of Generals Kearny, Mason, and Riley, and was a member of the Convention which drew up the constitution of California in 1859. He disappeared for a time from public life, following his profession as a lawyer on behalf of his Mexican clients in California, until the war of secession broke out, when he was induced to take service in the Federal army, with the rank of major-general. General Halleck's outward appearance by no means indicates the soldier, although he is not deficient in the dignity due to his rank; but whether on active service or not, his bearing more resembles that of a peaceful citizen than of a general officer. On the 22d of July, 1862, General Halleck was appointed Commander-in-Chief of all the troops in the United States.

ULYSSES S. GRANT.

GENERAL GRANT was born in 1828, in the State of Ohio. After being educated at West Point, he received his appointment as lieutenant in the 4th infantry in the year 1845, and served with great credit in the Mexican war. In 1847 he was appointed quartermaster of his regiment; but shortly afterward left the service and settled in the State of Illinois. When the civil war in America broke out, the command was given to him of the 2d volunteer regiment of Illinois. He was appointed a brigadier-general in 1861, and in the March of the following year was promoted to the rank of major-general, and was intrusted with the command of the army in West Tennessee.

JOHN CHARLES FREMONT.

GENERAL FREMONT was born in the year 1813, in the State of South Carolina, where his father, a native of France, had settled. As a youth he was noted as an excellent mathematician, and in his twentieth year was appointed professor of mathematics on board the man-of-war Natchez. He also accompanied various exploring expeditions in the West, fitted out by the United States Government. In the year 1838 he was appointed lieutenant in the corps of topographical engineers, and a few years afterward was intrusted with the command of very important exploring expeditions in the West. In 1845 he was promoted to the rank of captain, and made a third and extensive journey to Oregon and California. In California he took the command of the North Americans residing there, and in a few weeks cleared the northern part of the country from the Mexican troops, for which valuable service he was appointed Governor. In 1849 he succeeded in discovering a practicable route of communication for connecting California with the Eastern States of North America. This was his last exploring expedition previous to his settling in California, for which State he was elected Senator. Soon after the commencement of the war of secession he took service in the United States army, and was intrusted with an important command in Missouri.

THE END.

www.ingramcontent.com/pod-product-compliance
Lightning Source LLC
Chambersburg PA
CBHW031426230426
43668CB00007B/454